QUEER GENEALOGIES IN TRANSNATIONAL BARCELONA
MARIA-MERCÈ MARÇAL, CRISTINA PERI ROSSI,
AND FLAVIA COMPANY

LEGENDA

LEGENDA is the Modern Humanities Research Association's book imprint for new research in the Humanities. Founded in 1995 by Malcolm Bowie and others within the University of Oxford, Legenda has always been a collaborative publishing enterprise, directly governed by scholars. The Modern Humanities Research Association (MHRA) joined this collaboration in 1998, became half-owner in 2004, in partnership with Maney Publishing and then Routledge, and has since 2016 been sole owner. Titles range from medieval texts to contemporary cinema and form a widely comparative view of the modern humanities, including works on Arabic, Catalan, English, French, German, Greek, Italian, Portuguese, Russian, Spanish, and Yiddish literature. Editorial boards and committees of more than 60 leading academic specialists work in collaboration with bodies such as the Society for French Studies, the British Comparative Literature Association and the Association of Hispanists of Great Britain & Ireland.

The MHRA encourages and promotes advanced study and research in the field of the modern humanities, especially modern European languages and literature, including English, and also cinema. It aims to break down the barriers between scholars working in different disciplines and to maintain the unity of humanistic scholarship. The Association fulfils this purpose through the publication of journals, bibliographies, monographs, critical editions, and the MHRA Style Guide, and by making grants in support of research. Membership is open to all who work in the Humanities, whether independent or in a University post, and the participation of younger colleagues entering the field is especially welcomed.

ALSO PUBLISHED BY THE ASSOCIATION

Critical Texts
Tudor and Stuart Translations • *New Translations* • *European Translations*
MHRA Library of Medieval Welsh Literature

MHRA Bibliographies
Publications of the Modern Humanities Research Association

The Annual Bibliography of English Language & Literature
Austrian Studies
Modern Language Review
Portuguese Studies
The Slavonic and East European Review
Working Papers in the Humanities
The Yearbook of English Studies

www.mhra.org.uk
www.legendabooks.com

STUDIES IN HISPANIC AND LUSOPHONE CULTURES

Studies in Hispanic and Lusophone Cultures are selected and edited by the Association of Hispanists of Great Britain & Ireland. The series seeks to publish the best new research in all areas of the literature, thought, history, culture, film, and languages of Spain, Spanish America, and the Portuguese-speaking world.

The Association of Hispanists of Great Britain & Ireland is a professional association which represents a very diverse discipline, in terms of both geographical coverage and objects of study. Its website showcases new work by members, and publicises jobs, conferences and grants in the field.

www.legendabooks.com/series/shlc

STUDIES IN HISPANIC AND LUSOPHONE CULTURES

Queer Genealogies in Transnational Barcelona

Maria-Mercè Marçal, Cristina Peri Rossi, and Flavia Company

Natasha Tanna

LEGENDA

Studies in Hispanic and Lusophone Cultures 37
Modern Humanities Research Association
2019

Published by Legenda
an imprint of the Modern Humanities Research Association
Salisbury House, Station Road, Cambridge CB1 2LA

ISBN 978-1-78188-811-7

First published 2019

Copy-Editor: Dr Ellen Jones

CONTENTS

ACKNOWLEDGEMENTS

Brad Epps, I returned to academia when and where I did, specifically to work with you. You permeate these pages to a degree that the convention of mere citation could not possibly capture. So many of the ideas in this book emerged from our exchanges. For imparting your love of etymology, for challenging the normative in me, for insisting on the importance of close reading, for showing me how critical writing can be so queerly beautiful, thank you. I will long continue to have your voice in my mind and your words guiding my fingers as I write.

Thank you to the academics who have taught or mentored me. Particular thanks to my first Spanish literature supervisor Rosemary Clark, my unofficial mentor of the pub-going variety Dominic Keown, and my PhD advisor Stuart Davis. To Geoffrey Kantaris who first introduced me to Cristina Peri Rossi, Joanna Page, former Director of the University of Cambridge's Centre of Latin American Studies (CLAS), for her wisdom and level-headedness, Rory O'Bryen who supervised my first research dissertation over a decade ago, and Fabienne Viala, my MPhil thesis supervisor. Erica Segre, thank you for our snatched conversations about Peri Rossi. Louise Haywood, Georgina Evans, and Isabelle McNeill, thank you for our discussions about pace and pleasure in academia. Bob Davidson, thanks for regularly checking in with me from afar and by snail mail since my early days as a fresh-faced PhD student. The five o'clock club, including Maite Conde and Rhiannon McGlade, has brightened the end of many weeks. Many thanks to Helena Buffery and Bryan Cameron, the examiners of the doctoral thesis on which this book is based, for engaging with my work so rigorously. This book has no doubt benefitted from the privilege of discussions with you.

With their warmth and care, Julie Coimbra, Sam Mather, and Coral Neale made CLAS and the Department of Spanish and Portuguese in Cambridge such wonderful places with which to be affiliated. To my (former) peers at CLAS and the Department of Spanish and Portuguese, thank you for being part of such a supportive research environment. Special thanks to Viviane Carvalho da Annunciação, Liliana Chávez Díaz, Abeyamí Ortega, Sandra Velásquez Alford, Mara Polgovsky, Carlos Fonseca, Lucy Foster, Cherie Elston, Rachel Randall, Geoff Maguire, Adriana Massidda, Paul Merchant, Dunja Fehimović, Rebecca Fell, Ola Gocławska, Rachell Sánchez Rivera, Laura Kemp, Emily Baker, Lucy Bollington, Luis Castellví Laukamp, Parker Lawson, Tatiana Vargas-Ortiz, Erika Teichert, Benjamin Quarshie, and Hazel Robins. I am very grateful to Asiya Islam and Gavin Stevenson for welcoming me enthusiastically to the Department of Sociology very late in my PhD.

My doctoral research would not have been possible without funding from the UK Arts and Humanities Research Council (grant no. 1376944). In Cambridge, additional funds from St John's College, Christ's College, the Faculty of Modern and Medieval Languages, and the Department of Spanish and Portuguese enabled me to carry out fieldwork in Barcelona, Buenos Aires, and Montevideo. Thank you to Margarida Ullate i Estanyol, Neus Aguado, MariJo Vázquez, Meritxell Joan Rodríguez, and Ernesto Vera in Barcelona. While in Barcelona, I also met Cristina Peri Rossi and Flavia Company to discuss their work with them; I am grateful to them for their time.' To Marcela Baigros and José María Gómez Samela, thank you for adopting me for a few months in Buenos Aires. Marlene Flores, Roxana Rügnitz Garabedian, and Sandra Mattos Bidart, thank you for your warmth and friendship in Montevideo.

I am grateful to the Association of Hispanists of Great Britain and Ireland, the Spanish Embassy, and Legenda for the prize that led to this book being published. Particular thanks to Legenda's Managing Editor, Graham Nelson, for his enthusiasm and advice. My warmest appreciation to the anonymous readers who showed meticulous care in their reading of the manuscript. Thank you for your generous words and incisive suggestions for further reading. Many thanks to Ellen Jones for her careful copy-editing, and especially for spotting my penchant for scare quotes. The Institut d'Estudis Catalans and the Generalitat de Catalunya funded a three-month visiting studentship at the Centre de Recerca Teoria, Gènere, Sexualitat: ADHUC (formerly the Centre Dona i Literatura) at the Universitat de Barcelona during which I was able to carry out extensive archival research at the Fons Maria-Mercè Marçal in the Biblioteca Nacional de Catalunya, as advised by Noèlia Díaz Vicedo. At ADHUC I really found a home for my work thanks to Helena González Fernández, Director of the Centre, who has continued to offer me encouragement. It was through ADHUC that I met the wonderful Marta Segarra with whom Brad and I organised the 2016 Jornades Marçalianes in Cambridge.

Thank you to the Anglo-Catalan Society for a scholarship to present my work on Marçal at the 2014 Annual Conference in Cork. For their insights on my papers there or elsewhere, many thanks to Josep-Anton Fernàndez, Montserrat Lunati, Fina Birulés, Heura Marçal, Sara Torres, Marta Font, Elisenda Marcer, and Maria Sevilla. Eli Massana, thank you for your energy, encouragement, and endless insights — you are an inspiration. You have made some key reading recommendations and comments at crucial moments that have shaped this research directly.

I am deeply grateful to Nadia Sanmartín for allowing me to use an image of her brilliant and beautiful work, 'M.M.M', on the front cover of this book. I am grateful to the Catedral de Girona for permission to use an image of the Tapestry of Creation and to Heura Marçal for permission to use images from the Fons Maria-Mercè Marçal and to cite freely from Marçal's poetry. Thank you to the journal *Feminist Theory* for permission to include as Part I of Chapter Two a version of an article that appeared in the journal as 'Unravelling Compulsory Happiness in Exile: Cristina Peri Rossi's *The Ship of Fools*'. Thanks to Dominic Keown, General Editor of the Anglo-Catalan Society's Occasional Publications, for permission to use in

Chapter One an expanded version of a text that appeared in the publication, *Maria-Mercè Marçal: Her Life in Words* (2017), edited by Noèlia Díaz Vicedo, and to the Press of the Universidad de Sevilla for permission to use in Part II of Chapter Two an edited version of a text that appeared in Spanish in *Erotismo, transgresión y exilio: las voces de Cristina Peri Rossi* (2017), edited by Jesús Gómez-de-Tejada.

Thank you to all of my friends who have supported the writing of this book indirectly; there is not space to mention you all here. Things would have been a lot harder without Thomas Godard, my housemate for the longest time during the PhD — thank you for all of the kitchen chats. Particular thanks to Lucy Taylor, Josie O'Donoghue, Federico López Terra, Lucy Greaves, Molly Blackburn, CJ Mahony, Christine Doran, Rajandeep Singh, Wei Wei Wang, Michael Monteiro, Tom Muir, Zoe Twidle, Jody Walshe, Anna Bond, Vivienne Tong, Shriya Patel, Shruti Sharma, Payal Shah, Kashmira Mehta, Sheena Mehnon, Charlotte Thompson, Angela Tomlinson, Tiffany Page, Mirela Ivanova, and Faye Goldman for your support and energy. In Mexico, thanks to Erick Ephraín, Ángel González Cabrera, Ángel Rodríguez Vicente, Luis Alberto González, Bere, Pame, Ulises Elizondo Ascencio, and Martín Granados (que en paz descanse) for your friendship across decades, distance, and death. To the 'protesting people' in Cambridge for helping me to keep perspective: Mónica Moreno Figueroa, Ruby Zajac, Casandra Villava, Franco González, Gaby García Dunn, Lechugas, and Claudia Méndez Jaime.

During the process of transforming thesis to monograph, the support, care, and mere presence of a number of people kept me sane in ways that they may never fully know. For the morning runs and adventures that make life during teaching term immeasurably better, Caroline Egan, thank you. For long chats over cups of tea and for introducing me to the joys of adult education classes, Hettie Malcomson. For being such a supportive friend in so many ways during the strange experience of monastery living, Maya Feile Tomes. I was extremely lucky to start at Christ's at the same time as Harriet Lyon and Ed Zychowicz-Coghill, who have been most delightful companions. While at Christ's, I have also been cheered by the predominantly mealtime company of Ned Allen, Dai Jones, Carrie Vout, Emily Tomlinson, Mark Darlow, Mary Franklin-Brown, Dan Field, Tom Hawker-Dawson, Giovanni Mantilla, Sarah Radcliffe, Robert Hunt, Jane Stapleton, and Nick Gay. Ned, in particular, has weathered many an intense conversation. The lgbtQ+@cam initiative also provided much space for thought, action, and friendship. Special thanks to Sarah Franklin, Heather Stallard, Marcin Smietana, Robert Pralat, Diarmuid Hester, hakan sandal, and Lucy van de Wiel. Thank you to Esther for providing some emotional stability in turbulent times.

To Sameer for instilling in me a love of Spanish and of reading. To Akhil for prompting me to appreciate the importance of thinking critically. To Serrena for sustaining me with her unconditional love, warmth, care, and gentle presence. To my parents for their belief in the importance of education. It is because of them, and their example, that I learnt very early that rebellion starts at home.

Finally, to those who are most mingled in the words that follow. Joey Whitfield, my MPhil buddy of yesteryear, this book emerges some eleven years after we first met in undergraduate translation class. Thank you for the days in the tower, which

I will always remember fondly, despite everything. Without that space in which to hibernate, I'm not sure how I would have finished my PhD. Thank you (I think) for luring me back into academia after I had vowed not to return and for queering the queer in me in ways that I had never imagined. I dare say that anyone who reads my work in whatever form will also want to thank you for entreating me to do a bit of signposting.

Virginia Lucas (and Bilbo, Leopoldo, and Jules), thank you for welcoming me into your home, for your 'tratados sobre el tiempo', and for always challenging pernicious imperialist formations with perspectives from 'el sur' — the time we have spent together has been a true education.

Julia Powles, you were a whirlwind of an accomplice in stealing time and catching driftwood. Thank you for the endless flow of love, support, and patient encouragement, especially when I claimed not to need it. Thank you also for becoming an overnight Catalan and Latin American literature enthusiast.

I end with you, Estela, because you are where this research began. It is symbolic that Etna entered a queer genealogy in transnational Barcelona the day before my viva voce examination. That our periods of gestation — mine, of the thesis; yours, of Etna — coincided is a moving reminder of why the focus of this research is what it is. Thank you for humouring my obsessive step-counting, word-counting, and pomodoro-counting with a gentle belief in me, and for reading countless iterations of articles and conference papers in Spanish and Catalan without complaint, despite you finding my work 'a palo'. Above all, thank you for insisting on the power of friendship to overcome the inevitable pain of ruptures.

Natasha Tanna, Cambridge, August 2019

És com si [...] no fos sinó una còpia dolentíssima, una rèplica llunyana, d'aquell que jo pretenia fer.

Un esbós, tal vegada: hi ha a grans trets allò que volia dir, però essencialment incomplet.

— Sara T. in MARIA-MERCÈ MARÇAL's *La passió segons Renée Vivien*

[it is as if [...] it were only a terrible copy, a distant replica, of what I was trying to create.

A sketch, perhaps: it contains, broadly, what I was trying to say, but it is, essentially, incomplete.]

Genealogy is gray, meticulous, and patiently documentary.

It operates on a field of entangled and confused parchments, on documents that have been scratched over and recopied many times.

— MICHEL FOUCAULT, 'Nietzsche, Genealogy, History'

INTRODUCTION

> Queer, for me, was not a sign that I was getting rid of identity; rather, it points
> to the fact that it is spoiled, partial, never fully achieved, but sticky, familiar,
> and hard to lose completely.
>
> — HEATHER LOVE (2011: 185)

Queer Genealogies: Challenging the Anti-Social Turn

In queer theory, criticism, activism, and existence, the family as a social institution
is as contested as the notion of identity. Queer affinity is understood both
within and beyond a kinship matrix. Campaigns for same-sex marriage and legal
recognition of non-nuclear families see activists, often under the lesbian and gay
banner, demand entry into existing dominant forms of social organisation. This
so-called assimilationist approach sometimes changes the institution of the family
from within, but more frequently it broadens it and leaves it intact. In the wake
of Spain's legal recognition of same-sex marriage, for example, Alfredo Martínez-
Expósito laments the 'bourgeois and conformist normalisation' (2013: n.p.) of the
trajectory of LGBTQ+ politics and R. Lucas Platero Méndez (2005) brings the
feminist international critiques of marriage to same-sex marriage, arguing also
that lesbian women are often invisibilised within such political projects. A number
of contributors to Rosalía Cornejo Parriego and Kay Sibbald's special issue of the
Revista Canadiense de Estudios Hispánicos [Canadian Journal of Hispanic Studies] titled
'Un espacio *queer* — Queer Space' address the queer disruption of, and assimilation
into, heteronormative structures, with attention to both the deconstruction of
identities as well as their codification (2010: 1). Many activists and writers seek to
challenge radically the institution of the family, deeming it inherently conservative
and repressive.

Accordingly, some critics and writers have sought to imagine alternative models
of relationality beyond the family. Jack Halberstam ([2007] 2015), for example, calls
for the 'forgetting of family' (317). Others can be situated within queer theory's
so-called anti-social turn, seeking not only to move beyond the family, but beyond
future-oriented visions of sociality altogether. Lee Edelman's highly polemical *No
Future: Queer Theory and the Death Drive* (2004) draws on the work of Leo Bersani
and Jacques Lacan to herald an anti-future queer mode of being. Edelman argues
that more radical queer ethics are bound necessarily to the present:

> Far from partaking of this narrative movement toward a viable political future,
> far from perpetuating the fantasy of meaning's eventual realization, the queer
> comes to figure the bar to every realization of futurity, the resistance, internal
> to the social, to every social structure or form. (4)

In his call for an anti-reproductive mode of being that hinges on the denigration of the figure of the Child (capitalised in his text, as if doing so turns it into pure metaphor), Edelman dismisses queer family formations.

Many lesbian and feminist critics have challenged the anti-social turn spearheaded by Edelman. Maggie Nelson, for example, criticises Edelman for what she sees as the 'presumed opposition of queerness and procreation (or, to put a finer edge on it, maternity)' (2015: 16). She draws on Susan Fraiman's denouncement of 'heroic gay male sexuality as a stand-in for queerness which remains unpolluted by procreative femininity' (cited in Nelson 2015: 84). In response to Edelman's glamorous nihilism, Latinx critics such as José Esteban Muñoz in *Cruising Utopia: The Then and There of Queer Futurity* (2009) and Juana María Rodríguez in *Sexual Futures, Queer Gestures and Other Latina Longings* (2014), have proposed theoretical visions and alternative practices that insist on queer sociality, relationality, and futurity. Most significantly for this book, Edelman does not consider modes of reproduction and sociality that are not centred on children but that do, nonetheless, look to the future, including the relative permanence of writing.

In this book I look at writers and texts 'living on' and the ways in which they engage with the future within *and* beyond networks formed through biological procreation. As well as the queering of the biological family, I search for what Elizabeth Freeman describes as 'an embodied but not procreative model of kinship that has powerful resonances for theorising in a queer mode' ([2007] 2015: 303). She draws on Toni Morrison's historical 're-membering' in the African American context under and after slavery as a 'renewal of collective life' through bringing bodies together in new ways. It is my contention that these social and embodied models are frequently experienced, perhaps paradoxically, through texts. As the sociologist Les Back contends, 'writing is a profoundly social activity; it connects my thoughts to yours. In short, it lets them travel' (2016: 194).

Vital to the sociality of text and travelling thoughts is desire. Cristina Peri Rossi emphasises the interplay of literature and desire in the prologue to her *Poesía reunida* (2005), describing both the reader and writer as desiring beings:

> ¿hay alguna obra que no hable del deseo, que no surja del deseo, que no reclame el deseo? Para que un poema exista se necesitan, por lo menos, dos deseos: el deseo del poeta y el deseo del lector, convertido en sujeto deseante. (21)

> [is there any work that doesn't speak of desire, that doesn't emerge from desire, that doesn't appeal to desire? For a poem to exist there needs to be, at the very least, two desires: that of the poet and that of the reader, transformed into a desiring subject.][1]

In placing desire at the heart of literary creation and reception, Peri Rossi extends its erotic, sexual, or libidinal associations to elaborate a vision of literary desire. In this regard, Peri Rossi's words resonate with those of literary critic Kevin Ohi for whom 'to contemplate the writing of desire is also to contemplate the formation of a literary tradition' (10). Paying attention to how desire functions in texts is to pay attention to literary inheritance and, therefore, to the shaping of literary traditions, canons, and counter-canons.

For Ohi, the queer is 'an anarchic troubling of heteronormative lines of cultural transmission' (2015: 7). These are lines that often form and consolidate national literary canons. The troubling to which Ohi refers, enfolded in prior troublings of gender as a binary configuration, involves a questioning of kinship, temporality, and modes of communication. To be attentive to literary desire in the works in my corpus is to analyse the queer transmission of knowledge and practice beyond patrilineal, or indeed matrilineal, lines. The texts in my study diegetically enact the process of literary transmission as they contain within them real or fictional characters who are readers, writers, or both. In a number of cases, the textual relationship is highly erotic; in others, it is less so, desire being both erotic and other than erotic.

In the spirit of Back's travelling thoughts, in the texts that I study in this book, I saw an opportunity to trace a queer utopian genealogy through writers from different countries in a sort of global sisterhood, moving beyond both familial *and* national identity. Sisterhood, I say, despite myself. Genealogy, I say. The family persists, like the sticky identity about which Heather Love writes in the epigraph to this introduction. The more I read of and about Maria-Mercè Marçal, Cristina Peri Rossi, and Flavia Company, the authors whose texts I study in this book, the more I realise that try as they (and I) might to will the family away, to seek to depict relationality beyond it, the family often returns. In other words, the family *haunts* the queer, the lesbian, and so much more. It is to this haunting insistence that I respond, rather than a post-identitarian ideal held dear by many queer theorists and critics.

In *Escribir hacia atrás: herencia, lengua, memoria* (2008) [Writing Backwards: Inheritance, Language, Memory], Gina Saraceni reflects on genealogy and the relationship of the living with the dead through the Derridean notion of the spectre:

> espectro como presencia de lo ausente, como reaparición de algo que dejó de estar pero que sigue estando, como algo que ya fue y todavía no es: suerte de presencia anacrónica, de aparición intempestiva que desajusta y desarticula la contemporaneidad mostrando su deuda con el pasado, su actualidad inactual. (14–15)

> [the spectre as the presence of what is absent, as the reappearance of something that stopped being there and yet is still there, like something that was and yet still is not: a sort of anachronistic presence, an unruly apparition that disrupts and disarticulates contemporaneity, revealing its debt to the past, its no-longer-current presence in the present.]

Saraceni's words resonate with my central concerns about how approaches to inheritance may disrupt linear understandings of temporality and how other times, places, and people may erupt into the present. However much it may be criticised and berated, however anachronistic it may seem in some queer contexts, the family, no more than the nation, will not simply disappear. They persist, often queerly. Indeed, the texts of my corpus engage with our debts to the past and how the past continues to haunt the present through the present absences that move us.

Debates about the family have particular inflections in contexts in which the state has torn the social fabric and family apart and where family itself was and is a crucial site of resistance. Freeman, Sara Ahmed, and many writers of colour before them ask from what privileged position critics speak when they will the family to disappear. 'Family' is a word bound up in slavery, servitude, and submission — in Roman times '[f]amulus means domestic slave, and familia is the aggregate number of slaves belonging to one man' (Engels [1884] 2016: 42) — but it cannot be cast off with a gesture of the will. Indeed, while itself bound up in notions of servitude, the rhetoric of family is also part and parcel of a legacy of resistance to slavery in more recent times. In African-American (and other) cultures, for example, the rhetoric of family — brother, sister — is much more common and much more politically charged, especially given the forced destruction of familial bonds under slavery. Such terms are deployed to develop alternative kinship relations and to show solidarity, often across national borders.

In *Lazos de familia: cuerpos, herencias, ficciones* (2004) [Family Ties: Bodies, Inheritances, Fictions], Ana Amado and Nora Domínguez turn their attention to the Southern Cone, where Peri Rossi and Company were born. Writing of the political insistence on biological family ties in Argentina, they note that groups such as the 'Asociación Madres de Plaza de Mayo' [The Association of the Mothers of the Plaza de Mayo] and 'H.I.J.O.S. por la Identidad y la Justicia contra el Olvido y el Silencio' [Children of the Disappeared for Identity and Justice Against Forgetting and Silence], who fight for justice for the disappeared, 'cimientan la certeza del origen' (Amado and Domínguez 2004 : 16) [cement the certainty of origins]. For example, these groups encourage those whom they think might be stolen children of the disappeared given to right-wing military families under the dictatorship to have DNA tests to establish their 'true' biological origins. In this case, for from being a repressive force, the bonds of family are invoked in order to confront the painful legacy of the military dictatorship.

Writing in political contexts in which the deliberate rupture of the biological family was a systematic political tool of both totalitarian regimes and/or constitutional democracies under slavery (and indeed afterwards: the state can still decide whether children should live — or die), these critics and others have argued for the importance of 'la relación genealógica y familiar' (Ludmer 2002: 101) [genealogical and familial relations], affirming that the family is not inherently a conservative space filled with passive subjects blindly reproducing the modes of existence of previous generations. Many critics in such contexts call for a more nuanced approach to family. It is partly to their call for attentiveness to complex webs of relationality that this book responds.

Relating stories of familial and familiar relationships can contribute to imagining and enacting new alternative visions for these relationships. Amado and Domínguez argue that while stories about the family may seem anachronistic, 'los *relatos* familiares — sociales y también *representacionales* — parecen contener, paradójicamente, las coordenadas que exhiben lo social y cultural desde sus fisuras, e incluso revelar en su enunciado el germen de la resistencia o los dilemas de un cambio' (2004: 15–16, my emphasis) [family *stories* — as lived and as *represented* — paradoxically seem to contain the coordinates revealed in the fissures of the social and the cultural. They are stories that through their very telling seem to reveal seeds of resistance or the dilemmas regarding a change] (my emphasis). The use of the word 'relatos' here, the Spanish word for stories or tales, is germane. After all, I am dealing with literary texts. Such texts represent families, rendering them discursively, and can reveal their weaknesses and their 'fissures' to imagine new forms of relationality. Rather than a site of straightforward belonging or a site of oppression — what Engels called 'the composite ideal of sentimentality and domestic strife in the present day philistine mind' ([1884] 2016: 42) — , Amado and Domínguez see the family as an ambivalent space of 'enlace y separación, de atadura y corte, de identidad y diferencia' (2004: 14) [linkage and separation, tying and cutting, identity and difference].

The writing of family stories that reveal the fissures within the ambivalent space of the family resonates with Foucault's approach to genealogy. In order to explore inheritance and transmission within and beyond the family, I draw on his remarks on the importance of texts, writing, and symbolic structures to genealogy, beyond biological (or quasi- or pseudo-biological) formations. He opens his essay, 'Nietzsche, Genealogy, History' with the words cited in the epigraph to this book: 'Genealogy is gray, meticulous, and patiently documentary. It operates on a field of entangled and confused parchments, on documents that have been scratched over and recopied many times' ([1977] 1984a: 76). Textual entanglement, or intertextuality, is vital to all of the texts and intertexts in my corpus, some of which indeed become con-fused, fused together to the extent that they become indistinguishable.

Through genealogical study we can look to the future, but not necessarily in terms of progress and development, and look to the past but not necessarily as a continuous tracing back to comforting origins: 'el saber que se obtiene *escribiendo hacia atrás* es un saber de la precariedad y de la falta, de la interrupción y la incompletitud' (Saraceni 2008: 32) [knowledge that is obtained in the process of *writing towards the past* is knowledge of precarity and lack, of interruption and incompletion]. For Foucault, fragmentation is the very essence — a counter-essence, one might say — of genealogy. He writes: 'The search for descent is not the erecting of foundations: on the contrary, it disturbs what was previously considered immobile; it fragments what was thought unified; it shows the heterogeneity of what was imagined consistent with itself' (1984a: 82). Foucault proposes a reading of genealogy beyond a preoccupation with continuous lines and *origins*, as opposed to arborescent genealogies that tend to be, or at least *appear* to be, complete, linear, and mastered and to remit to a single, solid, stable trunk.

I deploy 'genealogy' as a critical concept, then, following Foucault's revival of genealogical analysis as a mode of 'counter-history', because the family lingers in these texts and kinship structures and terms are adopted and adapted within them. Bonds of family are often resisted, queered, and temporarily overcome in the texts, but new forms of living and relating do not necessarily totally destroy previous forms. María Teresa Vera-Rojas asserts that writers who challenge repressive institutions and the potential pitfalls of community groups do not simply advocate for these groups to disappear. She argues that the Chicana writer Gloria Anzaldúa, for example, 'no propugna la desaparición de las comunidades sino que nos invita a vivir en múltiples comunidades basadas en la diferencia, negociando entre todas ellas' (2012: 23) [does not advocate for the disappearance of community, rather she invites us to live in many communities formed around difference, negotiating between all of them]. I focus on such processes of negotiation of forms of belonging and inheritance.

Indeed, such a consideration of genealogy at a familial level also has implications for the notion of national origins and for how literature is related to place, be this the places where the authors were born, the places where they write, the places about which they write, or the places where their texts circulate. While this book's title situates it in Barcelona, the city where the writers have spent most of their lives and a key locus of LBGTQ+ activism and cultural creation, I am attentive to the authors' engagements with Montevideo, Buenos Aires, Paris, and Lesbos, amongst other locations. Through the works of the Catalan Marçal, Montevideo-born Peri Rossi, and Buenos Aires-born Company, all of whom engage issues of home, exile, and belonging through texts that play with fragmentation, interruption, and incompletion, I trace a diasporic and queer Foucauldian genealogy that differs from Wilfredo Hernández's notion of an 'autonomous' or 'indigenous' tradition of lesbian writing in Catalonia, which I outline in the next section. While a number of works on queer literature criticise the heteronormative basis of the nation-state, critics often continue to study authors by nation and/or language, categorising them according to their country of birth, or country of 'origin'. In our contemporary moment, marked by heightened tensions and impassioned feelings regarding making nations 'great again' and by fierce debates about belonging and who has the right to be where, my approach in this book shifts to a conception of place concerned with residence and movement.

Labile Locations: Transnational Barcelona

> S'estalonen l'infern i el paradís
> I el bressol i la tomba, i les paraules
> i el cos: país natal, exili.
> — MARÇAL ([1988] 2017: 391)

> [Hell and heaven,
> cradle and tomb, words
> and body: country of birth, exile.
> each is a crutch for the other.]

In English, sexuality has often been described in spatial terms, as in the description of heterosexual people as 'straight' and in the association (particularly in sexology in the late nineteenth century with its penchant for pathological categorisation) of other sexualities as 'deviant' (turning out of the way) or 'perverse' (turned about, turned away). As Eve Kosofsky Sedgwick points out, the etymology of queer links with crossing, with transversing as well as twisting: 'Queer is a continuing moment, movement, motive-recurrent, eddying, *troublant*. The word 'queer' itself means *across* — it comes from the indo-European root *twerkw*, which also yields the German *quer* (transverse), Latin *torquere* (to twist), English *athwart*' (Sedgwick 1993: xii). The notion of a subculture also spatialises those who are different, situating them underground (often literally), in a demi-monde. Queer people also often describe feeling 'out of place' in heteronormative milieux. The works in my corpus engage the spatiality of queerness on a macrolevel by combining considerations of lesbian/queer sexualities and migration, diaspora, or exile. Indeed, deploying the term 'queer' in non-Anglophone contexts is always already a transnational gesture, often reflecting a sense of exile within national culture (Córdoba García 2005: 21).

'Homonationalism' (Puar 2007) is a term that describes a supposedly queer sociality that takes an assimiliationist approach to an extreme. Counter to homonationalism, where LBGTQI+ subjects exemplify the ideal patriotic citizen rather than challenging the foundational exclusions and violence of the nation-state, for José Esteban Muñoz, it is vital that images of queer utopia are imagined beyond the nation: 'The *there* of queer utopia cannot simply be that of the faltering yet still influential nation-state' ([2007] 2015: 460). Muñoz imagines transnational connections while aware of the ongoing power and influence of the nation. Joana Sabadell-Nieto (2012: 72) argues that transnational connections are of heightened importance for women in the face of the continued and perhaps increasing power of discourses of nationhood that are often highly patriarchal.

The Argentine philosopher and activist Virginia Cano explains that she experienced her realisation of her lesbianism as a feeling of being foreign; she experienced it in English: 'Solía pensar: *"I'm gay"*. Incluso imaginé contar este (no) secreto en esta lengua. Quizás mi lengua madre no me permitía en ese entonces siquiera pensar en ello. Decirlo. O quizás fue algún tipo de profecía. El anuncio de cierta condición-extranjera' (2015: 20–21) [I used to think, 'I'm gay'. I even imagined telling this (open) secret in English. Maybe my mother tongue didn't allow me at that time to even think about being gay. To say it. Or maybe it was some kind of prophecy. The forewarning of a particular condition of foreignness].[2] Cano's words resonate with Anzaldúa's recounting of a student's misunderstanding of homophobia. The student believed 'homophobia' to refer to a queer person's 'fear of going home' (2012: 42). In these cases, queerness is figured as existing outside of the home and beyond the nation. The sense of deterritorialisation or foreignness has led, in some cases, to a reterritorialisation of the queer in altered form. For example, valeria flores, an Argentine teacher and activist, localises the 'queer' as 'cuir', as she details its manifestations in her country of residence (2013: 32, 35). However, the queer has also persisted in its Anglophone form in a variety of contexts.

Precisely for its impact beyond territory, some have deemed the term 'queer' neo-imperialist, a conceptual colonisation, potentially appearing 'classist' or 'elitist' outside the academy and particular political movements (Medhurst and Munt 1997: xi–xii; Fernàndez 2000: 16; Epps 2008). Indeed, one could argue that in its transnational reach, the queer mirrors the boundary-crossing power of the other spheres that the term 'transnational' brings to mind: the transnational corporations of neoliberalism. In 'Retos, riesgos, pautas y promesas de la teoría queer' [Challenges, Risks, Patterns and Promises of Queer Theory], Brad Epps writes that the generalisation of the term 'queer' should be awkward and uncomfortable (2008: 901). One could argue at length about whether or not 'queer' should be used beyond Anglophone contexts, and many have done so, but the reality is that despite criticism of the term and searches for alternatives, in many Hispanophone and Catalanophone contexts, it has stuck, uncomfortable as this may be.

I echo Chris Perriam's comments on the interrogation of terms about sexuality and representation of non-normative sexualities that combine the 'resonant and the irritant' (2013: 3) as part of a queer reading practice. It is, of course, ironic that theories that attend to the minoritarian and peripheral replicate a dominant Anglophone discourse. However, neither would it make sense to insist on purism, on only using concepts from a particular place in analysing works from that place. Carmen Romero Bachiller notes the limitations in deploying Anglophone terms and concepts, but concedes that it is nonetheless useful to engage with 'las herramientas analíticas que nos proporcionan, y hacerlos nuestros para abordar situaciones presentes' (2005: 149) [the analytical tools that they offer us, and to appropriate them in order to confront situations in our own present]. It is important to be attentive to the general — the theories circulating in a place — and to the particular manifestations and engagements with a general theory in a specific place. I follow Jorge Pérez (2010) in striving to highlight what non-Anglophone contexts bring to debates around queer theory and practice. One can recognise the transnational influence of the queer and appreciate its local manifestations; they are not mutually exclusive.

Let us move, then, to the local. Why Barcelona? I have turned to post-Franco Barcelona partly due to the city's prominence in the Catalan and Spanish LBGTQ+ movements during and after the dictatorship. Like the queer, Barcelona is both peripheral and the site of a certain centrality. It may be considered linguistically and culturally peripheral amongst visions of Spain frequently centred on Castile and Andalusia, but central in the sense that it is the capital city of Catalonia. As a city close to France with a port opening up to the Mediterranean, it has long seen itself as more European than the rest of Spain. The 'Front d'Alliberament Gai de Catalunya' [Gay Liberation Front] (FAGC) was the first gay organisation to be recognised and legalised in Spain in 1980 (and 'gay', at that time, was an umbrella term for non-normative genders and sexualities, as 'queer' claims to be today).[3] The FAGC was one of the main groups involved in the 1977 creation of the 'Coordinadora de Frentes de Liberación Homosexual del Estado Español' [Coalition of Gay Liberation Fronts in Spain] (COFLHEE), a coalition that campaigned for the legalisation of homosexuality in Spain. COFLHEE was created in the same year as the first gay pride march in Spain, which took place in Barcelona and was also organised by the FAGC. Two years later in 1979 homosexuality was legalised in Spain. However, discrimination against LBGTQ+ people continued under many guises. When several gay bars were closed in 1981 by the Civil Governor of Barcelona, who

FIG. I.1. 'Lo nuestro sí que es mundial' sign (1981) by COFLHEE

claimed to be improving the image of Barcelona in the run-up to the 1982 FIFA World Cup, a number of businesspeople in the city displayed signs designed by COFLHEE of the World Cup mascot, Naranjito, fanning himself alongside the slogan 'Lo nuestro sí que es mundial' [What *we* are is worldly] (see fig. I.1). The slogan, a word-play on the 'Copa Mundial' [World Cup], was an effort to connect activism in Barcelona with struggles taking place internationally. Beyond the 1970s and 1980s, Barcelona has continued to be at the forefront of LBGTQ+ activism in Spain, perhaps most notable in 1998 when the Catalan government was the first to pass regional laws in Spain on same-sex civil union (Perriam 2013: 1).[4]

As well as being a key locus of LBGTQ+ activist movements, Barcelona has been at the forefront of literary depictions of lesbian and queer desire in Spain. A series of novels and short stories published in the 1970s that depict sexual relations between women put Barcelona firmly on the map of queer literature. Hernández writes of authors from Catalan-speaking territories, such as Ana María Moix, Esther Tusquets, Carme Riera, and Ana María Matute as being part of what he describes (problematically, of course, given the tensions between Catalonia and the centralised Spanish state in Madrid) as an 'indigenous tradition' of contemporary Spanish gay writing (2003: 20) and as an 'autonomous Spanish lesbian tradition' (2003: 31). The main works depicting desire between women written in the 1970s are Tusquets's 'Trilogía del mar' [Sea Trilogy] 1978–1980, Moix's *Julia* (1970), and Riera's 'Te deix, amor, la mar com a penyora' [I Leave You, My Love, the Sea as a Token] (1975, henceforth 'Te deix') and 'Jo pos per testimoni les gavines' [Let Seagulls be my Witnesses] (1977). Hernández refers to a tradition started by Catalan novelists, most of whom wrote in Spanish (2003: 31). Again, the notion of an 'autonomous' Spanish tradition in Catalonia is rife with tensions. In this book, I focus on three writers who depict desire between women in Barcelona from the 1980s to the present to trace the twists and turns of what Hernández describes as an 'indigenous tradition', and, crucially, to complicate the very notion of indigeneity in this context.

In the spirit of Adrienne Rich's 'politics of location', captured in her call to '[b]egin with the material. Pick up again the long struggle against lofty and privileged abstraction' ([1984] 1994: 213), I situate the study in a particular, concrete, if labile location. However, I do this mainly to reveal how far-reaching genealogies can emerge from a supposedly single and specific site, a site that is, however, often vague, blurred, and disrupted. Appropriately enough for a queer thesis, the city of Barcelona itself features only in passing or incidentally in the texts and in my analysis. The passing and the incidental are consistent with the texts' interest in fragmentation and dispersion, recollection and belonging. Place, including mentions of Barcelona, is not straightforward in any of the texts; it is troubled, eluded, evaded, or ignored.

In Marçal's sole novel *La passió segons Renée Vivien* [The Passion According to Renée Vivien] (1994, henceforth *La passió*), the reader learns that Sara T., alter-ego for Marçal and focus of my reading of the novel in Chapter One, is from Barcelona. However, in the diegesis, she is mainly in Paris researching Renée Vivien. In Peri Rossi's novel *La nave de los locos* (1984, henceforth *La nave*), which I analyse in Chapter Two, Peri Rossi describes the trip of one of the characters, Morris, to la ciudad de B. (115). The city seems to be Barcelona, the place where Peri Rossi went into exile in the early 1970s and where she has long resided. However, it is not explicitly named. Instead, it is described as the 'Gran Ombligo' [Great Navel], and its citizens as 'ombliguistas' [navel-gazers]. In Company's *Querida Nélida* [Dear Nélida] (1988), set largely in Barcelona, the city seems to be an incidental backdrop to the relationship of the protagonists, Nélida and Celia. Nélida states in the letter that forms the prologue that the women's long-anticipated journey, around which the epistolary novel is constructed, only existed in 'una o dos habitaciones de esta Barcelona terrible' (12) [one or two bedrooms of this terrible Barcelona]. Their imaginings of the trip take place in a bedroom, suspended from daily life, and not rooted in a particular place. The women seem obsessively grounded in each other. However, the eponymous protagonist travels from Barcelona to Buenos Aires numerous times. Place being incidental and subordinated to the relationship in the novel could in itself be read as a comment on the queer transcending national boundaries. Indeed, the trip in the novel counters the novel's epigraph from Deuteronomy, which calls for the reader to remain within national boundaries.

In Company's *Melalcor* (2000), the protagonists are from the fictionalised Catalan village of Santa Canar dels Montons. The city where they attend university and to which their friends escape following an arson attack on their house seems to be Barcelona, but it is described simply as 'La Ciutat' [The City]. Eventually, the village misfits flee the policing of gender and sexuality. The protagonists end up living in Paris and their friends go to the UK. It is an escape from the 'local' that enables the protagonists to live freely in a cosmopolitan city that is not their own. In *Volver antes que ir* (2012) [Returning Before Departing], Company, who was born in Argentina, shifts her focus to her biological 'origins' in a journey from Barcelona to Buenos Aires. She reveals her longing to feel a rooted sense of belonging in the country where she was born, but ultimately the poem is a reflection on the impossibility of fulfilling such a desire.

Paradoxically, then, Barcelona is present in the texts in my corpus through its elusion, elision, and, indeed, illusions. Recalling the terms Saraceni uses to describe genealogy as spectral, we could consider Barcelona to be a present *absence* in the texts, distinctly unspectacular and indistinctly spectral. In a way, such a presence counters the spectacular touristic and consumerist visions announcing and selling Barcelona's charms to the world. What does the Catalan capital stand for today? Speculation, soaring property prices, and a boom in tourist apartments have priced many locals out of neighbourhoods such as Gràcia and Barceloneta. The mayor at the time of writing, Ada Colau, was a housing activist before she was elected mayor and she has introduced regulations to try to stem new building projects for tourist accommodation.[5] In many ways, Barcelona has been the victim of its perceived success after putting itself on the world stage with the 1992 Olympics. Oriol Pi-Sunyer (1995) has pointed to the difference between the vision behind the ill-fated Popular Olympics, in line with Barcelona's community-based working-class elements, and the Barcelona of the 1992 Olympics that involved high spending, an emphasis on spectacle, and so-called cleansing of the city. In Marçal's *La passió*, Vivien is described as a 'pantalla' (53) [screen], meaning a figure onto which people project their own visions and fantasies. In some ways, in my corpus the city of Barcelona has a similar function as a blank slate onto which people project their desires.

There are, of course, many Barcelonas, but what I hope to bring out in this book is a place where there are queer lives and loves in the city beyond the partnership of capital and 'lifestyle' behind formations such as the 'Gaixample', part of the trendy and upmarket Eixample where there is a concentration of pricey gay bars, clubs, and shops. Santiago Fouz-Hernández (2010) writes insightfully of Madrid's equivalent, Chueca, known locally as 'Chuecatown', and how in its gentrification it spatialises the sanitisation and commercialisation of queer politics. However, the transnational is not just about the flows into the city but also about how those in it relate outwards. I was drawn to Barcelona as a city in/from which to situate the study as it stands to me for the tensions between being a cosmopolitan, globalised city, as well as being a site of manifestations of a fiercely local identity, as evident in demands issued from the city for recognition of Catalonia as an independent nation-state. Indeed, at the time of writing, tensions between Catalonia and Madrid remain high after the centralised Spanish state's violent response to the Catalan independence referendum of autumn 2017, which was deemed unconstitutional by Madrid. Cosmopolitanism and a desire for statehood are not, of course, mutually exclusive. Part of the way in which Catalonia, as a nation, has often striven to differentiate itself from Spain is to assert its more outward-looking, international character.

I see Barcelona as an appropriate site to consider the increasingly intertwined local and transnational, including, in this case, probing links and crossings with Latin America through Peri Rossi and Company, born in Montevideo and Buenos Aires respectively. The publishing scene in Barcelona has long been important for Latin Americans, including exiled writers. In *Foreigners in the Homeland* (2000), Mario Santana addresses the very issue of Latin American writers and the creation/reception of their works in Spain, highlighting the fact that while many writers straddle literary categories based on nation and/or region, many national literatures only include the works of citizens born in the country in question (19). He asserts that 'literary geography [...] while conditioned by political and linguistic borders, is not coextensive with them' (12–13). Accordingly, he calls for critics to pay attention to the reception and circulation of texts (12).

To understand belonging (and non-belonging) in Barcelona, I focus on texts and ideas that circulate there. In *La passió*, Charles B. (based on French regionalist, Jean Charles-Brun), a writer with whom Vivien corresponds, comments on the character of cities being defined more by the circulation of texts and ideas in the city than by a concrete place. He contrasts 'París real' [real Paris] with 'aquella germinació d'idees i papers escrits que constituïa la cultura i que trobava a la capital el seu nucli magnètic' (100) [that germination of ideas and texts that constituted culture and that found its magnetic nucleus in the capital]. His sense of belonging stems from written texts where he can trace and write his own genealogy, rather than from the physical space of the city. Similarly, my readings and approach to literary historiography through these texts sees place as often discursively created.

In a similar vein to this slippage between real and textual or imagined place, the texts in this book combine literal movement and a metaphorical sense of being out of place that prompts writers to take refuge in writing. In *La passió*, the transnational space holds possibility and autonomy for Vivien and the Baroness Hélène (a woman of Jewish heritage and member of the Rothschild family) with whom she has an affair. The state of exile is considered a privilege akin to that of writing: 'La pertinença d'Hélène a la raça alhora privilegiada i execrada, cosmopolita i sense pàtria, havia suscitat en Pauline la visió d'un paral·lelisme amb la sort comuna dels poetes: l'exili' (78) [Hélène's place amongst that race that is simultaneously revered and deplored, cosmopolitan and without homeland, had aroused in Pauline the sense of a parallel with the common fate of poets: exile]. The novel is situated outside of Catalonia, but there are a number of hints that Marçal is also contemplating Catalan identity.

One example of Marçal's reflections on one place also being a reflection on her homeland of Catalonia is her reference to the possibility that distance may clarify one's sense of 'roots'. She explores this idea through the character of Charles, who lives in Paris. Charles notes that he feels more Parisian when he is in Montpellier and more Occitan when in Paris. When visiting Montpellier, where he is from, 's'arrapava a les arrels, però alhora sentia esfondrar-se aquell sentiment d'identitat que quan era lluny era tan nítid i inequívoc' (98) [he clung on to his roots, but simultaneously noticed that, when there, his feeling of identity, so clear and unequivocal when he was far away, vanished]. Similarly, Marçal moves away from the Catalan capital in the novel perhaps to better understand her (dis)identifications in Barcelona. In Company's *Querida Nélida*, the protagonists take refuge in the letters they exchange, allowing their imaginations to travel, despite never realising their long-discussed trip. In *Volver antes que ir*, Company longs to synthesise a coherent sense of Argentine national identity, having spent most of her life grappling with a diasporic identity in Barcelona. However, once she actually returns to Buenos Aires she describes feeling like a foreigner there.

In my analysis of *La nave* I consider how the possibility to feel a sense of belonging in exile depends on one's economic and cultural capital. Today it is impossible to invoke Lesbos, long associated with lesbian sexuality (indeed, the very word 'lesbian' refers to the island), without recognising that contemporary images of the island conjure not a paradise steeped in legends of Sappho, but overcrowded camps in which many migrants and refugees live in dire conditions. Cultural and economic capital are also at stake in Peri Rossi's first novel *El libro de mis primos* (1969, henceforth *El libro*) [The Book of my Cousins]. The older cousin Federico, himself a poet, runs away from his aristocratic family home to join the guerrillas. He is both the black sheep of his aristocratic family, and also not wholly trusted by the other guerrillas due to his belief in the political importance of poetry. He feels more at home in literature than in the family house *or* amongst his fellow guerrillas, some of whom see culture as bourgeois and irrelevant to revolutionary change. Place and belonging are complex issues for the characters in the texts, and in the authors' biographies, to which I will now turn.

Queer Biographies: The Transnational Authors

Cano laments that her years in academia have taught her that the prevailing view is that 'lo personal no sólo no se puede teorizar (al menos no "seriamente") sino que la teoría no es, *no puede ser,* personal, si es que quiere ser una "buena teoría" (es decir, una investigación teorética legitimada como tal)' (2015: 24–25) [the personal cannot only not be theorised (at least not "seriously"), but theory is not and cannot be personal if one hopes for it to be considered "good theory" (that is, theoretical investigation that is legitimised as such]. Cano, like many feminist writers, contests the notion of 'objetividad teórica' (32) [theoretical objectivity] which, in its claims to universality, often maintains the status quo, dismissing divergent experiences. Texts such as Anzaldúa's *Borderlands / La Frontera* (1987), with its blend of poetry, theory, autobiography, and history, along with many other feminist, postcolonial, and decolonial works, demonstrate that academic rigour need not be compromised, and can, in fact, be galvanised, through the acknowledgement and analysis of lived experience; indeed, it is an appreciation of a need to be attentive to subjective realities that gave rise to the feminist dictum that 'the personal is political'. Accordingly, I comment on the merging of biography and writing in the writers' lives where necessary, but I do not limit the readings to the biographical. I turn my attention to how the writers move others through their works and, as reader-writers, are moved *by* others. As such, I am attentive to the merging of the affective, the personal, the political, the theoretical, and the literary, if, indeed, these can be separated. In the spirit of paying due attention to the biographical, a few words about the writers' relationships with Barcelona. Just as place is complicated in their texts, so too do the authors have ambivalent relationships to the city.

Marçal grew up in Ivars d'Urgell, in the province of Lleida, hence the rural elements important to her poetry. However, she was actually born in Barcelona in 1952. Her parents decided to go to a hospital there, where there were more advanced facilities, due to a complication with an earlier birth. Although Marçal studied Classics at the Universitat de Barcelona from 1969, was heavily involved in political and cultural movements in the capital, gave birth to her daughter Heura in the city in 1980, and was living there at the time of her death in 1998, she described herself as a 'hoste permanent' in the city 'amb un ull posat en un improbable retorn als orígens rurals' (1995b: 170) [permanent guest [...] with an unlikely return to my rural origins always at the back of my mind]. Ever aware of the lure and allure of metropolitan centres, Marçal initially avoided the big Barcelona-based publishing houses, Edicions 62 and Proa, whose representatives believed that works could only become canonical if published and endorsed by those two main houses (Climent 2013: 15). The critic Laia Climent describes Marçal's rejection of the centralised model in which literary capital was associated with the paternalistic capital city: 'Marçal, situada contra aquesta actitud paternalista, va optar per una via descentralitzada. De Lleida a València sense passar per les plataformes barcelonines, s'hi erigia una literatura exquisida que s'escapolia de tota necessitat de ser venerada per la capital literària' (2013: 15) [Marçal, who was against this paternalistic attitude, opted for a decentralised path. She went from Lleida to Valencia without going through the Barcelona-based platforms. There, she constructed an exquisite body of work that escaped any need to be venerated by the literary capital]. In line with the attitude Climent describes, Marçal published her collected poetry, *Llengua abolida* (1989), with Valencia-based Tres i Quatre (Poesia 314). It has recently been republished with Barcelona-based Edicions 62 (2017) in an expanded volume to include Marçal's posthumously published poetry, a decision with which Marçal herself may have been uneasy. Even more recently (November 2018), the separate poetry collections *La germana, l'estrangera* [Sister, Foreigner], *Bruixa de dol* [Witch of Mourning], *Desglaç* [Thawing] and *Raó del cos* [The Body's Reason] were also (re)published by Edicions 62.

Marçal was a key figure in the Catalan feminist movement in the late Franco years and the transition to democracy. Her work received increasing critical attention after she won the prestigious Carles Riba prize in 1976 for her first collection of poetry, *Cau de llunes* [Den of Moons] (1977). The collection includes the poem 'Divisa' [Motto], which consists of what are arguably the most famous lines penned by the poet. They sum up the tenets of Marçal's activism:

> A l'atzar agraeixo tres dons: haver nascut dona,
> de classe baixa i nació oprimida.
>
> I el tèrbol atzur de ser tres voltes rebel. (2017: 19)
>
> [I am grateful to fate for three gifts: having been born a woman,
> working class and from an oppressed nation.
>
> And the turbid azure of being three times a rebel.]

As the poem suggests, Marçal campaigned for the rights of women, the working class, and the Catalan nation. Accordingly, in 1979, Marçal participated in the foundation of 'Nacionalistes d'Esquerra' [Leftist Nationalists], a socialist movement that aimed to unite a number of leftist groups who fought for Catalan independence. However, cultural militancy increasingly became Marçal's priority and by the 1980s her efforts were firmly concentrated in the literary sphere. From that time until her premature death in 1998, Marçal directed her energies towards her own writing and towards making connections between women writers of the past and present to trace a female literary genealogy. She was predominantly a poet, but it is her sole novel that is my main focus in this book. Her activities with the 'Comitè d'Escriptores' [Women Writers' Committee] of the Catalan PEN Club, founded in 1994, are an example of her efforts in the literary sphere. The three objectives of the group were to ensure that women writers of the past were remembered, to promote writing by women in the present, and to foster networks of Catalan and international women writers (Comitè d'Escriptores Centre Català del Pen Club, n.d.).

Peri Rossi moved from one dictatorial regime to another when she went into exile from Montevideo, where she was born in 1941, to Barcelona in 1972, during the last years of the Franco regime. She became 'naturalised' as a Spanish citizen in 1975, the year of Franco's death. The implication that a resident non-citizen is unnatural in the nation, itself etymologically linked with birth, is telling. Peri Rossi now holds dual Uruguayan and Spanish nationality. *La nave* was written during Spain's transition to democracy and published in 1984. At that time, Uruguay was still under military dictatorship, which did not end until the following year. Peri Rossi still felt herself to be living temporarily in Barcelona, unsure whether she would return to Uruguay if the military dictatorship ended. Like Marçal, who felt like a permanent guest in the city, Peri Rossi says that one of the reasons why she remained in Barcelona after the military dictatorship was over in Uruguay was that she felt uncomfortable in the city and that the discomfort helped her to write (Pérez-Sánchez 2007: 118). However, she was grateful for recognition from the Catalan literary establishment with the 'Ciudad de Barcelona' prize that she was awarded in 1992 for her collection of poetry *Babel bárbara* (1990), twenty years after her arrival in Barcelona: 'Me sentí como si me hubieran nombrada [*sic*] hija adoptiva o algo así, y cuando uno ha perdido la madre (la patria) aspira a ser bien querida por su madrastra' (2005a: 19) [I felt as if they had made me an adoptive daughter or something, and when one has lost one's mother (one's homeland), one aspires to be well-loved by one's stepmother]. It is revealing that Peri Rossi expresses her belonging with a kinship term often associated with a certain awkwardness or dislike, one that is based not on blood but on circumstance — Barcelona is her stepmother.

Company, for her part, moved to Barcelona from the Southern Cone in 1973 not long after Peri Rossi, but is almost two decades younger. She was born in 1963 in Buenos Aires to parents of Catalan descent. She wrote the works studied in this book between 1981 and 2014. *Querida Nélida*, while published in 1988, was written in 1981 (as noted on the inside front cover of the original edition), only two years after the legalisation of homosexuality in Spain in 1979.[6] The works thus span the early years of the legalisation of homosexuality and the legalisation of gay marriage in Spain in 2005. In the texts, Company looks at queer affinities within and beyond mainstream institutions. She has always striven to elude categorisation, which she sees as an ally to a commercialised publishing scene. She has been successful in avoiding, or at least complicating, literary categories based on regional or national identities. Her works can be found in bookstores under Catalan writing, Spanish writing, Latin American writing, with the same work appearing also under different genre sections. Unlike Peri Rossi and Marçal, Company does not overtly politicise her work. While Marçal and Peri Rossi's works are now canonical, Company is lesser known in academic spheres. However, her work was prominently on display in Cómplices, Barcelona's main LGBTQI+ bookshop, whenever I visited between 2013 and 2016.

Intimately connected to place, especially in the Catalan context, is language. This study draws connections between primary texts in Spanish and Catalan written in and between the Southern Cone of Latin America and in Catalonia. It also analyses intertexts in these languages, as well as in English, French, and Ancient Greek. What I bring to the foreground, then, are the imagined and literal journeys between places and how the idea of place is mobilised through the texts. The transnational webs of intertextuality in the works reflect the fact that national canons do not account for the reality of reading habits and connections made by readers. In a piece on contemporary Catalan lesbian literature in which she calls for an embrace of hybrid culture, Meri Torras writes about the multilingual interactions encountered by readers and writers between texts from different national traditions written in languages other than the reader/writer's native tongue(s) (2007: 135). Her perspective on the international texts within so-called national literatures resonates with that of Santana who argues that national literatures are 'both bound and open' (2000: 19). He argues that the concept of national literature should not be avoided altogether, but, as mentioned above, that it should not be defined exclusively in terms of works written by native-born citizens and that other influences, including texts that circulate in a place in translation, should be considered as part of the national literary scene (2000: 19).

The three authors in this study engage differently with the plurilingual situation in Catalonia. Marçal published only in Catalan, reflecting her political engagement in leftist movements for Catalan independence, Peri Rossi only in Spanish, and Company in both, often self-translating her works between the two. Translation was also important to Marçal, who includes in *La passió* lines of poetry from Sappho and Vivien translated into Catalan, and who translated into Catalan the works of authors such as Sidonie-Gabrielle Colette, Marguerite Yourcenar, Leonor Fini, Anna Akhmatova, and Marina Tsvetaeva. Peri Rossi is also a translator; she has translated a number of the Brazilian writer Clarice Lispector's works into Spanish. Marçal's novel thematises language and identity through Vivien, a transnational subject. She was born Pauline Mary Tarn in England but moved to *fin-de-siècle* Paris upon inheriting her father's fortune. There, she recreated herself as Vivien and adopted French as the language of expression in her works. Vivien also translated Sappho into French (1902). The centrality of language to Vivien's literary re-birth was perhaps one reason why Marçal was drawn to her, given the primacy of the Catalan language in conceptions of Catalan identity. It is evident, then, that transnational exchange, often via translation, is vital to the genealogies traced in these texts that often look beyond the author's direct milieu in order to reflect back on it. Similarly, translation has also been important to the impact of 'queer theory' beyond Anglophone contexts.

A Queer Genesis: Where Did This Begin?

When I first approached this project, my main aim was to foreground literary representations of erotic desire between women, often underrepresented in studies of queer sexualities, which have tended to privilege male homosexuality. In the Latinx, Latin American, Spanish, and Catalan contexts, I build on the research of critics such as Lourdes Torres and Inmaculada Pertusa (2003), Gema Pérez-Sánchez (2007), Jacky Collins and Nancy Vosburg (2011), and Rodríguez (2014), who have published important research into lesbian/queer Hispanic and Latina sexualities that does not sideline women. Rodríguez comments on the domination of queer studies by a focus on gay men. She asks: 'Is scholarship on bisexual women, lesbians, dykes, and gender-queer female-bodied subjects a less valued academic commodity because it is considered somehow less transgressive, less sexy, less public, or less relevant?' (2014: 15). In the light of the exclusions described by Rodríguez, some critics such as Terry Castle oppose using the term 'queer', which she describes as a 'pseudo-umbrella term' (1993: 12) that is not, in fact, sufficiently inclusive of women. She argues that the 'queer [...] makes it easy to enfold female homosexuality back "into" male homosexuality and disembody the lesbian once again' (12). To avoid the subordination of female desire to male desire she prefers to stick to 'lesbian' when talking about women desiring women. Collins and Vosburg do the same in *Lesbian Realities/Lesbian Fictions in Contemporary Spain* (2011).

While I agree that women are often invisibilised under the rubric of the queer, my approach differs from that of Castle, Vosburg, and Collins. I seek to visibilise and make a place for desire between women *within* the queer, with greater attention to the genealogy of queer theory, which emerged from and continues to engage with feminist and lesbian theory. In foregrounding women under the rubric of the queer, my work engages with, but temporally goes beyond, Pérez-Sánchez's *Queer Transitions in Contemporary Spanish Culture: From Franco to La Movida* (2007). I am seduced, as are many critics, by the liberational possibilities of a queer move beyond fixed notions of identity and belonging, which might foster affinities beyond the highly naturalised bonds and binds of family and nation, but I have also become acutely aware of the persistence and spectral power of the family and nation.

As this project progressed and through close reading of the three authors' works, I have shifted from the narrower initial focus on sex and sexuality amongst women to a broader understanding of desire that encompasses issues of queer textuality, representation, relationality, and literary transmission, not exclusively amongst women. Indeed, a number of the works that I study in this book complicate or 'queer' the male/female binary. The shift in my understanding of desire is part and parcel of a queer research process given that the queer is linked both to homosexuality and, more broadly, to anything and anyone different, strange, other, and non-normative. Indeed, there is an important body of work addressing the broadening of the notion of the queer beyond sexuality, including Janet Halley and Andrew Parker's compelling edited collection *After Sex? On Writing Since Queer Theory* (2011). The collection contains essays from a range of queer theorists; some embrace the wider reach of the queer, while others argue that it has become so broad as to become meaningless. This debate is not new; the wide applicability of queer theory has been contested since its conception. One example of critics' twists and turns in grappling with the term is the case of Teresa De Lauretis, the first critic to use the phrase 'queer theory' in a journal article 'Queer Theory: Lesbian and Gay Sexualities' (1991). A scant three years later she argues in the same journal that it has become 'a conceptually vacuous creature of the publishing industry' (1994: 297). However, I maintain that the powerful activist history of queer theory and praxis, and its potential to destabilise commonplace assumptions about inheritance, community, and belonging, remain useful for thinking about transnational literary influence and interplay, and how texts might rewrite social relations.

The book is structured by author. In Chapter One I turn to Marçal and her sole novel, *La passió*. In the novel, Marçal situates herself in a fragmented genealogy from the Ancient Greek lyric poet Sappho through to the English-born writer Vivien in *fin-de-siècle* Paris through to the Catalan scriptwriter Sara T., who carries out research in archives, libraries, and the streets of Paris in order to write a script for a film about Vivien. Marçal mobilises Lesbos and figures who specifically locate themselves in relation to Sappho and who write of erotic relationships between women. Marçal therefore traces a transnational genealogy of lesbian writing, merging literary and erotic desire. I bring *La passió* into dialogue with Carolyn Dinshaw's 'touch across time' (2001) and Freeman's 'erotohistoriography' (2005), both of which allude to a collapse of conventional chronology through affective connections with the past. I also draw on Elizabeth Meese's concept of 'lesbian : writing' (1992) that conjures forth a physical, embodied lesbian writer behind the text.

Chapter Two is on Peri Rossi, who has published a number of poetry collections and short stories about erotic desire between women. However, her novels tend to have male protagonists, as is the case with the novels that I focus on in Chapter Two: *La nave*, published in 1984 once Peri Rossi was in exile in Barcelona, and *El libro*, published in 1969 in Montevideo in a context of increasing authoritarianism in Latin America and heightened generational and political tensions in Europe and Latin America. In *La nave*, the protagonist, Equis, considered by critics to be both a (generic) man and a character with no fixed gender, is the principal reader/writer/ observer of the places through which he travels, the people that he meets, and, most importantly, the eleventh-century Tapestry of Creation, or Girona Tapestry, which is one of this highly intertextual novel's main intertexts. My analysis focusses on the novel's unravelling of the tapestry. I read Peri Rossi's textual pulling apart of the tapestry as a challenge to what Ahmed describes as the 'disciplinary technique' of happiness (2010: 8), which she associates with the normative timelines of conventional heterosexual relationships.

Some critics ascribe Peri Rossi's challenge to authority and exploration of exile to her physical exile and time in Barcelona. To challenge such a reading, I shift beyond the main temporal and geographical frame of the thesis to analyse her first novel, published before Peri Rossi had left Uruguay. *El libro* depicts the queering of patrilineal political inheritance through the relationship between two rebellious cousins in an aristocratic family, seemingly in Montevideo, though space in this novel, as in *La nave*, is blurred. In *El libro*, Federico, the elder of the two main cousins in the novel, flees his family to join a guerrilla group. He is a key reader-writer in the text, along with his young cousin Oliverio, who inherits Federico's papers and is charged with continuing his cousin's writing. Through fragmentation, allegory, and ambiguity, the novel contests authoritarian discourse without itself becoming a site of hegemonic meaning. In inviting the reader's collaboration, it ensures authorial legacy.

Chapter Three looks at the works of Company. In *Querida Nélida*, as in Riera's aforementioned emblematic works of lesbian epistolary fiction, 'Te deix' and 'Jo pos per testimoni les gavines', letters constitute the form of transmission of the memory of a broken, yet enduring, relationship. Unlike in Riera's texts (in which it is clear that the women have had a sexual relationship), the friendship between the two women, Nélida and Celia, is ambiguous. While it has erotic undertones, the lesbian is not explicitly invoked. Company wrote the novel, which is written in Spanish, in 1981, before the heyday of the queer and of the questioning of identity. The lack of clarity about the nature of the women's relationship, which seems to shift between friendship, love, and desire, is a manifestation of Rich's 'lesbian continuum' (1980: 648). The ambiguity of the relationship reflects how in 1980s Barcelona, as in other periods, friendship, for women, both was and was not a closet. The women, as the senders and recipients of the letters in Company's epistolary text, are representatives and/or surrogates of readers and writers. I analyse the temporal implications of obsession and melancholia in *Querida Nélida* via Carla Freccero's notion of 'queer spectrality' ([2007] 2015), as a mode of openness to 'ghostly returns' (197). I read the novel's emphasis on 'potentiality' in the light of Muñoz's 'utopian queer futurity' (2009).

Company published *Melalcor* in Spanish and Catalan in the same year; I analyse the Catalan text in this book. The novel troubles a binary vision of gender through its genderqueer characters. Their unconventional relationships challenge the sanctity of monogamy, marriage, the family, compulsory procreation, and ideas of love based on notions of possession. My analysis of *Melalcor* draws on Rodríguez's conceptualisation of queer affinities as existing in non-linear temporalities, such as ephemerality and simultaneity.

Textual transmission and inheritance are central to Company's *Volver antes que ir*, a lengthy narrative poem that she composed after discovering a childhood diary written by her late mother. Company says she wrote in 'argentino', her so-called mother tongue, which reflects her concern with her biological and national 'roots' in the poem. I look at Company's attempt to regain the sense of belonging of her childhood in Argentina and how she represents her frustrated desire through poetry and its 'interrupted' performance. In Company's semi-autobiographical *Por mis muertos* (2014) [For My Dead], written in Spanish, we read of an alternative line of inheritance via the 'bad' influence of aunts, biological and symbolic, in two short stories, 'La carta perdida de Andrea Mayo' [Andrea Mayo's Lost Letter] and 'Dos cuentos de amor' [Two Love Stories]. In the stories Company returns to lesbian desire, with a focus on inheritance and transmission within and beyond the family.

Notes to the Introduction

1. Translations are mine, unless otherwise stated.
2. Interestingly, these words were originally written by Cano in a letter in English, probably rendered differently from my translation into English here. Cano herself notes the logic of rewriting queerness in this shifting between languages (2015: 21).
3. The FAGC has operated with this name from 1975, but it existed clandestinely with other names from 1970, under Franco. It was first called the 'Agrupación Homófila para la Igualdad Sexual' (AGHOIS) [Homophile Group for Sexual Equality], which was the first gay and lesbian rights organisation in Spain, formed in response to the 1970 'Ley sobre peligrosidad y rehabilitación social' [Law of Dangerousness and Social Rehabilitation], which was created to control 'elementos antisociales' [antisocial elements] and to justify the repression of LBGTQ+ people. AGHOIS later became known as the 'Movimiento Español de Liberación Homosexual' (MELH) [Spanish Movement for Homosexual Liberation] and included groups in Madrid and Bilbao. After Franco's death, it took its current name, FAGC, paralleling international Gay Liberation Fronts.
4. In 1991, the group Gais Positius, a network for people who were HIV positive, was formed, the first mutual support group of its kind in Spain. In 1993, Barcelona hosted the International Lesbian and Gay Organisation (ILGA) conference. Madrid has since caught up, and perhaps overtaken Barcelona, in its prominence in the Spanish queer scene.
5. The question of tourism in Barcelona is very complex, especially as many residents benefit from the industry. It is somewhat paradoxical that a progressive mayor at once embraces Barcelona's cosmopolitanism, but also seeks to reconfirm 'native' places. I return to the tension between 'nativism' and 'internationalism' on the left in my analysis of Marxism in the 1960s and 1970s in the Southern Cone in Part II of Chapter Two on Peri Rossi's *El libro de mis primos* [*The Book of my Cousins*].
6. Homosexuality had been made illegal under Franco in 1954 through an amendment to the 1933 'Ley de vagos y maleantes' [Law on Vagabonds and Malefactors]. From 1971 it had been considered a mental illness rather than a criminal act in the 'Ley de peligrosidad y rehabilitación social' [Law on Dangerousness and Social Rehabilitation].

CHAPTER 1

Sapphic Literary Genealogies in Maria-Mercè Marçal's *La passió segons Renée Vivien* (1994)

> La literatura nos separó: todo lo que supe de ti
> lo aprendí en los libros
> y a lo que faltaba,
> yo le puse palabras.
> — PERI ROSSI ([1971] 2005a: 34)
>
> [Literature separated us: everything I found out about you
> I learnt in books
> and for the rest
> I thought up the words.]

Many critics of lesbian literary history have focussed on the invisibilisation or silencing of the lesbian subject. Castle outlines this trend in provocative terms: 'The lesbian is never with us, it seems, but always somewhere else: in the shadows, in the margins, hidden from history, out of sight, out of mind, a wanderer in the dusk, a lost soul, a tragic mistake' (1993: 2). In this chapter I argue that in contrast to the critical lamentation of lesbian texts as 'mutilades, censurades, reescrites' (Torras 2007: 141) [mutilated, censored, rewritten], which tends to lead to a fixation with recuperating an idealised past that supposedly came before this 'mutilation', in *La passió* Marçal celebrates fragmentation, which she depicts as oriented towards the present and future. Sara T. is considered an alter-ego for the author herself and also the main diegetic representative of the reader. Her name, which contains the Catalan word for now, 'ara', represents the present of the diegesis (1984–1985). Sara T. is a scriptwriter based in Barcelona who goes to Paris and Lesbos in the mid-1980s to research the figure and work of eponymous English-born poet, Vivien, who reinvented herself as a French writer in *fin-de-siècle* Paris. Sara T. carries out extensive research in Paris in order to write the script for a film about the poet who, in turn, looks back to the Ancient Greek lyric poet Sappho. Therefore, as well as its vital transtemporality, the novel also foregrounds a transnational genealogy. Castle's regretful references to the invisibilised lesbian in culture as 'a wanderer' and 'a lost soul', can be reformulated through the more affirming lens of creative transnational crossings and connections.

Vivien saw herself as an incarnation of Sappho, often referring to herself as 'Sapho 1900' (see title of Lorenz 1977). In the Western world, Sappho is the origin of lesbian literature and identity, with the island of Lesbos being the place of her birth. The continued use of the words 'Sapphic' and 'lesbian', even after the passing of millennia, suggests a contemporary desire to ground identity in history by tracking its genealogy back to the first recorded instance of its existence; this typically involves the notion of an unspoilt origin which is probed by Foucault via Friedrich Nietzsche in the essay 'Nietzsche, Genealogy, History':

> The lofty origin is no more than 'a metaphysical extension which arises from the belief that things are most precious and essential at the moment of birth.' We tend to think that this is the moment of their greatest perfection, when they emerged dazzling from the hands of a creator or in the shadowless light of a first morning. (1984a: 79)

The 'shadowless light' of an idealised origin contrasts with Castle's lesbian 'in the shadows'. Karla Jay, invoking a 'lofty origin', suggests that Vivien considered herself to be 'a Sappho to generations of young women yet unborn, in a kind of *unbroken* line of female succession' (1988: 37, my emphasis). Her insistence on the 'unbroken' signals a vision of female literary inheritance with stable classical foundations. Jay's statement echoes the Oxford English Dictionary definition of genealogy as 'a line of descent traced continuously from an ancestor'; a conceptualisation of genealogy that tends to revere the ancestor. In this chapter I ask what a Sapphic literary genealogy that embraces the shadows of which Castle writes, without seeking to obliterate them with a 'dazzling' light, might look like.

Sara T. visits Paris and Mytilene (the capital of Lesbos) to retrace Vivien's steps and Vivien, in turn, wanted to set up a poetry school on Lesbos in the early twentieth-century with her lover, Natalie Barney, to recreate the group of women that some claim Sappho founded there. As Margaret Reynolds notes, '[f]or Barney, Vivien, and other women, the search for authenticity took them back to Sappho's words and to Sappho's home. "Let us go to Mytilene," wrote Vivien, and "re-sing to an intoxicated earth / The hymn of Lesbos"' (2000: 293). The women travel across time and space through texts, but the physical place where the texts were created also holds great allure. In the Fons Maria-Mercè Marçal (FMMM) at the Biblioteca Nacional de Catalunya, which contains Marçal's notes and previous manuscripts of the novel from her ten year process of research and writing, I discovered that she had considered naming Sara T. Paulina or Paula T., emphasising the genealogy she traces with Pauline Mary Tarn (FMMM: box 8/5, folder 4, sheet 25). Marçal emphasises the need for a 'lenta confecció de la genealogia de la cultura femenina, d'una xarxa intel·lectual que situï cada nova escriptura d'una dona en *terra adobada*, amb sentit i referència respecte a l'obra de que l'ha precedida' (Marçal cited in Julià 2000: 366, my emphasis) [the slow compilation of a genealogy of cultural creations by women, of an intellectual network that situates each new work by a woman on *fertile ground*, with reference to and meaning in relation to the work that came before it] (my emphasis). Her mention of 'terra adobada' highlights the appeal of stable foundations.

Despite these bold statements that Marçal made when writing *about* literature, I will contend that through her focus in *La passió* on the fragmentary and discontinuous, she emphasises the impossibility of a continuous or unbroken line of succession. I will consider the Marçalian Sapphic genealogy in the light of Foucault's idea of genealogy as expressive of the tension between continuity and brokenness; he asserts that genealogy 'relentlessly disrupt[s] its pretended continuity' (1984a: 88). A key element in my exploration of Sapphic genealogy is the particularly fragmentary state of what remains of Sappho's work which, combined with the uncertainty about the biographical details of her life, makes the 'origin' of lesbian identity, literary and otherwise, partial and haunted by lacunae and the unknown. Sapphic fragmentation can be linked with the concept of 'l'esbós' in *La passió*. Marçal draws on the pun in the Catalan word for sketch, 'l'esbós', a play on Lesbos, to associate the originary topographical site of lesbian literature with the notion of the sketch — a finished but self-consciously incomplete work. The importance of the sketch to the novel becomes even clearer from Marçal's notes in the FMMM on possible titles for the novel. Jottings on the front cover of one of the full drafts of the novel suggest that she considered titles for the novel that included the wordplay on Lesbos and sketch, such as simply 'L'Esbós' and 'L'esbós de la memòria' (FMMM: box 11, item 2).

The novel is interspersed with fragments from Vivien's verses and some lines by Sappho. Readers also encounter multiple perspectives on Vivien's life through documents such as letters and diaries by a proliferation of historical and fictional characters who knew Vivien or were interested in her life or work. We are given the impression that the documents that make up the novel are texts that Sara T. comes across during research that she is carrying out following a rupture with her girlfriend. Sara T.'s truncated name, her amorous break-up — the broken heart — and the broken or fragmented texts she comes across, suggest the inevitability of break-ups, breakages, and a broken genealogy.

Through her fragmentary text Marçal highlights the importance of readers of today and tomorrow, whose imaginations are critical to the kaleidoscopic — from the Greek *kalos* 'beautiful' and *eidos* 'form' — process of twisting and rearranging the fragments of their predecessors in the formation of a Sapphic genealogy that anticipates the future. Their relationship to their predecessors is reminiscent of Meese's conception of 'lesbian : writing' described in her book *(Sem)erotics. Theorizing Lesbian : Writing* (1992), published a couple of years before *La passió*. Meese connects 'lesbian : writing' to 'queering' in the sense of 'twisting' (the etymology of the word 'queer' can be traced back to the Latin *torquere*, 'to twist', as mentioned in the introduction):

> Torque: the twisting and turning in the driving tension of my passion for you. Lesbian : vision is a torque differential machine, relating me to you. Because I am always approaching you/we who have no definition, the absence of definition consigns us to more writing, no endings, more talking, mountains without tops, threatening the de/nominative project of 'the known'. (1992: 94)

If 'lesbian' is taken to be an adjective and 'writing' a noun, the colon in 'lesbian : writing' symbolises the gaps in the text in which the reader may imagine the inevitably absent erotic desire between women that cannot be represented fully by words, but triggers the writing of more and more texts. The colon also prompts us to read 'lesbian' as a noun, and 'writing' as a gerund, signalling the reader's craving for a lesbian author behind the text. The similarly polysemous notion of 'lesbian : vision' — the lesbian could be the subject and/or object of the gaze in this formulation — and the 'kaleidoscopic' text are key here. Throughout the chapter I will make references to the novel's engagement with the visual, particularly through Sara T.'s screenplay — 'el text en absència que ordena tota la novel·la' (Julià 2013: 181) [the absent text that structures the entire novel] — and the idea of the sketch.

I begin by looking at how the reader-writer's desire to identify with the past may reveal a visceral longing for continuity with her predecessors both to overcome an apparently invisible or silenced lesbian history and to understand and consolidate her own existence in the present. I explore how in the desire to 'touch across time' (Dinshaw 2001: 203) to form a queer history, readers and writers in the Marçalian genealogy make *partial* connections with their literary predecessors, despite their yearning for *complete* identification. I then consider how the tension between continuity/wholeness and discontinuity/fragmentation is inherent to Sapphic writing through analysing critical responses to the extant fragments of Sappho's poetry. I go on to investigate how Marçal grappled with a sense of fragmentation in representation and examine how, in *La passió*, fragmentation or apparent brokenness is a source of great potential in her perception of 'lesbian : writing'. I analyse Marçal's approach to translation before contemplating what the collaborative reader-writer relationship that takes place in translation, rewriting, and writing means for writers' legacies in a Sapphic literary genealogy.

Desiring Identifications with the Past

> Some days I have little interest in the abstract 'Lesbian.'
> I want mine with skin [...].
> — MEESE (1992: 130)

At a forum on her book *Getting Medieval* (1999), Dinshaw relayed a comment by one of her students who noted that many people experience their first 'queer' encounter textually rather than sexually:

> As is true for many queers [...] my queer sexuality was first articulated not through a relationship with another body but rather through texts [...] I consumed such texts urgently . . . I was looking for a way to be queer, for a way to fashion my own identity [...] Queer history is my queer present. (Richard Kim cited in Dinshaw 2001: 202–03)

Similarly, we observe Sara T.'s urgent consumption of written accounts of Vivien's life as well as her work: '¿On cercar-te, si no en els mots, els teus, els dels altres, els meus mateixos, llançats, com una canilla mal ensinistrada, a la caça i captura d'un fantasma?' (91) [Where can I find you, if not in words — yours, those of others, my own — released, like an untamed pack of dogs, to hunt down a ghost?]. Indeed, texts are one way that readers and writers can connect with their 'spectral' predecessors in order to shape and understand their own existence in the present. In *The Apparitional Lesbian* (1993), published a year before *La passió*, Castle considers the 'ghosting' of lesbians in history. She views her essays as 'a kind of invocation: an attempt to call up [...] the much-ghosted yet nonetheless vital lesbian subject' (8). Castle describes as active search for these ghosts. In contrast, the language used by Sara T. highlights the ambivalence in her reaction to the ghostly figure of the writer from the past. The simile in which Sara T. likens her words and those of others to an untamed pack of dogs reveals the lack of control she has over them. She thus hints at the possibility of writers of the present also being h(a)unted against their will, or possessed by something or someone beyond their conscious control.

Sara T.'s 'ghost-hunting' thus tempers a pure emphasis on the active subject-agent in the quest for a literary past that is also implied by Kim's reference to 'fashion[ing]' his own identity. It is in this vein that Nietzsche critiques the over-emphasis on the volitional first-person subject in considerations of identity:

> a thought comes when 'it' wishes, and not when 'I' wish, so it is a falsification of the facts of the case to say that the subject 'I' is the condition of the predicate 'think.' *It* thinks; but that this 'it' is precisely the famous old 'ego' is, to put it mildly, only a supposition. (1989 [1886]: 24)

Some critics see Vivien as having been compelled to write by spirits, such as that of Violet Shilitto, Vivien's childhood friend who died in her twenties. Vivien did not go to visit her when she was on her death-bed as she was reportedly absorbed in her relationship with Barney. Her guilt at abandoning her childhood friend in her last hour seems to have tormented her throughout her life, leading her to scatter violets, as tokens of Shilitto, throughout her poetry. In the foreword to Teresa Campi's *Sul ritmo saffico: La vita e le opere di Renée Vivien* (1983) [On Sapphic Rhythm: The Life and Works of Renée Vivien], which introduced Vivien to Italian readers, Jean-Paul Goujon, a biographer of Vivien, described her as 'una autrice, la cui opera è un caleidoscopo dei suoi fantasmi personali' (12) [an author whose oeuvre is a kaleidoscope of her personal ghosts]. Again, the reference to ghosts conjures up the image of a sort of presence through absence that may be unwanted. However, it is also these 'ghosts' or visions that inspire Vivien's 'kaleidoscopic' work, an adjective which gives the impression of shifting, mesmerising rearrangements of beautiful fragments, including those of Sappho. Kaleido*scopic*, with '-scopic' from the Greek 'skopein', 'look at', also emphasises the importance of visual images for Vivien. Vivien may trigger the creation of the 'beautiful forms' through her act of writing — akin to a 'twisting', a 'queering' of the kaleidoscope — but the precise composition of the fragments is beyond her full control, both within her own work, and within the imaginaries of her readers.

In 'Sappho Enchants the Sirens' (1904) Vivien describes the sensation of feeling entangled in the seductive past. She refers to a sense of captivation beyond deliberative desire; the 'silvery nets' (cited in Reynolds 2000: 300) of the past are appealing and the writer may seek them, but they can also entrap her: 'The Past, more alive than the Present, and more resonant, will catch you in its silvery nets. You will be held captive by dreams and by long-vanquished harmonies' (ibid.). The notion of a living past hints at an 'affective connection — a touch across time' (Dinshaw 2001: 203) and 'the intentional collapse of conventional historical time' (ibid.), which are vital to Dinshaw's vision of queer history and community. Dinshaw sees the affective connection as 'an enabling concept with which readers could work in order to respond to their own situations — their places in space and time — and their needs and desires for a past' (ibid.). In the general plan for the novel that Marçal sent to the Institució de les Lletres Catalanes to request funding, she writes that the objective of the novel is not 'la recreació d'un ambient, que malgrat tot hi ha d'ésser com a teló de fons, una evocació del passat en tant que passat, que en tot cas ha d'ésser prèvia, sinó més aviat, un diàleg entre el present i el passat' (FMMM: box 9/8, folder 1, sheet 2) [the recreation of a milieu, which, in any case, has to be there as a backdrop, an evocation of the past as past, which has to exist anyway, rather it is a dialogue between present and past]. Therefore, Marçal's objective is not simply to recreate the lives and recuperate the works of writers who might have been side-lined or overlooked, but to make connections between the past, present, and future. Marçal's tactile reference to the backdrop of *fin-de-siècle* Paris as a 'teló de fons' [a backdrop, but, literally, a 'curtain in the background'] echoes Vivien's 'silvery nets', reinforcing the sense of 'touching' the past.

Similarly, Freeman, who writes about queer 'chronopolitics' as 'erotohistoriography: a politics of unpredictable, deeply embodied pleasures that counters the logic of development' (2005: 59) argues that 'social change itself enables, and perhaps even requires, that incommensurate temporalities — often most available to us via their corresponding aesthetic forms — rub up against one another, compete, overlap, crossreference' (2011: 31). The rubbing of words marks the works of Marçal, Vivien, and Sappho in *La passió*. Peri Rossi accentuates that Sappho seems ever-*present* for many contemporary poets: 'Safo es esa poeta que cuando no sabemos que es Safo creemos que es una poeta contemporánea. Y cuando sabemos que es Safo sentimos que somos contemporáneas de ella' (2007b: 15) [Sappho is that poet whose work we assume is written by a contemporary poet, when we don't know it is hers. And when we know it is hers, we feel like we are her contemporaries]. In this way, Sappho is repeatedly made 'contemporary'. Sappho is 'touched' by readers across time, and Marçal, via Sara T., reaches out to touch Vivien who in turn touches and is touched by Sappho.

The rubbing together of texts connects with the notion of literary affinity rather than a lineal sense of literary inheritance or influence. 'Affinity' literally means 'bordering on' from the Latin *ad*- meaning 'to' and *finis* meaning 'border'. The writers' words and texts border on and rub with the texts and words of what would conventionally be understood as their predecessors and successors. Beyond affinity, the rubbing together of texts evokes an erotic connection or identification. For flores, 'No hay escritura sin intercambio libidinal, una seducción por el acto de la palabra, un erotismo que se despliega en la propia práctica de un pensar escritural en el que nos habilitamos a comportarnos *como lo que todavía no somos*' (2013: 25, my emphasis) [there is not writing but libidinal exchange, an act of seduction through words, an eroticism that unfolds through the very practice of thinking through writing in which we enable ourselves to behave *as that which we have not yet become*] (my emphasis). Like Freeman's reference to texts facilitating social change, flores sees texts as making us behave more in tune with our imagined or desired futures. Elspeth Probyn also describes encounters between texts and how they prompt the creation of a communal, 'outside' space: '[they] commingle, their surfaces rubbing each other as they produce a momentary but richly interwoven outside' (2015: 153). For these writers, then, a libidinous experience of literature — described in terms of rubbing, touching, commingling, and seduction — permits them to imagine new ways of being, of relating both to other texts and to their own contexts outside the texts.

Castle signals a more affective than deliberative connection in her reference to Judith Roof's thoughts in *A Lure of Knowledge* on trusting one's instincts in making what Roof describes as lesbian identifications with a text. Roof writes:

> Even if I don't know precisely what lesbian is, I look for the lesbian in the text [...] probably because reading, even academic reading, is stimulated, at least for me, by a libidinous urge connected both to a sexual practice and to the shape of my own desire. (1991: 120)

A 'libidinous urge' is evident in Sara T.'s desire for Vivien. There is a tension in *La passió* between familiar family tropes and a desire to get beyond them. Sara T. seeks to identify with the past to overcome what Marçal has referred to as a feeling of 'orfenesa en què ens movem les dones que escrivim' (1985 cited in Llorca Antolín 2004: 223) [orphanhood in which we, as women who write, live]. Here, orphanhood refers to a perceived lack of female literary foremothers, to the apparent absence of a matrilineal genealogy. However, in the novel Marçal appears to probe the insistence of the mother-daughter relationship that endures spectrally, but is insufficient; rather than an inherited tradition, Sara T. seeks to overcome the isolation of literary 'orphanhood' through searching for a figure in the past with whom she feels affinity, rather than kinship. She is initially drawn to Vivien as she identifies with the feelings Vivien seems to express in her works — 'sé que en un primer moment em va atrapar per la identificació' (380) [I know that at first I was hooked because I identified with her]. The *feeling* of affinity and the *touching* across time are important as they suggest the interplay of sentiment and contact, of that which is psychologically or emotionally touching and physical touch. Lluïsa Julià, who in 2017 published the first biography of Marçal, describes Marçal's identification with Vivien in similar terms. Vivien is 'una poeta amb qui acabarà per identificar-se més que amb molta gent de la seva estricta contemporaneïtat' (2017: 332) [a poet with whom Marçal ended up identifying far more than she did with many of her direct contemporaries]. Just as Peri Rossi comments on Sappho's 'contemporaneity', Marçal creates a sense of contemporaneity with Vivien and Sappho through these literary 'touches across time'. In this way, these literary foremothers are spectres; they live out of sync with conventional notions of time in which past, present, and future are distinct.

However, once the initial elation of discovering Vivien's work has subsided, Sara T. wants more than words; she longs for a person in flesh and blood, for words to be corporeal. The desire for the writer's body recalls Meese's conception of 'lesbian : writing', which points to a physical absence: 'reading and writing are not enough [...] after the page has been signed, with just me and these words [...] I recall how the ecstasy of the letter — once the continual acts of re-memorization and reinfusion wane — eventually fades' (1992: 20–21). Sara T. confirms that her obsessive 'hunt' for Vivien resembles a lover's chase of a fading relationship: 'La Renée que jo m'havia forjat a imatge i semblança meva no podia desaparèixer sense deixar rastre... i vaig començar a perseguir-la, com una veritable enamorada' (382) [The Renée that I had forged in my image could not disappear without a trace... and I started pursuing her like someone truly in love]. The literary predecessor as lover, with the emphasis on affinity and passion rather than familiar tropes, overcomes views of sisterly or maternal relationships that may sometimes be utopian but that also tend to de-eroticise relationships between women.[1] Sara T. notes the disorientation she feels as she carries out her research into Vivien, also comparing her sense of a lost connection to a literary predecessor with the realisation of waning love:

> Cada cop em sento més perduda. ¿És encara, en realitat, un interès meu, en present, vull dir? ¿O simplement persisteixo en una via morta, per una absurda fidelitat a un interès pretèrit que no va saber treure cap a res? Allò que, de vegades, passa amb els amors: que ja no saps si van enlloc, però t'aferres al saber cert: d'on vénen, l'origen. (52)

> [I feel more and more lost. Is this really still a present interest of mine? Or am I simply continuing down a dead end due to an absurd loyalty to a past interest that led me nowhere? It is the same as what sometimes happens with love affairs: you no longer know if they are going anywhere, but you cling on to that certain knowledge of where they came from, their origin.]

The quotation suggests that when one cannot find points of reference in the present, or if the present is overwhelming, it can be tempting to cling to something in the past that seems certain; this is the structure of melancholy, and, indeed, one of the great Catalan motifs and stereotypes, *l'enyorança*.

We learn that Sara T.'s obsession with Vivien is, in fact, born of the difficulties that she is encountering in accepting a recent break-up: '(Entre parèntesis et confessaré que aquest amor per una morta m'ha servit de contrapès per a l'altre amor, més perillós per a mi, potencialment molt més obsessiu.)' (382) [(as an aside, I will confess that this love for a dead woman has been a counterbalance for a love that is more dangerous for me, and potentially much more obsessive)]. It is telling that the other love is bracketed and set apart; Sara T. tries to displace it from her life. Unable to process the loss that her break-up signifies, she projects her desperation onto the figure of Vivien. She seeks consolation in the past in which she looks for a *familiar* figure in order to suture her heartbreak in the present: 'qui és, però, ella, en realitat?: només un fantasma que em permet, per uns moments, de creure que hi ha un camí, en algun lloc, al marge de tu' (213) [but who is she really? Just a ghost who allows me, momentarily, to think that there is a path, somewhere, beyond you]. She summons Vivien's presence through her obsession with Vivien's words in order to sideline or bypass the all-consuming sadness of her dwindling relationship.

Meese explores the turn to a textual body to deal with the absence of a physical body: 'The pleasure in/of writing as engagement stands in for other pleasures — a kiss or an embrace; perhaps just a touch [...] So when her lover is no longer or not ever there, the writer returns to writing' (1992: 19). For Sara T., a persistent longing for *familiarity* paradoxically leads to a sense of defamiliarisation, causing her to feel even more lost. Her fractured bond with the past cannot be unbroken, nor can her recent relationship. Her feelings recall the disposition of Vivien, who struggled to deal with her break-up from Barney and longed to return to an idyllic Sapphic past on Mytilene. According to Goujon, for Vivien, literature was 'il luogo [...] dove si congiungono l'amore impossibile e l'impossibile ritorno al passato' (Goujon 1983: 12) [the place where impossible love and an impossible return to the past join together]; she also endeavoured to cope with a broken genealogy, and a broken heart through her poetry, which looked back to that of Sappho.

Sara T.'s trip back to Mytilene, looking for traces of Vivien, prompts reflections on five different types of 'enyor' (which could be roughly translated as 'longing') that merge, for her, into one, as she thinks simultaneously of Vivien and of Arès, a woman with whom she has recently broken up. The different types of longing she feels include 1) a longing based on a clear memory and expectation of a return to a person whom you feel belongs to you. This sort of *enyor* anticipates a physical encounter, 'demana el tacte [...] [...] El relleu suau d'un rostre sota els dits extasiats' (212) [it entreats touch [...] the smoothly sculpted relief of a face beneath ecstatic fingers]; 2) a pained longing 'travessat de fantasmes' (ibid.) [filled with ghosts] for a love that banishes a deep sense of guilt (presumably for not conforming to societal/familial expectations); 3) a melancholic longing based on the denial of being separated from your lover that involves absorbing a fantasy version of the other into yourself: 'Vius perquè vius en mi' (213) [you live on because you live in me]; 4) a more neutral memory of something that was and no longer is; 5) a longing for something that could have been and never was, for a 'paradís perdut que mai no s'ha posseït' (ibid.) [a lost paradise that has never been possessed]. In her list of the types of longing, Sara T. describes the ways in which she experiences the distant and more recent past and her engagement with the figure of Vivien, and the other loves in her life. Through describing the collapse of all of the forms of longing that she lists into one, she illustrates the desire expressed by Meese in the epigraph to this section. Meese refers to a desire for the 'abstract' lesbian, and the 'flesh and blood' lesbian, and the slippage between these desires.

As an aside (we are between brackets, once more), given the semi-autobiographical nature of the novel, it bears noting that in her biography of Marçal, Julià reveals that while Marçal was carrying out research into Vivien's life, she was going through a difficult period in her relationship with Fina Birulés, who corresponds to Arès in the novel (2017: 341). Goujon, a biographer of Vivien with whom Marçal corresponded after the publication of the novel (their correspondence was published in 2014 in *El senyal de la pèrdua* [The Sign of Loss]), said it was clear why Marçal was interested in the figure of Vivien; both of them were deeply passionate about women and about literature. He remarks that Marçal's work and life are engaged in a continuous and deep exchange: 'l'obra ens remet sense parar a la vida, i la vida a l'obra, en un continu moviment de vaivé' (cited in Julià 2017: 341) [her work never ceases to refer us to her life, and her life to her work, in a continuous to and fro]. By acknowledging her need for the past through the figure of Sara T., Marçal does not partake in the short-sighted or self-deceiving reassurances described by Love. Love writes that queer critics tend to 'disavow their need for the past by focussing on the heroic aspect of their work of historical recovery. Like many demanding lovers, queer critics promise to rescue the past when in fact they dream of being rescued themselves' (2007: 33). Love's 'demanding lovers' resonate with Sara T.'s description of herself as chasing Vivien with the intensity of 'someone truly in love'. Marçal's engagement with writers of the past is, as she herself emphasises, a dialogue, not simply a heroic gesture of recuperation and salvation on her part; her novel reveals that the contemporary writer needs the works of writers of the past as much as writers of the past need hers.

For Marçal, then, literary desire, i.e. efforts to create and situate oneself in a genealogy with Sappho and other Sapphic writers, becomes merged with erotic desire, i.e. amorous obsession with writers of the past. In this sense, Marçal's search for literary predecessors in a canon largely made up of male heterosexual writers, a search that she described as a search for symbolic mothers, is less a search for predecessors, and more a search for contemporaries, whose presence is conjured in a quasi-erotic mode in what Dinshaw describes as 'an extended now, a shared contemporaneity' (2007: 110). In an interview, Marçal says of her own research into Vivien that it was 'una mena d'enamorament a distància. M'interessava ella, era com un mirall en el qual jo m'interrogava' (FMMM: box 17/4, item 15) [a sort of long-distance falling in love. She interested me, she was like a mirror in which I interrogated myself]. She also writes in a letter to Goujon that 'en el llibre, hi ha una recerca de mi mateixa' (2014b: 75) [the book contains an investigation into myself]. What she conceives of as a search for symbolic mothers is more akin to a search for symbolic lovers, and, indeed, a search for herself.

I have shown how the lesbian reader-writer's desire for a tangible past can manifest itself as a 'libidinous' longing for a literary predecessor with whom she can totally identify. We have considered how the reader-writer may attempt to consolidate a fractured genealogy, seeking continuity with a coherent, idealised past in order to feel more secure in an uncertain present. We have seen, then, that Sara T.'s engagement with Vivien's texts is followed by a desire for an embodied encounter; she strives to bring Vivien back to life in the present. However, as I will show below, she also battles against her desire to freeze a fixed image of the poet. I will explore the importance of images and the senses in navigating the tension between stillness and movement in the next section.

Motion Pictures: Visualising the Past

> El futuro es la sombra del pasado
> en los rojos rescoldos de un fuego
> venido de lejos,
> no se sabe de dónde.
> — PERI ROSSI ([1994] 2005a: 620)
>
> [the future is the shadow of the past
> in the red embers of a fire
> that has come from some place faraway,
> no one knows where.]

At Vivien's tomb, Sara T. reflects on how she might bring Vivien back to life: '¿Com donar-te cos, encarnar-te, arrelar-te, fer que la meva sang recorri la teva ombra i, sense substituir-la, la converteixi en vida, en saba, en moviment?' (91) [How can I give you a body, make you flesh, root you, make my blood run through your shadow and, without taking its place, convert it into life, sap, movement?]. Sara T.'s reference to using her own body to transform Vivien's shadow into life and movement corresponds to her writing a screenplay about Vivien. While envisioning her film about Vivien, her *projection* of Vivien's life into the future through a motion picture — a moving image that involves motion and emotion, an image that moves both on the screen and that moves the viewer psychologically — Sara. T. strives to feel closer to an embodied Vivien. The reference to both root and sap indicates the tension between evoking the figure of Vivien, but not fixing it.

Marçal's notes in the archive reveal her concern with the interplay of the textual and the visual, with stillness and movement, with how images of places might evoke moving bodies. Her jotted ideas point to the centrality of photos and images to her conception of the novel. She writes: 'Escenes a partir de poemes de Renée' [scenes based on Renée's poems], 'Qui té les fotos, presentació de les fotos: la narradora!!!' [Who has the photos, presentation of the photos: the narrator!!!], 'el guió s'estructurà a partir de fotos' [the structure of the script will be based on photos], 'Una foto s'anima' [a photo comes to life] (FMMM: box 8/5, folder 3, sheet 8); the reference to a photo coming to life signals the nature of film or motion pictures as, quite literally, pictures in motion. Amongst her notes is a draft for the beginning of a screenplay that she had written, suggesting that she thought about including parts of Sara T.'s script in the novel (FMMM: box 8/5, folder 4, sheets 2–6).

As she was working on the novel, Marçal started teaching herself film-making techniques and giving film-making classes in 1986 at the school where she taught (Julià 2017: 343). The draft screenplay in the archive includes technical cinematographic vocabulary and detailed visual descriptions of imagined scenes or places based on location-specific research. For example, the title credit sequence begins with a description of a 'travelling-panoràmica' of Vivien's flat: 'És un pis gran, ampli i de sostre alt, construcció principis de segle. La decoració és d'un artifici peculiar i ombrívol [...]' (FMMM: box 8/5, folder 4, sheet 4) [It is a large apartment, spacious and with high ceilings, built at the beginning of the century.

The décor is strange and shadowy [...]]. It is evident that carrying out research in the city is an attempt to get closer to an embodied sense of the poet: 'El jo-narradora acut a París per trobar "el paisatge", el "cos" de Renée/Pauline' (FMMM: box 9/8, folder 1, sheet 2) [The first-person narrator goes to Paris to find the 'landscape', the 'body' of Renée/Pauline]. In the archive I found a document that reveals Marçal's concern for the senses, a major part of this embodied encounter. At the side of a draft outline of the novel, she wrote 'vista' [sight], 'olfacte' [sense of smell], 'gust' [taste], and 'olor' [smell] (FMMM: box 11, item 2). While she does not mention touch here, it is evident that she wanted the readers' experience not to be purely mental, but corporeal too, as in Laura Marks's later concept of 'haptic cinema'. The sensory experience described by Marks, in which 'memory may be encoded in touch, sounds, perhaps smell, more than in vision' (2000: 129), is an apt description for Marçal's process of researching and writing the novel.

The importance to Marçal of creating a landscape is evident from the abundance of visual material in the archive, such as photos of the streets frequented by people including Vivien, her housekeeper, Barney, and Colette. While the place descriptions in the screenplay mention colours and brightness they also emphasise textures, in line with what Marks has described as the 'multisensory quality of perception' (131). We might consider this evocation of touch through visual media from the past in the spirit of what Tina Campt describes as a 'haptic temporality' (2017). For Campt, photographs are 'deeply affective objects that implicate and leave impressions upon us through multiple forms of contact: visual contact (seeing), physical contact (touching), psychic contact (feeling), and, most counter-intuitively of all, the sonic contact [...] that requires us to listen to as well as view images' (2017: 72). In a sense, then, photos enable a form of communication with the past as seeing, touching, hearing, and feeling them prompts a creative response; the photos speak to us and we/Marçal/Sara T. speak back. As well as the photos of Paris in the archive, we can find Marçal's sketches of different neighbourhoods in Paris, with attention to how they fit together (see fig. 1.1 and fig. 1.2 from FMMM: box 10/4, folder 3). We might consider Marçal's preoccupation with moving beyond the indexical photos to gain a sense of the spatiality of the places through which Vivien and her acquaintances moved as evidence of her desire to inhabit another time, to feel herself into being amongst Vivien and her contemporaries.

Marçal's simultaneous preoccupation with visualisation and awareness of its limitations is also apparent from her initial ideas for the novel's title. As well as the aforementioned titles containing 'l'esbós', Marçal considered a number of titles that referred to Venus of the Blind, drawing on a book of Vivien's poetry of that very name, La Vénus des aveugles (1904). Other titles considered by Marçal included 'Venus de cec' [Venus of the Blindperson], 'Venus al país dels cecs' [Venus in the Land of the Blind], and 'la Venus de l'ull borni' [One-eyed Venus] (FMMM: box 8/5, folder 3, sheet 7). Sigrid Weigel's idea of women's 'double focus' (1985) illuminates these titles. In her chapter titled 'Double Focus', Weigel argues that women should always have a 'sideways look' in which 'at least half their field of vision' must 'concentrate [...] on the so-called "woman problem"' (1985: 71). She describes the development of a more aesthetic focus in cultural creation that, nonetheless, can only be gazed

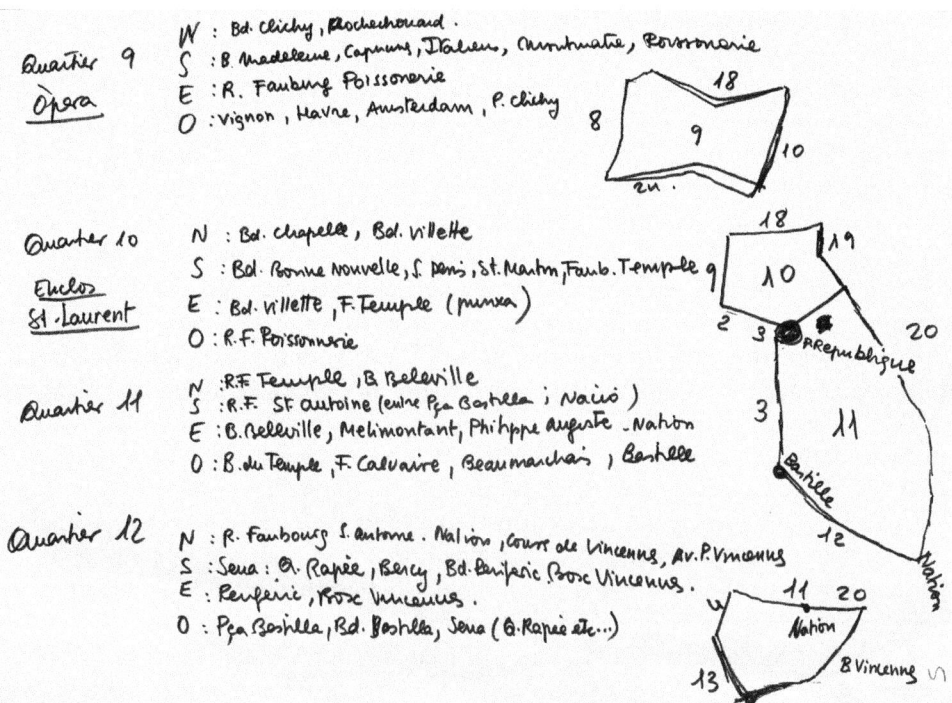

FIG. 1.1. Sketch of Paris by Marçal (c.1984)

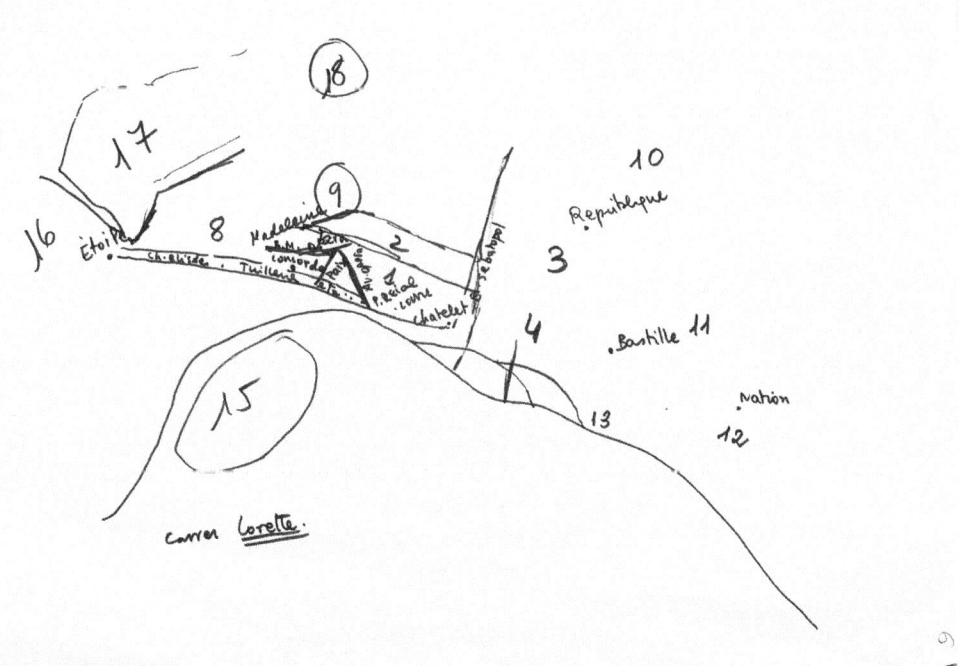

FIG. 1.2. Sketch of Paris by Marçal (c.1984)

upon 'out of the corner of *just one eye*' (1985: 71, my emphasis). For Weigel, social engagement should underpin aesthetic concerns until such engagement is politically redundant, i.e. women's full emancipation has been reached. The Catalan writer Montserrat Roig drew on this concept in the early 1990s when she referred to women's 'mirada bòrnia' [one-eyed gaze]. With this gaze, women could look outwards with one eye that 'no tenia sexe' [had no sex] (2001 [1991]: 139) while always maintaining an inwards gaze too, that is, a gaze that did not forget women's identity *as* woman. That is to say that for Roig, it was imperative that women not lose sight of women's exclusion in many spheres. Marçal's 'ull borni' may be a reference to Roig's 'mirada bòrnia' and, in turn, to Weigel's 'double focus'. If we read *La passió* with this double focus in mind, our attention is drawn to Marçal's aesthetic engagement with Vivien's work *and* to her political and personal interest in the challenges of maintaining relationships between women in societies hostile to them or where models and modes for such relationships were lacking. In such contexts the development of the relationship is somewhat improvised, without the standard milestones of heteronormativity. This is described in the novel as an experience at once liberating and overwhelming. For example, Sara T. writes of the tensions with her former girlfriend about whether they would live together and their differing expectations of the relationship.

Returning to the titles listed above, in Marçal's notes there seems to be a draft of part of the novel titled 'La mirada' [The Look], in which we can observe why Marçal might have considered the titles. In the draft she writes about the narrator's failure in evoking the figure of Vivien, describing how the narrator of the novel is not omniscient:

> No és que mai es proposés d'estrafer amb aquest l'ull omniscient i invisible de déu per damunt de les seves criatures [...] ni tan sols un simulacre d'aquest ull, estràbic i miop, empresonat en triangle. El lloc de l'ull era, d'entrada buit, buidat, com el d'un gran gegant borni — Odin o Cíclop [...] Quan la darrera paraula d'aquest relat ha estat escrita, l'ull seguia igualment buit. (FMMM: box 8/5, folder 4, sheet 1)

> [The objective was never to emulate with that eye the omniscient and invisible eye of god over his creatures [...] nor even to create a simulacrum of that eye, short-sighted and cross-eyed, trapped in a triangle. The place of the eye was, from the start, empty, emptied, like the eye of a one-eyed giant — Odin or Cyclops [...] When the final word of this story has been written, the eye will remain just as empty.]

Marçal goes beyond highlighting the partiality of the narrator's perspective, their impossibility of getting or giving a full picture. The single eye of the goddess of love is not an all-seeing eye, not the Eye of Providence, but neither is it simply an eye with limited, partial vision. The eye is empty and this emptiness is compensated for by the words of others, for whom the narrator seems to be a vehicle, a cipher. Marçal writes about words striving to compensate for the narrator's inevitable blindness: 'Només el buit s'amaga darrere la Venus dels cecs | Però les paraules segueixen intentant omplir-lo' (FMMM: box 8/5, folder 4, sheet 1) [Only an empty space hides behind Venus of the Blind | But words keep trying to fill the space].

As a scriptwriter, Sara T. struggles with similar concerns to the 'blind' narrator. She is aware of the insufficiency of her efforts, but nonetheless desires to discover more about Vivien, to give a clear image of the poet. Sara T. retraces the poet's steps. She describes the thoughts that run through her mind as she approaches Vivien's tomb, a physical site for the memorialisation of loss:

> de quina manera *redreçar-te* a tu, més enllà d'aquest estrany joc d'encaixos, de peces movedisses [...] Peces canviants i indòcils, que ballen i s'encarcaren, fugen i s'apropen, desapareixen i es recreen, en contínua metamorfosi. Peces mòbils fetes amb fragments de peces fixes, trossos de papers esquinçats i restaurats [...] cases que han estat enderrocades, carrers que han canviat de nom. I els teus mateixos escrits, màscares sobre màscares sobre màscares. (91, my emphasis)

> [how can I *straighten you*, beyond this strange puzzle with moving pieces [...] Shifting and untamed pieces that become loose and stiffen, flee and come closer, disappear and reappear, in continuous metamorphosis. Moving pieces made with fragments of fixed pieces, tattered and restored bits of paper [...] houses that have been demolished, streets that have changed name. And your own writings, masks upon masks upon masks.] (my emphasis)

The use of the verb 'redreçar' in this passage, which again recalls a kaleidoscopic process, is significant. It can be read as *another* address to someone (re-adreçar), i.e. an apostrophe in the sense of an address to an absent or imaginary person or to a personified abstraction, thus signalling an absence and marking a loss. 'Redreçar' can also be interpreted as the verb 'to straighten'; Sara T. strives to make Vivien's life conform to her projection of it. She wants to tame the 'wild' fragments that hint at how Vivien lived and interacted with those around her. Frustrated with the palimpsestic nature of the clues she comes across, in documents and on the streets, Sara T. attempts to make Vivien's life cohere into a comprehensible narrative.

As the passage shows, the 'metamorphosing' fragments of the past resist Sara T.'s ordering, normalising impulse; Vivien 's'ha convertit [...] en metàfora de l'inaccessible' (380) [has become a metaphor for the inaccessible]. The impossibility of the permanent coherence of a welter of fragments moulded into Sara T.'s desiring vision of Vivien and the apparent inaccessibility of the past cause her to feel disorientated. Nonetheless, she continues to claw desperately at the *familiar* vision of Vivien that she has created in her mind as a result of reading Vivien's poetry, despite the persistent defamiliarisation in the form and content of the documents she encounters during her research. Sara T. initially sees Vivien's texts as a mirror of her life in order to consolidate her sense of self in the present, but she eventually comes to realise that this first seeing is an illusion, a fantasy, a specularisation of the spectral that involves her projecting her desires: 'la seducció havia començat per aquella mena de miratge-miracle del mirall' (381) [the process of seduction had begun with that sort of mirage-miracle of the mirror]. She thus comes to learn the fallacy of seeking a mirror-image of herself in a seemingly single figure in the past for self-validation in the present. The novel enacts Love's call for allowing figures in the past with whom we long to identify to turn their backs on us. Love writes of queer critics (I would extend her remarks to apply to writers of fiction, also) who look back to queer figures of the past and struggle to cope with the past's resistance to our touch, which may be more like a clutch: 'Turning back towards them seems essential, but it also demands something that is, in the end, more difficult: allowing them to turn their backs on us' (2007: 43). As Love argues, and Marçal demonstrates in the novel, we can make these images move, as Sara T. does, but we must also allow the images to move *away* from our range of vision, out of our lines of vision; we must accept at least a partial blindness.

Sara T.'s relationship to her literary predecessor is unavoidably *queered*, in the sense that it involves twisting, turning, and rearranging fragments rather than simply looking back to the past for a ready-made, full reflection, on which to base her self-perception and her relationships in the present. The 'peces mòbils fetes amb fragments de peces fixes' (91) [moving pieces made with fixed pieces] that frustrate her at Vivien's grave are unavoidable. She realises that, as Dinshaw asserts, the 'touch across time' involves 'partial connections' (2001: 206) and a connection with and through parts; the past cannot provide all the answers for Sara T.'s present. The 'touch across time' is precisely that — a touch, not a grab. A partial touch, a partial, or even imagined, gaze. Meese draws on Jacques Derrida to make a useful distinction between identity and resemblance: 'in the resemblance of one thing to another, there is always an absence [...] There is resemblance but not identity [...] So that at the heart of the very description which is supposed to give us lesbian presence, lesbian identity, this absence lingers' (1992: 13): the empty eye gazes on.

Moving images, as images that move on a screen and move out of reach, slipping away from our grasp, out of sight highlight the tension between craving wholeness and continuity and the realisation of the impossibility of this desire. The tension between desiring a total image while simultaneously being aware of the impossibility of this task is also evident in critical responses to the seductive figure of Sappho and her work, particularly in approaches to the translation of her fragments to which I will now turn.

Sapphic Fragmentation, Sapphic Translation

> DEFINICIONES
> PALIMPSESTO. — Escrito debajo de una mujer.
>
> — PERI ROSSI ([1971] 2005a: 31)

> [DEFINITIONS
> PALIMPSEST. Written underneath a woman.]

> WHAT HAVE YOU DONE WITH MY POEMS? [...] I can no longer read my own writing. It isn't surprising that so many of you have chosen to read between the lines when the lines themselves have become [...] mutilated [...].
>
> — JEANETTE WINTERSON's 'Sappho' (1994: 51)

The figure of Sappho and her work that is extant resists association with conventional notions of perfection in an original wholeness. In the twelfth century, the Byzantine grammarian John Tzetzes of Constantinople declared in frustration, 'time has frittered away Sappho and her works, her lyre and songs' (1110–80 CE, cited in Poochigian 2009: xliv). We can read fragments of her poetry, salvaged from damaged papyri but it is estimated that ninety percent of what Sappho wrote has been lost or remains undiscovered (Duffy 2009: vii). Thus, for a present day reader, as for most of her readers throughout history, Sappho and her fragmented texts are in a process of becoming.

The process is mediated by others through citation; many of her words have reached us through quotations in the works of scholars (Reynolds 2000: 18). A recent discovery of Sappho's words in 2004 took place at the University of Cologne where it was found that a papyrus of previously uncertain authorship contained parts of three poems by Sappho (Poochigian: xliv). Foucault's aforementioned depiction of genealogy as palimpsestic, operating on 'documents that have been scratched over and recopied many times' (1984a: 76), could readily double as a description of Sappho's oeuvre. To borrow from Peri Rossi's words in the epigraph to this section, there is a palimpsest written underneath Sappho. Sappho *is* a palimpsest. flores considers queer/cuir writing to be inherently palimpsestic:

> Como palimpsesto teórico y poético, la escritura cuir no trata de historias, biografías e identidades premoldeadas, más bien insiste en el ejercicio incesante de la pregunta y la crítica, animada por el malestar de la clasificación, deshaciendo la solidaridad entre los géneros. Su opción por la ruptura y el desvío compone una galaxia de significantes y no una estructura de significados; no tiene principio, pero sí diversas vías de acceso [...]. (2013: 32)

> [As a theoretical and poetic palimpsest, *cuir* writing is not about preconceived (hi)stories, biographies, and identities, rather it insists on the incessant process of questioning and critique. Stimulated by an unease about classification, it undoes the fixed relationship between genres. Its preference for rupture and deviation creates a galaxy of signifiers rather than a structure of meanings; it has no beginning, but multiple access routes]

For flores, queer writing blurs genre categories and revels in the multiplication and interplay of many levels and layers of meaning. Many express pleasure in the fragmented nature of the discoveries of Sappho's words as it permits a collaboration with her through the multiple access routes to her palimpsestic lines: 'it is in Sappho's broken fragments that the modern woman poet could reinvent Sappho's verse and thus inscribe feminine desire as part of an empowering literary history of her own' (Greene 1996: 4). I will return to creative collaboration and the porous boundaries between genres below.

It is important to note that the palimpsestic Sappho cannot be contained in an exclusively women-centred or lesbian sphere. Although Jay draws our attention to Sappho as a figure who has represented 'all the lost women of genius in literary history, especially all the lesbian artists whose work has been destroyed, sanitized, or heterosexualized in an attempt to evade what Elaine Marks identifies as "lesbian intertextuality"' (1988: 64), her fragments lend themselves to both queer and heteronormative manipulation. In Vivien's novel *A Woman Appeared to Me* (1982 [1904]), Vally (a nickname for Barney) expresses her outrage at the tale of Sappho committing suicide after being shunned by her male lover, Phaon: 'Haven't they invented the legend of an idiotic infatuation for the swell Phaon, a legend whose stupidity is equalled only by its lack of historic truth?' (68). Vivien underlines Barney's dismissal of interpretations that dispute Sappho's lesbian desire through her choice of words; alternative visions to that of Sappho as representative of desire between women are spurned as invention, legend, idiocy, and stupidity. The character of Barney concedes no space to ambiguity, despite the speculative nature of her own readings of Sappho's desires. Jeanette Winterson's Sappho, whose words appear in the epigraph to this section, refers to her mutilated lines, pointing to the symbolic violence to which Sappho has been subjected in a heteronormative dismissal of the ambiguity of her extant work. Many scholars, including Ovid, lauded her work but often refuted or downplayed its homoeroticism (Poochigian 2009: xiv). Sappho, often praised for foregrounding the first person voice in her works, focussed on her own feelings as a desiring subject rather than on the object causing them, hence the ambiguity of those she or the voice in her poems desired.

Lesbian desire in modern Catalan letters, as in many of its early literary appearances (or apparitions), was, to begin with at least, ambiguous and implicit. Amongst works in Catalan, it is worth mentioning the short story 'Carnestoltes' (1907) [Carnival] by Víctor Català (the masculine pseudonym of Caterina Albert). The story ambiguously depicts the intensification of the bond between a Marquise and her maid. Outside on the streets in the Carnival parades, crowds are wearing masks and costumes, while inside the apartment the women disguise their affection as obligation and mask their desire. Before they have acknowledged their love for each other, the maid dies. The story is thus associated with death, and indeed with Lent, a time of fasting (the love was never consummated) and penitence, which will follow the Carnival. The story leaves open whether the Marquise will regret her feelings, or regret not having expressed them. Another relatively early text depicting lesbian characters is Ana María Matute's *Los soldados no lloran* (1964) [Soldiers Don't Cry]. It is set largely in rural Catalonia during the Civil War and includes ambiguous references to a relationship between the narrator's mother, Elena, and a woman called Dionisia who share a house. Dionisia, in particular, is depicted as morally reprehensible for deviating from the alleged norms of femininity; she works on a boat, smuggling and dealing drugs.

The ambiguity of some representations of lesbian desire has led to naively short-sighted or deliberately homophobic readings of lesbian texts. For example, when Riera was awarded a prize for 'Te deix' one of the judges approached her to comment on an orthographic mistake in her short story, stating that she had missed off the accent from the name of one of the lovers (in Catalan the masculine version of the name Maria is Marià) (Riera 2004a: 251). It is a short story written in the form of a letter from a younger woman to an older woman looking back on an erotic relationship that they stopped due to the younger woman's father's outrage and the older women's concerns about her position as a teacher. However, it is not evident until the end of the story that the older character is a woman, Maria. The absence of an accent holds the key to the text. Similarly, in Sappho's Fragment One, the goddess Aphrodite asks Sappho who it is that she desires but, as Glenn Most notes, 'by a freak of the transmission, even the answer to the question whether the lover is male or female depends upon a single, badly transmitted letter' (cited in Greene 1996: 33).

However, a text does not need to be ambiguous for critical homophobia to rear its head. Until Marçal portrayed lesbian characters in her novel, the unequivocal lesbian elements of some of her poetry were frequently ignored by mainstream critics. Referring to criticism of her novel, Marçal states that

> és el primer cas, pel que fa a la meva obra, que la crítica oficial ha parlat de lesbianisme, tot i que en general no han concedit al tema el lloc nuclear i motriu que té en el llibre. Es molt curiós, i m'agradaria tenir-ho més analitzat, l'estrany proteccionisme cap a la meva persona, o cap a la meva imatge, que ha funcionat en els altres casos, fins a forçar interpretacions de poemes d'una forma increïble: pura miopia o voluntat de neutralització d'un discurs dissonant? (cited in Mérida Jiménez 2011: 104)

> [it is the first time, with regard to my work, that official critics have spoken of lesbianism, even though, in general, they have not given it the central place that is has in the novel. This strange protectionism of me, or of my image, which took place in the other cases to the point of forcing interpretations of poems in an unbelievable way, is a very odd phenomenon, and I would like it to be further analysed: is it pure shortsightedness or a desire to neutralise a dissonant discourse?]

It is clear, then, that Marçal, now considered part of the Catalan canon, is admitted to it with her sexuality 'neutralised'. Even with a novel as undeniably Sapphic as *La passió*, lesbian sexuality can be sidelined.

The homophobia and misogyny of the critical establishment weighed on Vivien also. To avoid it, she published with the male pseudonym René before adopting the feminine form of Renée, and she was also the subject of critical protectionism after her death. Her papers came to be in the possession of the French historian and archaeologist Salomon Reinach, referred to in the novel as 'el savi Salomó' [The Wise Salomon]. Jay writes that he deposited them in the Bibliothèque Nationale in Paris, where they were to be sealed until the year 2000 (1988: xii). Apparently her lover, Barney, disagreed with this decision, but Reinach asserted that he wanted to protect Vivien's literary reputation and the personal reputation of those who had known her intimately. There remains some confusion about the whereabouts of this archive (Rubin 2011: 374). Sappho, Vivien, and Marçal, then, were all subjected to 'neutralisation'.

Having outlined the homophobia, protectionism, or convenient oversight of critics, I now turn to other key figures who influence reader reception of works: translators. The majority of readers of Sappho (myself included) approach her extant work in translation, thus the transmission of her words through time and space depends heavily on the approaches of translators of her work.

Some critics and translators strive to impose order, structure, and intelligibility on Sappho's fragments, seeking to straighten and complete the figure of Sappho, as Sara T. initially seeks to do with Vivien. Aaron Poochigian, who translated a 2009 edition of Sappho's poetry into English, writes: 'though Sappho's remains are usually fragments that are themselves fragmentary, I have done my best to create a sense of completeness and, on occasion, translated supplements proposed by scholars' (xlv). Stanley Lombardo, who translated a 2002 English edition, recognises the value of Page duBois's proposed shift in *Sappho is Burning* (1995) from a focus on reconstitution of a lost whole to recognising 'our momentary and receding relationship to the shattered fragments of the past' (Lombardo 2002: xxvi). Nonetheless, he announces that he has 'engaged in some kind of reconstitution, as a translator *must...*' (xxvi, my emphasis), going on to state that he 'felt *compelled* to order and arrange [the pieces] into a collection with some kind of esthetic coherence' (xxvi, my emphasis). The sense of obligation in the phrase 'compelled to' smacks of 'compulsory heterosexuality', as formulated by Rich (1980). Lombardo's words echo those of Sara T. when she acknowledges the temptation to simplify Vivien's life for her screenplay. She describes 'la sensació d'intentar encerclar, delimitar i definir allò que és complexitat i moviment i que constantment tens la sensació que se t'escapa de les mans' (379) [the feeling of trying to enclose, delimit and define things characterised by complexity and movement, things that you feel are constantly escaping your grasp]. Again, the reference to hands trying to capture and restrict evokes a clutch or grab, rather than a 'touch' across time.

Translations that aim to paint a coherent picture of a complex subject or to complete a fragmented work negate the powerful potential for language to communicate multiple layers and scatterings of meaning. Marçal's collage of Vivien's words includes the lines: 'Què m'importa que el vent dispersi els meus versos en els replecs més foscos del fosc univers: ja que sols he cantat per a la meva sola joia' (394) [Why should I care if the wind disperses my verses in the darkest folds of the dark universe, given that I have only sung for my own joy]; Vivien does not lament the scattering of her words. I return below to Vivien's claim about the primacy of feeling in writing, over and above communicating clear meaning. I will focus first on the darkest folds of the complex figure of Sappho. Reynolds points out that the transformation of Sappho's name in different languages reflects the concomitant 'simplification' of her figure internationally. In both Ancient and Modern Greece, 'if you hear a native speaker say her name, she comes across spitting and popping hard p's. Ppppsappoppo. We have eased off her name, made her docile and sliding' (2000: 2).

Translation as a corrective, completing act imposes the translator's would-be univocal reading, stultifying the consideration of other perspectives. It also betrays the translator's lack of faith in the imagination of the reader. In his influential text on translation, 'The Task of the Translator' (1999 [1923]), Walter Benjamin emphasises the importance of the 'mode' of communication in texts, above 'meaning' and 'sense':

> Fragments of a vessel which are to be glued together must match one another in the smallest details, although they need not be like one another. In the same way a translation, instead of resembling the meaning of the original, must lovingly and in detail incorporate the original's mode of signification, thus making both the original and the translation recognizable as fragments of a greater language, just as fragments are part of a vessel. For this very reason translation must in large measure refrain from wanting to communicate something, from rendering the sense. (79)

Pamela Gordon echoes Benjamin in her introduction to Lombardo's translation,

'Instead of trying to weave the fragments too closely together, why not take each one as it comes, remembering that a poem can resonate with other poems without becoming an entry in a single narrative?' (2002: xvii).

It is precisely 'mode' and 'resonance' that Anne Carson considers critical in her translations of Sappho, in which she strives to suggest the musicality of the text, reminding us that Sappho's poetry was originally sung. In what are considered the original texts, Sappho's words appear without breaks; all the letters run together. Carson does not emulate this, but she does attempt to conjure the lost *voice* and *music* of the lyric song: 'I have sometimes manipulated its spacing on the page, to restore a hint of musicality' (2003: xii). She also retains the plurality of potential meaning by maintaining a sense of fragmentation through the use of brackets and blank spaces to indicate missing text. For her, translation is 'no reason you should miss the drama of trying to read a papyrus torn in half or riddled with holes or smaller than a postage stamp — brackets imply a free space of imaginal adventure' (x). She goes on to note, 'I like to think that the more I stand out of the way, the more Sappho shows through' (ibid.); she does not want to obscure the palimpsest that is Sappho. Carson, then, strives to maintain the figure of Sappho as 'other', rather than absorb her into the English renderings of her fragments.

For Benjamin, a respect for otherness is vital to translation, which he believes should consist of the othering of the target language. He cites Rudolf Pannwitz who laments that the translator often: 'preserves the state in which his own language happens to be instead of allowing his language to be powerfully affected by the foreign tongue' ([1923] 1999: 81). Reynolds also celebrates Sappho's 'distance' from us, asserting that 'Sappho and her work should be thought of as something strange, foreign and remote; something that is ultimately unrecoverable, in spite of all the many layers of invention by later writers' (Reynolds 2000: 16). As well as using brackets and spaces to simulate missing text to maintain the fragmentation of the extant parts of Sappho's poetry, Carson includes transcriptions of the discovered Ancient Greek text alongside the English translations to remind us of the otherness of Sappho's writing, and our distance from it.

Attempts to retrieve Sappho's 'authentic' words and to uncover her text from layers of invention or alteration through transcription and translation often overlook the fact that as Sappho's poetry was originally sung, there is not an 'original' written *text* at all, but an 'original' *voice*. As Reynolds warns, 'Sappho has no authentic voice in any language, even her own' (2000: 16). Carson reminds readers of her translation of Sappho's fragments that 'whether or not [Sappho] herself was literate is unknown' (2003: ix). Therefore, even prior to the act of translation, Sappho's voice has undergone a transformation in being transformed from voice to text. It is significant that as Sappho has become more well-known through text, she has been increasingly associated with an Attic culture that was not hers; she sung in Aeolic dialect.

In contrast to the tendency to associate Sappho with the language of Athens, in Vivien's poetry she emphasises a simultaneous desire for Sappho, but awareness of her distance from her. In Vivien's poem 'Desembarcant a Mitilene' [Disembarking in Mytilene], translated by Marçal, we read: 'Del fons del meu passat jo torno cap a tu | Mitilene, a través dels segles dissemblants' [From the depths of my past I return to you | Mytilene, across disparate centuries]. Vivien emphasises resuscitation, but seems aware of the *song* and *echo*, the aural quality that cannot be as penetrating as in the past: 'Lesbos [...] fes que ressuscitin de nou lires i cants [...] Tu que l'eco conserves de les lires i els cants' (Vivien, translated by Marçal in Julià and Marçal 1998: 36) [Lesbos [...] resurrect lyres and songs once again [...] You who conserve their echo]. Vivien recognised the transformation in Sappho's appropriation by other literatures and often used the Aeolic spelling of her name, 'Psappha', considering the name 'Sappho' to be 'a bourgeois denigration of her ideal' (Jay 1988: 70). The standardisation of the peninsular, peripheral Aeolic by central Attic culture has symbolic resonance with the situation of Catalan in Spain. Reynolds contests tales that claim that the repeated sacking of the library at Alexandria by barbarians was responsible for the loss of the majority of Sappho's works. She believes that Sappho's Aeolic dialect contributed to her work being undervalued and largely lost, because the dialect was considered 'provincial' and an 'arcane taste, not worth the labour of retranscription' (2000:18).

Many critics have noted that the figure of Sappho is better known than her work and words. In the case of Vivien, both her work and her figure are little known. It is significant that Marçal chose Vivien as the subject for her novel, especially given Vivien's relative obscurity. In terms of Vivien's contemporaries in *Belle Époque* Paris, she is particularly overshadowed by her lover, the more extroverted Barney, often known as 'the Amazon', whose many tumultuous relationships are recounted in Djuna Barnes's lesbian cult classic, *Ladies Almanack* (1928). Vivien is also lesser-known than Colette, who depicted Vivien in her novel *The Pure and the Impure* (1932). Marçal's decision to focus on the figure of Vivien, who in turn drew attention to Sappho's peripheral language (relative to Attic Greek), reveals Marçal's interest in apparently marginal or peripheral figures, perhaps a consequence of her concern for the Catalan language and its status.

Returning to approaches to translation, a respect for otherness in translation accords with Gayatri Spivak's argument in her essay 'The Politics of Translation' (1993), in which she draws on Benjamin's aforementioned piece to highlight the importance of recognising untranslatability. She posits the recognition of untranslatability against an imperialist assumption that everything 'other' can be accessed and known, an attitude which she describes as 'confidence in accessibility in the house of power, where history is waiting to be restored' (195). The assumption is particularly relevant in the case of Sappho given the colonial context in which a large part of the modern discoveries — or rediscoveries — of her fragments took place.

In 1895, two students from Queen's College, Oxford, heard news of farmers turning up pieces of papyrus as they ploughed new fields in Egypt. Excavators from Germany, France, and Britain turned up at the site. The students, backed by the Egypt Exploration Fund, travelled there and realised that the land had been a rubbish heap of a town from the period of Hellenistic Egypt. After quarrels with local workers, they sent the scraps of papyrus that they found back to Oxford, where many crates still remain in the basement of the Ashmolean Museum (Reynolds

2000: 19). Interestingly, Vivien (and Barney) started writing in Paris at around the same time that more of Sappho's work was discovered in Egypt, prompting new interest in her work (Jay 1988: 61). Spivak's comments on imperialistic visions of history as awaiting restoration recall Foucault's assertion that 'genealogy does not pretend to go back in time to restore an unbroken continuity that operates beyond the dispersion of forgotten things' (1984a: 81). By not striving to complete the fragmented text in a reparative act, we acknowledge that we do not have mastery over knowledge or history; 'forgotten things' are an inescapable part of the past.

However, simply forgetting is not the most productive way forward either. Linda Bishai summarises Nietzsche's critique of history as such: 'the essence of truly living occurs *in the space between remembering and forgetting.* In other words, we must remember in order to know who we are, and forget in order to become what we may be' (2004: 133, my emphasis). Marçal manages to evoke this 'space between remembering and forgetting' in her poetry. The first poem in Marçal's last collection of poems, *Raó del cos*, published posthumously in 2000, describes the forgotten things in history through poetically rendering 'forgetting' as a material thing:

> Amb fils d'oblit
> cus la memòria
> la sargidora cega.
> (2017: 461)

> [With threads of oblivion
> the blind seamstress
> sews memory.] (2014a: 19)[2]

Similarly, a place between knowledge and memory on the one hand, and unknowing and forgetting on the other, is vital for Meese's conception of the project of writing the lesbian. She evokes a similar image to the blind seamstress in her reference to Penelope in the *Odyssey*, who weaves and undoes a shroud in order to delay choosing a suitor to remarry:

> I want this word to be a place where my story is not known to myself, to any-one; where the story of the other remains also a mystery, always being solved or written — made and unmade every day like Penelope's handwork. *A place between the ecstasy of desire and passion, and of arrest, silence, not knowing.* (1992: 18, my emphasis)

Marçal also sees weaving and unweaving as representative of women's desire:

> Mans de dona
> teixeixen
> i desteixeixen
> un desig
> translúcid
> (2017: 477)

> [Women's hands
> weave

and unravel
a translucent
desire] (2014a: 43)

The fragmentation of Sappho's extant texts offers 'in-between' spaces for sewing memory out of threads of oblivion. However, Sapphic incompletion has proved vulnerable, reflecting a tension between respect for the otherness of the unknown and an imperialist desire to access the past and make it cohere. Having considered approaches to translations of Sappho and Marçal's evocation of memory, forgetting, and desire, I will now consider how Marçal weaves and unweaves her translations of Vivien's lines into *La passió*.

Translation and Genealogy: Renée Vivien according to Maria-Mercè Marçal

Com si em vingués de tu
la carn, la sang
de les paraules.
— MARÇAL ([2000] 2017: 491)

[As if it came from you to me
the flesh, the blood
of words.] (2014a: 65)

Catalan activist, researcher, and teacher Mercè Otero Vidal's essay 'Patchwork lèsbic' [Lesbian Patchwork] (2011), which appears in a book on lesbian literature in Catalan, describes her reading history. The reference to a patchwork once more evokes the notion of a textile composed of numerous fragments from different sources. She describes how she sought out and read works that were significant for her identity as a lesbian woman. An active search for fragments and their piecing together into an individual's 'patchwork' is vital in lesbian identity formation. We have seen that the reader is central in the creation of their own personal genealogy from fragments they discover. Where, then, are these fragments found?

The title of Otero Vidal's essay hints at the transnational nature of these fragments through the use of the English word 'patchwork'. Her literary references can be traced back to multiple sources, in multiple places, in multiple languages. Among others, Otero Vidal mentions Joanna Russ's *The Female Man* (1975), Denis Diderot's *La Religieuse* (1796), Ursula Le Guin's *The Left Hand of Darkness* (1969), Riera's 'Te deix', and the works of Marçal. Otero Vidal's recollection of books that have contributed to her patchwork of literary intertexts recalls Halberstam's 'arqueologia carronyera' mentioned by Torras in her earlier piece on lesbian identity in Catalan literature (2007: 141). Halberstam's queer methodology is a 'scavenger methodology [that] uses different methods to collect and produce information on subjects who have been deliberately or accidentally excluded from traditional studies of human behaviour' (1998: 13). It involves searching in diverse places for examples of queer writing. I posit that translation is vital to the scavengers. Torras highlights the transnational oeuvre by which readers and writers are inspired, and the importance of translation for access to those works:

> Una de les generositats de la tasca de traducció [...] rau en fer-nos *avinents* textos en principi al·liens, donar-nos la possibilitat *d'incorporar-los* a la literatura pròpia, per tant, *d'apropiar-nos-en.* (2007: 135, my emphasis)

> [One of the generous acts of the task of translation [...] lies in bringing *closer* to us texts that were once alien, in giving us the possibility of *incorporating these* texts into our own literature and, therefore, *appropriating them.*] (my emphasis)

In a sense, Torras's vision of translation differs from that of Benjamin and Spivak outlined in the previous section. Where Benjamin, Carson, and Spivak emphasise the need to reveal a sense of otherness and distance in approaching texts in translation, Torras emphasises the need to 'apropiar' the texts, which in Catalan conjures the sense of 'appropriating' them, i.e. making them one's own, and moving closer (*més a prop*) to them.

Translation is essential to *La passió*. In line with Freeman's conception of aesthetic forms that rub together, Marçal incorporates Vivien's words, translated into Catalan, in a somewhat chaotic form of *collage* in the closing section of the novel, the 'Monòdia final' [Final Monody]. In an article titled 'Maria-Mercè Marçal: tradició/traducció/creació' [tradition/translation/creation], Caterina Riba Sanmartí describes how Marçal's creative work blurs the distinction between recuperation, translation, and creation: 'La tasca de recuperació i la de creació es fusionaren i acabà convertint la seva pròpia obra en espai de trobada' (2015: 471) [The task of recuperation and creation fuse and she ends up turning her own work into a space of encounter]. Traditionally, a monody is a composition for one voice and Marçal indicates in her note at the book's end that all the words used are Vivien's. However, she lends her 'voice' to Vivien's words, which appear here jumbled and rearranged, emphasising rather than resolving the internal contradictions in the poet's verses. Indeed, these contradictions are exposed through the juxtaposition or 'trobada' [encounter] of textual fragments and lines that seem to state contrary views. For example, 'Sovint no temo res sinó l'oblit' (386) [I often fear nothing except oblivion] followed by 'Estic cansada, res no vull sinó l'oblit' (394) [I am weary, I want nothing but oblivion]. Marçal describes her practice of translation as renovation (FMMM: box 13, folder 1), rather than completion. In this regard, her approach differs from those of a number of translators of Sappho whom I considered above. While her approach does not seem to align with Spivak's call to maintain a sense of distance and otherness of the source text, neither does it make the texts 'cohere'. In this regard, her work reflects Benjamin's philosophy of translation in which the primary focus is not to transmit 'meaning'.

Marçal's incorporation — from the Latin *incorporare*, 'to form into a body' — of Vivien's words in her text results in the creation of a multiple, fragmented body of text, and a complex, contradictory, rather than a coherent subject. Similarly, Vivien incarnated Sappho through 'borrowing' her words, as Reinach details in *La passió*: 'es creu una Safo abandonada i s'expressa en conseqüència, manllevant a voltes expressions al vocabulari de la poetessa que admirava, de la qual es creia sens dubte una encarnació' (239) [she believes herself to be an abandoned Sappho and this impacts her way of expressing herself, sometimes borrowing expressions from the words of the poet she admired, of whom she no doubt thought herself a incarnation]. For Vivien, translation goes hand in hand with incarnation. Marçal translates the words of Vivien who sees translation as becoming the other: 'Sóc més que teva: sóc tu mateixa. Tradueixo el somriure i l'ombra del teu rostre' (Vivien translated by Marçal in Julià and Marçal 1998: 52) [I am more than yours: I am you. I translate the smile and shadow of your visage]. Importantly, then, it is a *partial* incarnation filled with *shadows*.

Nonetheless, Vivien and Marçal's apparent recognition of the impossibility of fully incarnating or incorporating the other did not stop the authors from attempting to do so, just as Sara T. struggles with her longing to make Vivien cohere. Marçal describes translation as a gesture of desire and passion, using metaphors of consumption. It is not simply motivated by a desire for the poem to reach others but by 'un altre impuls més primordial, que s'assembla a l'amor o a la passió que cerca apropriar-se en certa manera del text, *menjar-se'l o ésser menjat*, convertir el jo en tu i el tu en jo' (Marçal 1991 in FMMM: box 13/1, folder 1, sheet 3 2, my emphasis) [another more primordial impulse that is similar to love or passion that looks to appropriate the text in a way, *eat it or be eaten by it,* to convert me into you and you into me] (my emphasis). Like Vivien, she highlights the process of becoming the other that she considers to be inherent in translation.

Riba, evidently unaware of Marçal's own conceptualisation of translation as consumption, attributing it to Mercè Ibarz, describes the 'canibalisme literari de Marçal' (2015: 479) [Marçal's literary cannibalism]. Riba also describes Marçal's relationship with her literary predecessors in digestive terms: 'La poeta les engoleix, les devora, les fagocita i les converteix així en carnatge íntim de la seva escriptura' (2012: 85) [The poet swallows, devours, and engulfs them and, in that way, converts them into the intimate carnage of her writing]. Riba sees in Marçal's body of work the bodies of writers of the past. Riba draws on Oswald de Andrade's 'Manifesto Antropófago' [Cannibal Manifesto] (1928) of Brazilian modernism, which conceptualised literary cannibalism as a mark of admiration and respect. Emphasising translation as an embodied process of transmission, De Andrade describes it as a blood transfusion (Riba 2015: 479). Riba also highlights Susan Bassnett's description of Augusto de Campos's approach to translation as 'a physical process [...] a devouring of the source text, a transmutation process, an act of vampirisation' (1998: 155).

In the light of translation as transfusion or cannibalism, it is revealing to turn to the title of the novel. The title echoes in its structure and wording the Gospels, such as 'The Passion of Our Lord Jesus Christ According to St John', which describes the Passion of Christ on the cross that precedes his rebirth. Furthermore, the novel opens with a section titled 'Introit'. The 'introit' is sung at the beginning of the Eucharist which, according to the Catholic Church, involves transubstantiation: the transforming of the bread and wine into the body and blood of Christ. By opening the novel with an 'introit', Marçal draws our attention to how writers such as Vivien attributed to Sappho a 'quasi-religious significance' (Jay 1988: 72) and wanted to resuscitate them through translation as a form of transubstantiation.

The notion of translation as a blood transfusion recalls Benjamin's comments on the translational 'afterlife' ([1923] 1999: 72). In her analysis of Benjamin's philosophy of translation, Emily Apter argues that Benjamin's 'genetic paradigm' shifts emphasis from the notion of an 'original' to 'textual reproducibility' (Apter 2006: 223). She argues that '[i]n this scheme, the significance of origins and originality cedes to grander concerns over the work of art's messianic perpetuity' (ibid.). Benjamin's focus on translational afterlives 'implicitly devalues the original, suborning the source text (and its privileged status as *primum mobile*) to the translation (now elevated to the position of midwife in the obstetrics of translatability)' (Apter 2006: 224). In Apter's words we read yet another reference to birth: the text is reborn through translation, just as the writer is reborn through new readings of their works. Apter and Benjamin propose a process of translation as akin to De Campos's transfusion, akin to the vampiric consumption, feeding, and rebirthing of texts; crucially, the texts that are reborn are different to the 'originals'. In shifting the focus from textual origin to the text's resurrection, these critics and philosophers emphasise futurity. Such approaches to translation, which may adapt and renovate without a *totalising* gesture, reveal and revel in the contradictions in the source text and, as such, they too evoke Foucault's conceptualisation of genealogy, which 'opposes itself to the search for "origins"' (1984a: 77).

In her notes written in preparation for her participation in an event in Ireland on translation, Marçal describes translation as a transnational gesture of love and recognition. Writing of her *own* works being translated, she says: 'No cal dir que sempre és gratificant el fet d'ésser objecte d'amor [...] Lorca — quan li preguntaven per què escrivia contestava: para que me quieran' (FMMM: box 13, folder 1) [It goes without saying that it is always gratifying to be an object of love [...] when Lorca was asked why he wrote, he would reply: so that people will love me]. She believes external recognition to be particularly important in the case of so-called minority languages such as Irish and Catalan: 'ésser traduït és potser la millor manera d'ésser reconegut i traduir la millor forma de reconèixer' (ibid.) [to be translated is possibly the best way of being recognised, and to translate the best way of giving recognition]. However, beyond a gesture of recognition, she believes translation to be vital to enriching and broadening readings of texts, specifically poetry in this case:

> Hi ha aspectes primordials en un poema que el vinculen a la llengua d'origen, però en desaparèixer aquests, altres que potser quedaven en un lloc secundari o amagat prenen més relleu i bullen amb més intensitat. Això és especialment important en cultures de llengües minoritàries on, sovint, la propia situació de precarietat i/o de repressió, el context de resistència pot ser propens a supervalorar alguns aspectes més directament lingüístics o destacables des del punt de vista "local" i ésser cec a altres característiques potser més interessants, i que apareixen quan els treiem fora del seu propi context. (FMMM: box 13, folder 1)

> [There are primordial elements in a poem that link it to the language in which it was originally written, but when these disappear, other elements that were perhaps secondary or hidden become more prominent and throb with more intensity. This is especially important in the cultures of minority languages where, often, the very situation of precarity and/or repression, the context of

resistance might lend itself to the overemphasis on some more directly linguistic aspects or those which stand out from a 'local' point of view, and a blindness to other characteristics that are perhaps more interesting, and that appear when we take them out of their own context.]

Marçal thus acknowledges that 'minority' cultures and languages may be inclined to be inward-looking due to a preoccupation with their own precarity. To counter an inward-looking tendency, she dialogues with the works of Sappho and Vivien and translates them into Catalan in her novel, thus prompting Catalonia to reread itself and also permitting new readings of their works. Her reflections and practice of translation as both an act of love and a disruption of purely local concerns is similar to the words of Apter who also sees translation as a way of overcoming individual and collective narcissism of the sort that Peri Rossi describes in 'El Gran Ombligo' [The Great Navel], a city akin to Barcelona in *La nave*. Apter writes:

> Cast as an *act of love*, and as an *act of disruption*, translation becomes a means of repositioning the subject in the world and in history; a means of *rendering self-knowledge foreign* to itself; a way of denaturalizing citizens, taking them *out of the comfort zone of national space*, daily ritual, and pre-given domestic arrangements. It is a truism that the experience of becoming proficient in another tongue delivers a salubrious *blow to narcissism*, both national and individual. (2006: 6, my emphasis)

Of course, however metaphorical Apter's intention here, the idea of a 'comfort zone of national space' is not universal and should not be taken for granted: in Catalonia, especially given the recent violence of agents of the centralised Spanish state during and following the last referendum, it would be short-sighted to describe this space as a 'comfort zone'.

I have shown in this section that translation as digestion, incorporation, becoming the other, and othering the self does not necessarily mean forming a complete or coherent image of other writers and their works, appropriating them in an imperialistic gesture, or simplifying them, as has frequently occurred with the figure of Sappho. The process can, on the contrary, stop the international perspective on a nation being reduced to particular concerns, instead being appreciated in its complex diversity. In contrast with the approach of those translators who sought to complete the extant fragments of Sappho's songs, Marçal's translation practice is at once an act of incorporation and of recognition of the other and of the self, be this an individual or a nation, as *other*, and as inaccessible as a whole. Similarly, in her transposition of Vivien to the script/screen, Sara T. must confront the fragmentation of the figure of Vivien and her work.

The Sketch of a Sketch: Fragmentation and the Unfinished Work

In the novel, Sara T. struggles initially to come to terms with the 'forgotten things' in Vivien's life. When she finishes her screenplay, she writes a letter to a friend noting the script's 'incompleteness':

> És com si [...] no fos sinó *una còpia dolentíssima, una rèplica llunyana*, d'aquell que jo pretenia fer. Un esbós, tal vegada: hi ha a grans trets allò que volia dir, però essencialment incomplet. Això, que potser només és la constatació de l'inevitable, en aquest cas és més greu. Perquè un guió ja és sempre, en si, un esbós. Així doncs el meu text no arriba sino a ser *l'esbós d'un esbós.* (378, my emphasis)

> [It is as if [...] it were only *a terrible copy, a distant replica*, of what I was trying to create. A sketch, perhaps: it contains, broadly, what I was trying to say, but it is, essentially, incomplete. This phenomenon, which is possibly an affirmation of the inevitable, is more serious in this case. Because a script is always in itself a sketch. Therefore, my text becomes no more than *the sketch of a sketch.*] (my emphasis)

Reference to her finished text as a 'terrible copy', a 'distant replica', and a 'sketch of a sketch', reveals that Sara T. feels that she is unable to conjure with words the life of Vivien that she hoped to portray. Vivien represents, for Sara T., incompleteness and fragmentation, but she also leads her to go beyond considering incompletion to be solely a particular feature of Vivien's life and work. Sara T. concludes that her 'sketch of a sketch' is a more marked manifestation of the inherent 'incompleteness' of all representation, that inevitably simplifies and carries over, impossibly, as in metaphor, or re-presents the reality that it depicts. In her consideration of 'lesbian : writing', Meese also acknowledges the 'failure' inherent in representation: 'As with lovers, in the relationship of language and act or event, there is always failure. Nothing is what/as it seems (semes). Could it be, I worry, that what I say is not what I mean at all?' (1992: 94).

Marçal, who was first and foremost a poet, appears to have come to grapple increasingly with the limits of representation in reflecting her world. Her first books of poetry — *Cau de llunes* (1977), *Bruixa de dol* (1979), and *Sal oberta* (1982) [Open Salt] — align, as Noèlia Díaz Vicedo argues (2014: 59, 61), with the notion of poetry as the ordering of chaos, chaos from which a subject emerges. Marçal herself compares the poem to the symbol of the mirror: 'Crec que és una recerca de la identitat, però d'una identitat completa. Ens hi reconeixem sencers, en el mirall. Aquest construeix i reflecteix la imatge d'una certa aparença de coherència' (cited in Díaz Vicedo 2014: 42) [I think that it is a search for identity, but a complete identity. In the mirror, we recognise ourselves as whole. This constructs and reflects the image of a certain appearance of coherence]. The desire for order is apparent in the majority of Marçal's poetry through her adherence to traditional forms such as sonnets, sestinas, and Sapphic stanzas. In *Terra de Mai* (1982) [Neverland/Land of Mai, with Mai being the name of one of Marçal's lovers] she describes a climactic utopian fusion of female bodies which leads to a sense of feeling rooted and at one with the natural world, as in 'Sextina-mirall' [Sestina-Mirror]. Here, the tree, often associated with genealogy (the family tree), is altered through the addition of a woman clinging on to it:

> Cap foc no s'arbra com tu dins la terra,
> dins de l'espai atònit del meu sexe
> on es dreça el deler contra la runa.
> [...]
> Arrapada a l'arrel d'aquest gran arbre,
> cap foc no s'arbra com jo dins la terra. (2017: 244)

> [No fire plants itself like you in the earth,
> in the astonished space of my sex
> where desire is built against the rubble.
> [...]
> Clinging to the root of that large tree,
> no fire plants itself like I do in the earth.]

In Marçal's poetry she eventually abandons classical forms, reflecting her growing awareness that an apparently complete identity is merely the illusory and alluring unity of an inescapably fragmented subject. *Terra de Mai* or 'neverland' is perhaps a reference to utopia, which remits both to 'no place' (*ou* + *topos*, Greek for 'not' and 'place') and also to a better place (*eu* + *topos*, Greek for 'good' and 'place). Marçal states that poetry is 'el mirall on es reconeix, unificada i dotada de sentit, per un instant la vivència fragmentària i sense forma' (Marçal cited in Riera 2010: 257) [the mirror where one can see a fragmentary and formless experience unified and endowed with meaning for an instant]. She recognises that the comforting unity of the image in the mirror, and of the family tree, is ephemeral.

In *La germana, l'estrangera* (1985), perhaps a play on Audre Lorde's *Sister Outsider* (1984) published the previous year, Marçal experiences giving birth as a fracturing of the bond with the foetus, which accords with her rupturing of familiar family tropes. She renders such tropes strange: 'jo contemplava aquell bocí de mi | esdevingut, ja per sempre, estranger' (2017: 282) [I contemplated that piece of me | that had become forever foreign]. The fracturing of self and other in Marçal's later poetry may be considered in the light of Monique Wittig's call for the splitting of the self as a radical act of resistance to patriarchal language. Wittig's emphasis on violence within language and in desire between lesbians challenges the stereotypical visions of maternity and sorority in which relations between women are frequently presented as soft and nurturing. For Wittig, the splitting of the subject is part and parcel of the act of lesbian love: 'I see your bones covered with flesh the iliacs the kneecaps the shoulders. I remove the muscles . . . I take each one between my fingers the long muscles the round muscles the short muscles' ([1973] 1975: 31). Wittig enacts what she considers to be a specifically lesbian violence through language, shattering the female subject-as-object of patriarchal language that is behind the standard first person pronoun, 'je'. Her trademark split pronoun in *The Lesbian Body* ([1973] 1975) — j/e — symbolises her rejection of the dominant social order.

Marçal confronts the literal collapse of patriarchal influence after the death of her father in 1984, about which she writes in *Desglaç* (1989). It leads to a period of melancholy, but also to a questioning of the pressures for heteronormative conformity inherent in patriarchal law. It prompts her to imagine the possibilities of rebirth through her love for another woman. In 'Sota el signe del drac' [Under the Sign of the Dragon], Marçal notes her ambivalence at the time of her father's passing, which she sees as both an ending and a beginning. It offers potential for new ways of being: 'la desintegració aparent és també la possibilitat de *fluir*. Enllà queda la rigidesa, l'encarcarament, els moviments d'autòmata, la repetició compulsiva i mecànica dels gestos. Camí *fluid*, de nou sense esquemes ni pautes' ([1989] 2017: 5–6, my emphasis) [apparent disintegration is also the possibility to *flow*. Rigidity, robotic movements, and the compulsive and mechanical repetition of gestures are left behind. A *fluid* path, without structures and guidelines once more] (my emphasis). Her father's death heralds a new fluidity beyond the mechanical and often compulsive force of habit. Thus, it does not appear incidental that Marçal started researching and writing her sole novel, the anomaly in her oeuvre, in the year of her father's death. It seems to be the outcome of her grappling with and pushing at the limits of poetry that aimed to depict an ordered reality. In the novel, she probes the cohering effect of writing, exposing instead its potential to fragment. In the author's note, Marçal describes *La passió* as having 'alguna cosa de trencaclosques a mig fer. I alguna cosa, encara, de *collage*' (396) [the feel of a half-finished puzzle. And, more than that, the feel of a collage], echoing Sara T.'s earlier comments on the sense of incompleteness of her work.

In *Raó del cos*, Marçal's confrontation with the limitations of the rigid poetic structures of her earlier collections see her turn to free verse and experimental forms. The idea of 'l'esbós d'un esbós' [the sketch of a sketch] ties in with the limits of representation that Marçal addresses in a very short poem in the volume in which she reflects on the limits of language which cause the poet to feel in a sort of double exile:

> Porta entre mar
> i mar
> la paraula:
> exili de l'exili. (2017: 484)[3]

> [Door between sea
> and sea
> the word:
> exile from exile.] (2014a: 53)

Words may lead to an awareness of one's distance or 'exile' from the unified subjectivity that they purport to represent and to one's distance from one's imagined reality. 'L'esbós d'un esbós' [the sketch of a sketch] and 'exili de l'exili' [exile from exile] chime with Goujon's interpretation of Vivien seeking 'refuge' in the illusion of words and a 'love of love' when love itself proves destructive to her: 'parole finirono col diventare la sua grande illusione, così come *l'amore dell'amore* prese il posto dell'amore' (Goujon 1983: 13, my emphasis) [words ended up being her big illusion, just as *the love of love* took the place of love] (my emphasis). Similarly, Meese considers 'writ[ing] (of) the lesbian' to involve 'speaking metaphorically about metaphor, or representationally of representation' (1992: 8). Marçal's increasing sense of the distance between words and reality resonates with Vivien experiencing love through the *illusion* of love in texts. Both women illustrate Meese's association of lesbian desire with metatextual alienation in language.

Marçal's shift from a notion of poetry as coherence to poetry as revealing the limits of such coherence reflects the root of the word 'poetry', which is connected to 'heaping up' or 'piling up' (in contrast with prose, which refers to moving straight ahead). The heaps and piles may be an attempt at order but they often bring disparate elements together. In the case of *La passió* we observe an intermixing and blending of genres, of order and disorder, of poetry and prose. Indeed, Julià suggests that rather than considering *La passió* to be a novel, 'potser seria millor definir-la com un text de textos' (2013: 174) [perhaps it could be better defined as a text of texts]. As well as the poetic prose of the novel, it contains extracts from poems and, as we can see particularly in the 'Monòdia final', prose composed of lines of poetry by Vivien and Sappho. While *La passió* is widely regarded to be the sole novel of a poet, Cinta Massip sees the novel as 'pure poetry': '[Marçal] no va deixar mai d'escriure poesia. Pensa que *La passió segons Renée Vivien* és poesia pura! [...] Tot i ser posada al servei de la narrativa, per damunt de tot hi ha el seu món poètic' (cited in Climent 2013: 121) [Marçal never stopped writing poetry. Just think, *La passió* is pure poetry! While it serves the narrative, above all there is a poetic world].

Reflecting the merging of poetry and prose, in some early notes for the novel, we see a draft of a letter by Sara T. in which she writes of struggling with the novel form as it seems too 'solid'. It appears from the notes that she is flitting between writing a screenplay and writing a novel. She describes being drawn back to 'lengthy poetry', or, indeed, as in the title of one of Vivien's works, to 'Poèmes en prose' [Poems in Prose]:

> La novel·la se'm segueix negant... tinc una estranya dificultat amb aquest gènere; no puc sostreure'm a la impressió de fals que em provoca *tota versemblança sòlida i acabada*. I si fujo d'això, em trobo tornant a la poesia, a *una poesia allargassada*, que en perdre la concisió, perd també una de les seves qualitats essencials: ja la vida en la poesia em sembla massa aigua en cistella, però *la seva fragmentarietat, la seva fulguració breu, em sembla que correspon més al vívid llampec dels instants forts*, aquells que, al meu entendre, mereixen perdurar. (FMMM, box 8/5, folder 4, sheet 7, my emphasis)

> [the novel continues to elude me.... I have peculiar difficulties with this genre. I can't get beyond the feeling of falsity that all *solid and complete verisimilitude* provokes in me. And, if I flee from that, I find myself returning to poetry, to *a lengthened form of poetry* that loses its concision, and also one of its essential qualities: it's hard enough as it is to fit life into poetry, but *its fragmentation, its brief splendour, corresponds better to the vivid lightning flash of intense moments*, those which, as I see it, deserve to last.] (my emphasis)

For Sara T., text in prose gives an impression of being fixed and complete, whereas concise and fragmented poetry is more suited to evoking the intense moments that she sees as worthy of being immortalised through writing. Sara T.'s reflections on genre offer an explanation for the fragmented form and poetic style of Marçal's novel. The use of visual metaphors in Sara T.'s description of the 'splendour' of poetry that can better represent the 'lightning flash' of strong feeling also hint at why she turned to the visual medium of cinema in writing a screenplay about Vivien. Indeed, in a letter to the Institució de les Lletres Catalanes requesting a grant to write the novel, Marçal describes the script as 'el "gènere" incomplet per excel·lència' (box 9/8, folder 1, sheet 9) [the incomplete genre *par excellence*].

As well as a sense that fragmentation can better evoke moments of intense feeling, Sara T.'s eventual acceptance of the fragmented script results partly from a realisation that the sense of incompleteness is what characterised the life and works of Vivien, as well as her own. Of Vivien, Sara T. states:

> Allò que em sembla crucial és la seva lúcida i gens resignada consciència d'esbós, és a dir, d'incompleció, i, alhora, la intuïtiva certesa que qualsevol intent de plenitud real seria fal·laç: només el somni — el desig? — pot omplir aquest buit, aquesta ànsia immoderada i desmesurada, sempre decebuda, de totalitat i d'absolut. I, estretament lligada al somni, al desig, la literatura. (378)

> [What seems crucial to me is her lucid awareness of the sketch, that is, of incompletion, which lacks any feeling of resignation, and, at the same time, the intuitive certainty that any attempt at real plenitude would be deceptive: only dreams — desire? — can fill that gap, that excessive yearning for totality and the absolute, which will always be unsatisfied. A yearning closely linked to dreams, desire, literature.]

Sara T. comes to acknowledge that the sketch is a symbol of an ambivalent incompleteness; it may provoke a longing for an impossible wholeness, but it is simultaneously seductive, as suggested in a line by Vivien, translated by Marçal in *La passió*, in which she writes, '[l]'encís tan dolorós dels esbossos m'atreu' (378) [the painful charm of sketches attracts me]. Sara T. comes to understand, through Vivien, that the gaps in a sketch can be filled through the dream-filled desire that prompts the writer to write, seeking a sense of plenitude that will be forever just out of reach. Accordingly, Sara T. ultimately accepts the difficulties in approaching the fragmented figure of Vivien.

Reflecting on such difficulties in confronting a queer past, Love argues that negative affect in queer histories should be embraced for its potentially disruptive force. She critiques what she sees as an emphasis on positive affect in queer historiography. She writes:

> negative or ambivalent identifications with the past can serve to disrupt the present. Making connections with historical losses or with images of *ruined* or *spoiled identity* in the past can set into motion a gutting 'play of recognitions,' another form of effective history. (2007: 45, my emphasis)

Love goes on to explain that the queer historian 'cannot help wanting to save figures from the past, but this mission is doomed to fail' (Love 2007: 51); it is, as Sara T. puts it, 'sempre decebuda' [always unsatisfied]. However, through the process of approaching the ruins of the past, writers may be able to save themselves, nonetheless.

In the archive, I found a draft of a letter written by Sara T. to her friend

Chantal that resonates with the ruins of a Foucauldian fractured genealogy, with Halberstam's aforementioned 'scavenger methodology' (1998: 13), and with Love's call not to shy away from ruins. Sara T. writes: 'I jo vetllo les precioses *ruïnes* de Pauline. I el meu amor per ella, el meu culte, és el de l'arqueòleg que extreu glòria de *la mort*, que arrenca de l'oblit les cendres i la pols i les pedres *mutilades*' (box 8/6, folder 6, sheet 28, my emphasis) [I watch over the beautiful *ruins* of Pauline. And my love for her, my cult, is that of the archaeologist who extracts glory from *death*, who pulls from oblivion the ashes, dust and *mutilated* stones] (my emphasis). The ashes, dust, and mutilated stones resemble Love's 'negative affect', and Sara T. is able to extract 'glory' from them. Marçal uses similar terms in *Raó del cos* as she reflects on facing death. In response to Maria-Antònia Salvà's 'D'un cactus' [About a Cactus] she writes:

> entre les pedres dures
> de cega desmemòria que endures,
> et sé. I saber-te em dóna terra, arrel.
> (2017: 475)

> [among hard stones
> of blind forgetfulness you endure.
> I know you. And knowing you gives me earth, roots.] (2014a: 39)

She recognises her literary predecessor in the gaps between stones of 'forgetfulness' or 'unmemory', gaps that, in keeping with Foucault's fragmented genealogy, enable her to root herself in a literary genealogy with Salvà. The blind 'unmemory' echoes the blind seamstress in the lines that open *Raó del cos*.

There is another draft letter in the archives, the 'Carta final' [Final letter], which is a draft for the chapter in the novel titled 'Papers privats de Sara T. (10)' [Sara T.'s Private Papers (10)]. In the letter in the archive, Sara T. explains that representing a single moment in words is, for Renée, like 'una gran Sinècdoque impossible, en que la part ocupa il·lusioriament el lloc del Tot' [a great impossible Synecdoche in which the part deceptively appeared to occupy the place of the Whole]. She goes on to say that Renée seems to have perceived herself to be living precisely '[e]n la tensió d'aquesta impossibilitat' (box 8/6, folder 7, sheet 44) [in the tension of this impossibility]. Like Sappho, then, Vivien inhabits a sort of limbo between wholeness and fragmentation. In the novel itself, Sara T. reflects that '[e]ls mots que pretenen salvar la fissura no fan sinó representar-la, recrear-la i refer-la un i altre cop' (379) [the words that try to remedy the fissure only serve to represent it, recreate it, and remake it over and over again]. We can see that the fragments, the mutilated parts that stand in for a whole, are a site of both tension between the desire for totality and the impossibility of a total representation, and a celebration of the possibilites afforded by fragmentation. The spaces in the sketch, in ruins, the absences they contain, the shadows, make them exemplary of Meese's 'lesbian : writing', which triggers further writing:

> Hers is a profitable absence, produces 'more' writing, the undecidability of which permits, indeed requires, us to produce other writings, other likenesses, diversity, change. [...] In/completion motivates our compulsion, our obsession, and, better still, our passion for the return, the repetition as reappearance of

the lesbian-in-writing, who, in coming *again*, comes a second and a third time
as though recalling that illusory, shadowy first time, and, of course, the first
(mythically originary) Lesbian. (Meese 1992: 17–18)

Literature and imagination flourish amongst the fragments, which prompt the
writer to shuttle between the ancient past and the present. In Vivien's novel,
A Woman Appeared to Me (1904), the character of Barney states 'I, to realise my
dream of passion, must collect *scattered* perfections, in order to unite them into a
harmonious whole created by my dreams' (4). Desiring dreams fill the gaps in the
sketch. For Meese, via Barthes, the unsaid is highly erotic: 'absences, or suggestions
of the unseen, are even more erotic than presence or what is revealed. [...] the space
between, the suggestion of what is there but not yet there, the visibly invisible,
makes erotic claims' (1992: 99). The epigraph to the Columna Jove edition of Riera's
collection of short stories, which takes as its title that of the most well-known story
in the collection, 'Te deix', is a 'Fragment mai no escrit de SAFO' [Fragment never
written by Sappho] that bears out this notion of the erotic claim of space:

> ('Escolliré per sempre més la teva
> absència, donzella,
> perquè el que de veritat estim
> no és el teu cos
> ni el record del teu cos
> tan bell sota la lluna;
> el que de veritat estim
> és l'empremta que has deixat
> sobre l'arena.')
> ([1975] 2005: 9)
>
> [('I will choose forevermore your
> absence, fair maiden,
> because what I truly love
> is not your body
> nor even the memory of your body,
> so beautiful under the moonlight;
> what I truly love
> is the print you have left
> on the sand.')]

Here, the absence of a woman is praised, not their physical body or even a memory
of it, but its trace, the marks it has left in the margins, bracketed off, like this
epigraph, leaving a space to be filled with imagination. Counter to Meese's desire
for a lesbian 'with skin', perhaps what the reader wants is not a body, but evidence
of the effects of that body on the world; a lesbian trace.

In *La passió*, Vivien mourns her works having left the sphere of texts that reach us
in an incomplete state as they leave 'espai per al no-dit, per a l'irreal, per al somni,
per al vertigen' (89) [space for the unsaid, for the unreal, for dreams, for dizziness].
Similarly, Marçal writes in her notes that she wants the novel to be 'un tot procedent
de fragments. Sensació d'incomplet i d'acabat' (box 2/5, folder 3, sheet 2) [a whole
created from fragments. A feeling of being finished, yet incomplete]. Fragmented
works call for the deployment of imagination and Vivien and Marçal want their

work to belong in this category of texts that invite readers' collaboration; the reader must investigate, like Sara T. Indeed, the word 'investigate' has similar associations to the word 'esbossar', meaning 'to sketch' in Catalan. 'Investigate' comes from the Latin *investigat*, meaning 'traced out'. Marçal is evidently attracted by the potential of self-consciously fragmented representation for encouraging a personal readerly response to the text.

In the author's note she states that she wanted to give 'una perspectiva múltiple, complexa, fins i tot a voltes contradictòria [de Vivien] i del seu entorn' (396) [a multiple, complex, even sometimes contradictory perspective on Vivien and her surroundings]; the disjointed nature of her novel expressly calls for a multitude of interpretations of Vivien's life. She hopes to encourage contra-dictions, other sayings, counter sayings. She refers to *La passió* as 'un punt de partença, un escarit esquema inicial' (ibid.) [a starting point, a bare first outline], thus emphasising the role of the reader in building on the sketch she provides. She explains how she intended the apparently chaotic style of the novel to impact on the readers:

> He cercat també que les lectores i els lectors s'endinsin en la història no pas d'una manera lineal, sinó que aquesta es vagi construint en la seva ment a partir de dades fragmentàries [...] tal com ens sol arribar la informació sobre els éssers i els esdeveniments del present o del passat. (ibid.)

> [I have endeavoured to make readers delve into the story not in a linear way, but in such a way that the story comes together in their minds through fragmentary pieces of information [...] just like we usually find out about beings and happenings in the past and present.]

For Marçal, incoherence or contradiction in the text make it a more realistic encounter with the present and the past that calls for intimate engagement.

Marçal does not accord, then, with Maria Àngels Cabré's call for Catalan lesbianism to be represented conventionally: 'el que volem és tenir bons llibres entre les mans amb els quals les lectores lesbianes puguin créixer, madurar, estimar, enamorar-se, desenamorar-se i tantes altres coses sense haver de llegir entre línies' (2011: 37) [what we want are good books with which lesbian readers may be able to grow, mature, love, fall in love, fall out of love and so many other things without having to read between the lines]. Cabré's unwillingness to read between the lines implies a desire for more linear narratives suited to the passive, conventional reader accustomed to conduct manuals. Marçal, on the other hand, suggests that the 'essence' of what a text purports to represent may lie elusively between the lines, between the fragments, in the very shadows lamented by some critics of lesbian literature. At the start of the novel, the narrator confesses her 'ingènuament inesperada sensació de fracàs' [naively unexpected feeling of failure] (15) in capturing what is 'essential' to Vivien, comparing herself to a photographer who cannot fully capture a landscape no matter how many photos he takes:

> com el fotògraf neòfit que hagués intentat de trobar tots els angles i punts d'enfocament d'un paisatge, i al final se sorprengués de tenir a les mans només unes dotzenes de cartrons que deixen a fora allò de més essencial que a ell li sembla saber què és. (ibid.)

[like the neophyte photographer who has tried to find all of the angles and focus points of a landscape, and ends up being surprised to be left only with dozens of camera rolls that do not capture what is most essential in the landscape, an essential element that he believes himself to know.]

I have shown, then, that readers are invited in Marçal's novel to consider what is implicit, rather than explicit in the text — to 'endinsar-s'hi' [delve into it]. Much as Sara T.'s relationship to Vivien is queered when she attempts to 'straighten' Vivien, the reader's relationship with implicit meaning in the text — from the Latin, *implicitus*, 'entwined' — involves a delving into the text rather than a superficial encounter with an explicit text — from the Latin *explicitus*, past participle of *explicare*, 'to unfold' — , a 'straightened' text. In this sense, Marçal's text exemplifies flores's statement that:

> entre saber lesbiano y lengua tortillera no habrá relación de claridad ni luminosidad sino entrelíneas a desplegar, gestos furtivos a desenterrar y pasadizos a transitar. No hay aquí texto llano, translúcido, fácil y militante a la típica usanza; sólo retos de lectura y una provocación a la re-escritura. (2013: 27–28)

> [between lesbian knowledge and *tortillera* (a slang word for lesbian) language there will not be a bright and clear relationship, but spaces to unfold between the lines, furtive gestures to excavate, passages to travel. Here there is no flat, translucid, easy text, easy to deploy politically, but reading challenges and a provocation to rewrite the text.]

For flores, as for Marçal, reading 'lesbian' texts is and *should be* a challenge, an encounter with shadows and in folds. Reading between the lines and travelling *through* the shadows in the text provokes the reader to rewrite them. What, then, does this infinite process of rewriting mean for the authorial legacy of Sapphic writers?

The Reader is Born (and the Author Lives On)

> Oblideu-me, que sóc una ànima passatgera...
> — Vivien (cited in Marçal 2008: 394)
>
> [Forget me, for I am a passing soul...]

The first section of *La passió* (after the 'Introit') ends with Amédée, a poet and friend of Vivien, reading a newspaper announcement of her death (50); subsequently we read multiple, partial, often contradictory depictions of her life. As Julià notes (2013: 182), it is significant that the date of Sara T.'s last letter to Chantal explaining that she has finished the screenplay and enclosing a copy of it is 21 November 1985 (377), which is seventy-six years to the day after *Le Figaro* reported Vivien's death (19). The same date comes to mark both Vivien's death and her rebirth through the perspectives of others on her life. On the one hand, the '*segons* Renée Vivien' [*according to* Renée Vivien] (my emphasis) of the novel's title suggests attribution. The reader might expect from the title that Vivien will be a key narrator. On the other hand, the word 'segons' highlights the subjectivity of a narrative as one version amongst many possible versions; and so it is that Vivien turns out to be present in the novel primarily as the *object* of the narrative, present largely through the words of others.

It is significant that Sara T. is at Vivien's grave as she struggles to make sense of the poet's life from the fragmentary textual clues that she has discovered during her research. The aforementioned scene at the cemetery can be read as a staging of the reader's grappling with the death of the author as a unified, coherent, single subject with mastery over meaning. Vivien's death in *La passió* allegorises the loss of authorial control over the narratives of her life; her passing is vital for her incorporation in the present.

Critics often credit Sappho and her contemporaries with giving birth to the lyric 'I' and to subjectivity in poetry. However, as Yopie Prins argues, via Jesper Svenbro, in Sappho the written 'I' emerges at the moment of death. Svenbro situates Sappho in a context of emerging literacy and claims that 'Sappho understands that, as a consequence of writing, she will be absent, even dead' (cited in Prins 1996: 45). He cites Sappho's Fragment 31 as representative of death by writing and consequent birth by reading: 'the poem is triangulated in such a way that Sappho may be revived by the voice of a reader, who lives in a future when she will be dead' (Prins 1996: 45). The final lines of Fragment 31 are:

> I am and dead — or almost
> I seem to me
> (Sappho translated by Carson 2003: 63)

For Svenbro and Prins, the death of authorial voice permits and, in fact, is necessary for the rebirth of the text, and the author, in the reader.

I am not meaning to conjure the death of the author in the Barthesian sense of the separating of the work from its real-life author and the context of its creation. In his 1967 essay, Barthes argued that interpretation of the text should be separated from considerations of authorial intention and biographical context, a concept popularised as 'the death of the author'. What we see in the works of Vivien, Marçal, and Sappho is an authorial death in order that the author may, paradoxically perhaps, live on. Sappho expresses this sentiment confidently in 'I declare':

> someone will remember us
> I say
> even in another time
> (Sappho translated by Carson 2003: 297)

So, whereas Svenbro and Prins associate the poetic 'I' with death, the 'I' in the lines above is sure of authorial legacy. Despite Vivien's nonchalance in the words cited in the epigraph to this section — '[o]blideu-me' [forget me], she exclaims — her works also reveal a concern for legacy. The following lines, translated by Marçal, appear towards the end of the novel in the 'Monòdia final':

> *Vosaltres, belles noies, per qui jo vaig escriure...*
> *Vosaltres que estimava, ¿llegireu els meus versos,*
> *en els futurs matins d'un univers nevat*
> *o en capvespres futurs de roses i de flames?* (382)

[You, beautiful girls, for whom I wrote...
You whom I loved, will you read my verses
on future mornings in a snowy universe
or at future twilights of roses and flames?]

Having previously claimed to be writing for her pleasure alone and having willed readers to forget her, here Vivien states that she was writing for hypothetical women of the future whom she loves. Vivien has evidently picked up on Sappho's images of flames, flowers, and poetic inspiration as mentioned in the following fragment. We can observe Sappho's fear of invisibility for those who do not leave a legacy through artistic creation, which implies that the reverse is true of those who do leave such creations; the 'Pierian spring' is a symbol of poetic wisdom (Poochigian 2009: 16):

Dead you will lie and never memory of you
will there be nor desire into the aftertime — for you do not
share in the roses
of Pieria [...]
(Sappho translated by Carson 2003: 115)

Poetry is therefore a way of living on, of ensuring some sort of afterlife. In her essay, 'Sappho's Afterlife in Translation', Prins, like Carson, is attentive to the contrast between oral and written culture. She asserts that Sappho's immortality specifically requires the death of her *voice*; her legacy is, perhaps paradoxically, assured by the 'passing' of her song: 'In a simultaneous conversion of voice into text and text into voice, what remains is pure "white" pages that are not mere transcriptions of song but the inscription of an idealized voice that leaves no textual trace' (1996: 36).

If we take the passing of the author's voice as being a condition for their 'remaining' to be the case, Vivien's line in the epigraph to this section on being a 'passing soul' is not, as it might first seem, conducive to forgetting her. Sara T.'s reference to Vivien's 'glotis paralitzada' [paralysed glottis/vocal cords] recalls Sappho's speaking through her voicelessness: 'Aquesta pluralitat de missatges pòstums atribuïts a una agonitzant amb la glotis paralitzada és un fet significatiu i gens banal. Renée ha estat un d'aquells personatges mítics que funcionen com una pantalla: tothom hi projecta el propi imaginari' (53) [This plurality of posthumous messages attributed to a dying woman with paralysed vocal cords is a significant and not at all unimportant fact. Renée has become one of those mythic characters who functions as a screen: everyone projects their own imaginary onto her]. The depiction of Vivien as a blank screen on which readers' imaginations are reflected (reminding the reader of Sara T.'s transposition of Vivien's life onto the screen) emphasises the status of the reader as the writer, as the creator of a narrative. In this way, jouissance and ecstasy overcome the potential fixation or 'paralysis' of the writer.

The idea of Vivien as a blank screen and the 'white' pages of Sappho's song recall the entry for Sappho in Wittig and Sande Zeig's *Lesbian Peoples: Material for a Dictionary* (1980) — a full blank page. The blank page is both an acknowledgement that so little is known of her life and that so little of her work is extant, which has made her the site of legend and invention. The page also highlights her ghostly presence in absence that lends itself to spectral returns, to disrupting conventional temporality. The blank page can also prove provocative: in the sense of 'before the vocal' and in the sense of inviting or asking for inscription.

Writers living on through the memories of their readers are an example of an alternative form of legacy to motherhood. In the account of her relationship with Vivien that Kerimée writes for Reinach in *La passió*, she explains that she has decided to write precisely because she has produced neither children nor artworks: 'No sóc artista ni he tingut fills. [...] ¿La paraula escrita pot ser, simplement, aquesta altra memòria que perdura més que nosaltres i dóna un xic de treva a la nostra mort?' (249) [I am not an artist and I haven't had children [...] Could the written word simply be this other memory that lasts longer than we do and offers a small truce to our deaths?]. We have returned to procreative metaphors. The word 'genealogy' comes from the Greek *genea*, meaning race or generation, which in its original meaning is linked to the inheritance of characteristics through blood/genes which has a certain inescapability and inevitability about it, as in a familial blood line. Sara T. writes of her power to give life to the past, referring to texts as 'vampires' and recalling De Andrade's conception of translation as a blood transfusion: 'Estrany poder aquest de donar o no donar sentit als personatges del passat, de ser sang o no per a aliment d'aquests rars vampirs que són els textos que necessiten nodrir-se de nosaltres' (382) [This strange power to give or not give meaning to figures from the past, to be or not be blood with which to feed these strange vampires that are the texts that need to feed off us]. Sara T.'s reference to the texts from the past needing to be fed by readers illustrates Marçal's emphasis on rhizomatic affinity or alliance as a counter-point to arborescent genealogy with its consecutive generations.

The Deleuzo-Guattarian rhizome offers a more horizontal, egalitarian pattern than the tree of knowledge and its branches. In the Translator's Foreword to *A Thousand Plateaus* (1980) Brian Massumi states that the rhizome 'synthesizes a multiplicity of elements without effacing their heterogeneity or hindering their potential for future rearranging (to the contrary)' (1987: xiii). In its incorporation of disparity, the concept of the rhizome can be likened to Foucauldian genealogy that 'show[s] the heterogeneity of what was imagined consistent with itself' (1984a: 82) and the Marçalian reaction of fragments. The fragments in the Marçalian Sapphic text represent possibility and potentiality, an entity always in the process of becoming. Through fragmentation, meaning is not reified; new meanings emerge, transitively and simultaneously. Gilles Deleuze and Félix Guattari state:

> A rhizome has no beginning or end; it is always in the middle, between things, interbeing, *intermezzo*. The tree is filiation, but the rhizome is alliance, uniquely alliance. The tree imposes the verb 'to be,' but the fabric of the rhizome is the conjunction, 'and . . . and . . . and . . .' (25)

For Deleuze and Guattari, the 'rhizome is an antigenealogy. It is a short-term memory, or antimemory' (21). I would argue that the notion of an 'antigenealogy' is perhaps too binary and antagonistic, would suggest instead a twisting, bending, turning genealogy. Not an anti-memory, but a partial one. Considered in this way, genealogy shifts from a teleological obsession with the past to a realisation that both the past and the present feed into each other.

As Sara T. asked the absent Vivien earlier in the novel, '¿Com [...] fer que la meva sang recorri la teva ombra?' (91) [How can I [...] make my blood run through your shadow?]. She is willing to give her blood but, as a reader, she is also 'vampiric', she chooses which texts to feed on. Sara T. thus notes that there is an interdependency between herself, as a reader, and Vivien. The reader seeks identification with the writer, as we noted earlier, but the writer also needs the reader to bring their 'vampiric' texts to life, texts that are nourished by readers' minds, which ensures their continued legacy. Meese also highlights the importance of both reader and writer in producing 'lesbian : writing' together:

> Through writing I call out the lesbian *in me*, and *in you* as you read my letters. [...] Of course, you can decide to read or to put the book down. You agree or disagree, defining a lesbian reader as you go. *Together, we create* templates, texts, for lesbian : love. (1992: 137, my emphasis)

In her 'Lectura comentada' [Recital with Commentary] at the beginning of *Diàlegs gais, lesbians, queer/Diálogos gays, lesbianos, queer* (2007b), a book that collates the papers from a multidisciplinary Catalan conference on queer culture and activism, Peri Rossi refers to Octavio Paz's notion of poetic tradition constructed by the individual, in contrast with genealogy in familial terms:

> Paz dice [...] que cada poeta inventa su tradición, y quizás es la única cosa que podemos inventarnos, porque como la familia real no la podemos inventar, no podemos inventar a nuestros padres y nuestros hermanos, tenemos el derecho de inventar a quienes nos precedieron. (15)

> [Paz says [...] that each poet invents their own tradition, and perhaps it is the only thing we can invent for ourselves, given that we can't invent our real families, we can't invent our parents and siblings, we have the right to invent those who came before us.]

The notion of inventing one's literary genealogy rather than inheriting it can be linked with the Sapphic emphasis on community formation by affinity rather than collectivity through kinship. Sappho, in her role as educator rather than purely as a biological mother,[4] offers a radical reimagining of community distinct to the family, etymologically marked by notions of patriarchy, authority, and control, as discussed in the introduction to this book. Marçal's calling into question of masculinist visions of history through problematising the proper name in *La passió* can be considered in light of collectivity beyond the family. Sara T.'s name is partially withheld throughout the novel and she is an alter-ego for Marçal, Vivien is a pseudonym for Pauline Tarn who has numerous nicknames — 'Pauline, Paule, Paulette. Segons el dia i el matís' (31) [Pauline, Paule, Paulette. It depends on the day and context] — and many other characters are referred to with multiple names. The disruption of the proper name is a challenge to identity inherited through a bloodline that usually provides a surname or the 'name of the father'.

Reynolds states that '"Sappho" is not a name, much less a person. It is, rather, a space. A space for filling in the gaps, joining up the dots, making something out of nothing' (2000: 2). It is this 'space', recalling the blank screen and blank page, that Marçal believes needs to remain a space and also be filled repeatedly and temporarily to form a dynamic genealogy of women writers, not simply as individuals, but as a network. We could say that in Marçal's vision of genealogy, the women are coordinates joined with dotted lines rather than points absorbed into continuous lines:

> no es tracta de parlar de les escriptores d'una en una, de forma aïllada, tal com massa sovint apareixen les obres de les dones, com suspeses en el buit, desvinculades de qualsevol genealogia femenina i només inserides de forma sovint excèntrica en l'univers cultural heretat, falsament neutre, sinó que la nostra idea és la d'establir les possibles coordenades d'un espai *entre* que permeti un moviment, un recorregut, un viatge que poguéssim fer en comú. (Marçal 1999 cited in Llorca Antolín 2004: 229)

> [it is not about talking about women writers one by one, in isolation, just as women's works all too often appear, as if suspended in a void, disconnected from any female genealogy and only inserted in an often eccentric manner to the inherited cultural universe that falsely claims to be neutral. Our idea is to establish the possible coordinates of an in-between space that permits a movement, a route, a journey that we can go on together.]

Marçal is aware that it is not sufficient simply to rescue single women authors from oblivion because, when recuperated individually and in isolation, they are frequently regarded as 'exceptional' cases. This is doubly so in the case of women representing lesbian desire in their works. Sara T. states that Vivien searches for a genealogy of women that is a '[g]enealogia invisible que uneix indestriablement femenitat, revolta i dolor' (105) [an invisible genealogy that indestructibly unites femininity, revolt, and pain]. This is one reason why many writers look to the past to consolidate their identity in the present, to situate themselves within an existing counter-tradition. Accordingly, intertextuality is crucial in the works of these reader-writers. However, in Marçal's references to the 'in-between space' and 'movement' suggest that she is also wary of fixing writers in set canons of influence.

Despite struggling to identify directly with Vivien, Sara T. nonetheless strives to connect with her, and she acknowledges that their art is the only way of them 'meeting' across time, across an 'abisme' [abyss], another reference to the space between writers: 'sé que Renée i jo ens havíem de trobar així: per damunt d'aquest abisme que els temps i l'oblit han intentat d'establir entre nosaltres' (384) [I know that Renée and I were meant to meet like this: over this abyss that time and oblivion have tried to create between us]. She comes to see their meeting across time as a productive encounter. It is a way of levelling the playing field, rather than adopting the paralysing attitude of idealising her literary predecessor. She writes: 'L'equilibri només es fa possible a través d'aquesta mena de superació — momentània — de la mort que és un poema, un llibre, una pel·lícula... i que cadascuna ha intentat des de la seva banda' (384) [Balance is only possible through this momentary overcoming of death that a poem, a book, a film represents... and that each woman has to attempt from her side]. Writers and readers need each other; Benjamin's 'afterlife' that commences through translation also occurs through reading which is, in itself, an act of translation, of rewriting. In the introduction to a collection of essays on translation in relation to Marçal, Mireia Calafell and Torras write:

> Llegir, interpretar i traduir són noms diferents per a operacions molt properes, indestriables, que es podrien recollir sota el paraigua de la reescriptura; allò que al capdavall dóna vida al text, en reconeix l'existència, el fa ser text que ens fa ser, perquè en definitiva són els textos que ens llegeixen a nosaltres. (2013: 16)

> [Reading, interpreting and translating are different names for very similar and inextricably entwined processes that could be grouped under the umbrella term of rewriting. That which, at the end of the day, gives life to the text, recognises its existence, the making of the text that makes us, because it is definitely the texts that read us.]

The reference to texts 'reading' readers, more than readers reading texts resonates with Marçal describing to Goujon the process of reading Vivien as an attempt to understand herself. In a poem dedicated to Vivien, Marçal acknowledges this two-way process between writer of the past and their reader-writer, keeping each other alive:

> Dues dones: alhora
> fer néixer i néixer, vives
> en el nom i en la carn. (2017 [2000]: 476)

> [Two women:
> giving birth and being born, alive
> in name and flesh.] (2014a: 41)

Rather than displaying a longing for a lost 'whole', Marçal seems to see both Lesbos and 'l'esbós' as sites of potential as they call for creative engagement, for repeated comings-into-being. It seems to be with an eye to future transformations that Marçal brings together chaotic fragments in her novel. For Marçal, fragmented texts are part of a Foucauldian genealogy that counters 'a history whose perspective on all that precedes it implies the end of time, a completed development' (1984a: 86–87), and instead acknowledges the potentiality of the future and of readers' imaginations. In the Marçalian depiction of the search for Sapphic literary genealogy, rather than completely identifying with one figure in the past, readers and writers experience multiple, transnational *identifications* that are necessarily partial and transient. Their perpetual interpretation of textual fragments holds new meanings relevant to changing times and identities. By allowing 'l'esbós' to remain 'un esbós', by revealing and drawing attention to the interstices between fragments, and by leaving space for multiple interpretations, Marçal permits Sapphic texts and authors a certain form of immortality as they are shaped by those who read them.

Notes to Chapter 1

1. This is not to say that the maternal is not erotic, but it is not conventionally depicted as such. For a recent account of the potential eroticism of motherhood, see Nelson (2016). See also Julia Kristeva's chapter 'The Passion According to Motherhood' (note the parallel with the title of Marçal's novel and, of course, with the gospels) in *Hatred and Forgiveness* (2012).
2. *Raó del cos* was translated into English by Montserrat Abelló and Noèlia Díaz Vicedo as *The Body's Reason* (2014). I have used their translations in this book.
3. I would like to thank Montserrat Lunati for drawing my attention to the echo in this poem in

a comment on a version of this paper given at the Anglo-Catalan Society Conference in Cork, September 2014.

4. Some of Sappho's poems seem to suggest that she had a daughter, Kleïs, though this has not been proven (Poochigian 2009: xii).

CHAPTER 2

Affect, Authority, and Inheritance in Cristina Peri Rossi

Part I: Unravelling Compulsory Happiness in Exile: *La nave de los locos* (1984)

> Soy ambigua — dice la poesía —
> como toda revelación.
> — PERI ROSSI ([1979] 2005a: 395)
>
> ['I am ambiguous', says Poetry,
> 'like every revelation.']

A number of feminist critics of Latin American women writers in exile have suggested that women in exile may flourish as they are freed from the traditional gender restrictions imposed on them in their home countries. For example, Kate Averis argues that distance from home may offer 'a new space of agency' and 'a site of creativity' (2014: 3). In a similar vein, Amy Kaminsky describes women's 'discovery within the self of a capacity to survive and grow in the new environment' (1993: 37). Concepts such as 'creativity', 'agency', 'growth' and 'transcendence' abound in these two critics' considerations of women's experiences in exile. The argument that women may enjoy more freedom for self-creation away from their country of birth accords with Rosi Braidotti's Deleuzian theory of subjectivity in which she posits that 'a joyful nomadic force' (1994: 8) is the best basis for a forward-looking feminism.

Braidotti calls for a 'nomadic consciousness', which she describes as 'the kind of critical consciousness that resists settling into socially coded modes of thought and behaviour' (1994: 5). Although she deploys the concept of nomadism in a figurative sense, stating that it is 'the subversion of a set conventions that defines the nomadic state, not the literal act of travelling' (1994: 5), the literal and figurative are deeply interconnected, and at some points merged, in her work. For example, while she notes that she is not referring to the literal act of travelling, she talks about a non-unitary subjectivity as being 'embedded and embodied' and warns against speaking from 'nowhere' (1994: 4). Indeed, the title of the book in which she outlines her position — *Nomadic Subjects: Embodiment and Sexual Difference in Contemporary Feminist Theory* (1994) — emphasises embodiment and the nomadic *subject* rather than metaphorical nomadism.

The fluidity between the figurative and the literal in the unsettled thought about grounded lives that characterises Braidotti's theorisation of nomadic subjectivity offers us a useful lens through which to consider the combination of 'nomadic thought', i.e. the challenging of dogma, and literal movement in *La nave*. The novel, written by Peri Rossi in exile in Barcelona and published in the same year that Marçal started her research into Vivien, is often cited as a key example of experimental Latin American exile writing. In her analysis of Peri Rossi's oeuvre, Claire Lindsay has contested some critics' reductive and problematic alignment of Peri Rossi's literary exploration of the exilic condition with her physical exile. For example, Gustavo San Román argues that Peri Rossi's later work, in what he describes as her 'Spanish phase', explores 'wider psychological and political issues' (cited in Lindsay 2003: 21) than her work written in Uruguay, which he considers to be relevant to a narrower local situation. Similarly, Kaminsky describes writers in exile being 'freed into a perspective of universality' (1987: 149). In contrast, Lindsay argues that even in Peri Rossi's early work that seems firmly rooted in Uruguay, the author writes in the mode of an alienated writer in the Kafkaesque space of symbolic exile, critiquing society from a psychological, rather than necessarily physical, distance (2003: 29–30, 34–35). Lindsay's reading has much in common with Braidotti's figurative use of the nomad. Braidotti's theory proves particularly compelling in the analysis of works written from *or* about exile, symbolic or otherwise, that call into question the authoritarian discourse of military regimes.

La nave was originally published around twelve years after Peri Rossi fled from Montevideo to Barcelona in exile. She left Uruguay just before the military took power, marking the start of a twelve-year dictatorship. The literary response of many left-wing writers of the Southern Cone to authoritarian regimes in the 1970s was to trouble conventional monolithic linear narratives in an attempt to expose and challenge the regimes' control of language and manipulation of reality. *La nave* is a powerful example of the disruption of teleology in which ambiguity and the proliferation of meaning prevail. Peri Rossi contests centralised authority as the site of creating and controlling meaning. Like *La passió*, the novel is characterised by fragmentation and formal experimentation. It consists of chapters describing the expansive, meandering travels of the protagonist Equis [X or Ecks] — a perpetual wanderer who, like Peri Rossi, seems to be a political exile — and those he meets on his journey without any firm direction. The novel relentlessly complicates binaries such as movement and stasis, drift and grounding, freedom and control, as Mary Beth Tierney-Tello has demonstrated (1996: 173–208). In its subversion of convention and challenging of social norms, it is a powerful precursor to Braidotti's theorisation of the unsettled and unsettling force of nomadism.

La nave can be read as a feminist *bildungsroman* — Pérez-Sánchez describes it as 'a pedagogical journey towards a feminist awakening' (2007: 126) — due to Equis's growing awareness of privilege and oppression during his endless journey. It explores the connections between gender, sexuality, nomadism, and power through accounts of Equis's travels, including his encounters with a sex worker and groups of women travelling from an unspecified country where abortion is illegal to London to undergo the procedure. The novel begins and ends with descriptions of Equis's dreams, which emphasise the feminist enlightenment that he has undergone as a result of his diasporic travels; at first ambiguity overwhelms him, but by the end of the novel he welcomes it.

Interspersed through the tales of the characters' diasporic wandering are descriptions of 'El Tapiz de la Creación' [The Tapestry of Creation] (see fig. 2.1) that Equis sees in the Cathedral of Girona in Catalonia. The tapestry is a medieval depiction of the biblical story of Genesis and of agricultural activities that take place in different months of the year. The depiction of agricultural cultivation is significant for my analysis of nomadism given the settled conditions under which agriculture developed as opposed to the hunter-gathering survival activities with which nomads are usually, often misleadingly, associated. The representation of days, seasons, and months in the tapestry is relevant to my argument about the temporal discipline of the settled 'good life'.

The descriptions of the tapestry stand out as they are written in italics and scattered onto separate pages to the rest of the novel. My analysis focusses on how Peri Rossi's ekphrastic text picks at the worldview depicted in the tapestry. Her weaving of the wandering outcasts into the tears and seams of the tapestry disrupts both conventional narrative and the societal convention espoused by such a worldview. However, the recurrent presence of the tapestry's happy vision in the novel suggests that it cannot be dismissed outright. I argue that closer study reveals that there are openings to a more dynamic cosmic vision within the tapestry itself. I draw on some background information about the piecing together of the parts of the tapestry that had been lost, and its undoing and redoing in various reconstructions (Calzada i Oliveras 1980: 196). It is, in fact, a misnomer to call this work The Tapestry of Creation as it is not, technically, a tapestry, but a 'brodat', an embroidery (Calzada i Oliveras 1980: 179); the confusion could be symbolic for my reading of the novel. Just as the ways in which 'compulsory happiness' upholds the timelines of heternormativity are often invisible, the so-called tapestry actually has an invisible support behind it; the threads do not hold themselves together but are held together by an invisible piece of fabric, thus making it more difficult to unravel.

In the last chapter I described how there is little known about Sappho because her works were found in fragments and in citations in the works of others. I also described how many have wanted to 'complete' Sappho's work, to make it 'cohere'. The same can be said of the tapestry, on both of these fronts. For the 'universal' man to whom the narrator in La nave alludes, the tapestry is said to be an image of order and harmony: 'Todo en él está dispuesto para que el hombre se sienta en perfecta armonía' (20) [Everything is so arranged that man can feel in harmony with the design] (13).[1] However, its history, and the little that is known of it — it has not even been possible to establish the size of the original piece (Calzada i Oliveras 1980: 204) — paint a different story.

Peri Rossi's emphasis on diasporic, eccentric, and unsettling ways of writing and being offers further tools for conceptualising, grounding (paradoxically, perhaps) and, indeed, questioning a celebration of 'nomadic consciousness'. The novel,

FIG. 2.1. 'El Tapís de la Creació' (eleventh century)

written before the affective turn of the mid-1990s, is a form of creative theorising that offers provocative interventions into what would later become philosophical debates about affect, feminism, and queerness. Crucially, my reading of the novel complicates Braidotti's coupling of 'joy' and 'nomadism'. I argue that Peri Rossi highlights the deceptive charm of imperative positive affect which may function as a disciplinary force that implicitly buttresses heteronormativity. I consider Peri Rossi's unravelling of the tapestry in the light of Ahmed's compelling critique of happiness as a disciplinary technique in *The Promise of Happiness* (2010). Ahmed takes as a point of departure the commonly uttered and usually covertly manipulative statement, 'I just want you to be happy' (19). She argues that happiness has come to be a disciplinary force at the service of global capitalism that leads subjects to believe that following a particular path that is marked by certain milestones to be reached by certain times in life (heterosexual marriage, property ownership, children, accumulation of material wealth), will lead them to a happy and good life.

Ahmed explicitly challenges Braidotti's call for joy for the exclusions it may unwittingly enact (Ahmed 2010: 87, 214–16). Ahmed is particularly critical of Braidotti's alignment of 'negative passions' with a 'reactive mode', of pain with passivity (Ahmed 2010: 215). My suspicion of positive affect, following Ahmed, differs to that of critics such as Gabriela Mora (1995) and Lucía Invernizzi Santa

Cruz (1995), who emphasise the order and harmony of the novel. Invernizzi Santa Cruz argues that the novel 'protege del caos' (1995: 147) [protects us from chaos]; she describes the novel as being similar to the tapestry in that it is '[un] espacio en el que reuniendo la pluralidad en un orden, se recupera el perdido sentido del centro y de la unidad y se recompone la totalidad fragmentada y dispersa' (ibid.) [a space in which, through bringing together plurality in an order, the lost meaning of the centre and of unity is recuperated and a fragmented and dispersed totality is reconstituted]. I argue, in contrast, that Peri Rossi embraces chaos, chance, and the unpredictable, rather than seeking to minimise such forces in order to follow a predetermined path. She does not seek to recuperate a sense of centredness and unity but to reveal the exclusions upon which such apparent harmony relies.

Below, I explore how the diasporic wandering of the novel's characters resonates with Braidotti's later account of 'joyful nomadic subjectivity'. I then consider how the struggles and suffering that the characters, principally Equis, experience and observe on their paths to feminist enlightenment call into question imperative positive affect. I argue that Peri Rossi's probing of disciplinary happiness is reflected formally in the scattering of the tapestry amongst tales of 'wretched' wanderers. I go on to reflect on the risks of retaining the ideal of 'nomadic subjectivity', even when it is decoupled from joy, highlighting the ease with which new exclusions may emerge in feminist theory. In the final turn of my nomadic argument, I call into question the association of home with stasis, and diaspora or exile with transgression.

From Joyful Nomadic Subjectivity to Disciplinary Happiness

In one scene in the novel, Equis arrives in a new city and sees a local woman who reminds him of someone he has met previously. He politely asks her to have coffee with him. She agrees, but soon regrets the decision as her prejudices surface. She considers Equis to be, first and foremost, 'un extranjero' [a foreigner]. Peri Rossi explicitly links the 'ex' of 'extranjero' with Equis, exile, excess, estrangement, the expelled, the errant, all terms that point to dispensable or *ex*cluded elements of a *x*enophobic society. Eventually, the woman, displaying no empathy at all, assumes that Equis is mad and runs away from him. She describes her irritation at Equis's incursion into her day: 'Ahora me va a contar toda la historia del hospital, su internación, cómo huyó y yo tendré que llamar a la policía, con lo que detesto meterme en problemas' (30–31) [That's it, she thought, now he's going to tell me his clinical history, how he escaped from the hospital, and I'll have to call the police. How I hate getting involved with other people's problems...] (26). Her routine life takes priority over his pathologised desire for human connection.

In the same chapter, the narrator comments on the fact that Equis has at times found it difficult to get a job due to the fact that 'la extranjeridad es una condición sospechosa' (28) [people suspect a foreigner] (23).[3] With echoes of Simone de Beauvoir's dictum on 'woman' — 'one is not born, but rather becomes, woman' ([1949] 2011: 330) — the narrator remarks:

> [e]l hombre sedentario — el campesino o el hombre de ciudad que viaja sólo ocasionalmente, durante sus vacaciones o por asuntos de familia — ignora que la extranjeridad es una condición precaria, transitiva, pero también intercambiable; por el contrario, tiende a pensar que algunos hombres son extranjeros y otros no. Cree que se nace extranjero, no que se llega a serlo. (28)

> [Those who live always in the same place — the countrymen or city-dwellers who only travel on holiday or for family reasons — do not realize that foreignness is a temporary situation, one that can be altered; in fact they assume that some men *are* foreigners and others not. They believe that one is born — and does not become — a foreigner.] (23)

Equis himself points to the incidental nature of his 'foreignness' when the woman in the café asks him if he is a foreigner: ' — Sólo en algunos países — le contestó — y posiblemente no lo seré durante toda la vida' (29) ['Only in some countries', he answered, 'and hopefully, I will not be one forever'] (24). A journalistic piece by Peri Rossi on her own nomadism, written in 1989, echoes Equis's response. She writes, 'Yo, que soy un poco nómada, me he acostumbrado a vivir en los hoteles, perífrasis de la vida. Los hoteles me hacen recordar que estoy en tránsito por la vida: no soy, sino estoy. No tengo, sino usufructo' (2005b: 48) [I am a little nomadic, and I have got used to living in hotels, which are periphrases for life. Hotels remind me that I am in transit through life: I am not here permanently, but temporarily. I do not *own*, but *borrow*]. The references to 'borrowing' and 'transience' contrast with the sense of entitlement Equis notices in those who feel themselves to be anchored rightfully in a particular place. In some ways, then, Peri Rossi's novel shares Braidotti's celebration of 'nomadic subjects' and her disdain for 'very settled, anchored, sedentary people [who] are amongst the least empathic, the least easily moved, the most self-consciously "apolitical"' (1994: 35). However, a closer reading of the novel led me to question the imperative tone of Braidotti's insistence on positive affect in her conceptualisation of feminism as a 'joyful nomadic force'.

The lure of a happy path to the good life is represented in the novel by the tapestry seen by Equis. The central part of the tapestry depicts the creation of the world by the Pantocrator (i.e. Christ represented as ruler of the universe, from the Greek for 'ruler over all'), who is situated in a circle in the centre. As Josep Calzada i Oliveras has noted, the Pantocrator in the centre of the tapestry is a merging of the Cosmocrator and the Chronocrator, the implication being that he is responsible for creating and controlling both the universe and time (1980: 199). Around the circle containing the Pantocrator are representations of light and dark, day and night, creatures of the sea and sky. The positioning of the elements around the Pantocrator symbolises his control over their rightful time and place. The sense that each creature has an assigned place in the universe that is part of a greater order is emphasised by the prominent decorative lines that radiate out from the Pantocrator, dividing the segments of the tapestry. The depictions around the edge of the tapestry of the tasks typically undertaken in the different months of the year, such as ploughing, sowing, and harvesting, seem to promote a vision of happiness based on stasis or the following of a fixed path.

The narrator notes that the design of the tapestry is the product of 'esa religiosidad medieval capaz de construir un mundo perfectamente concéntrico y ordenado' (20) [a religious system, a world, that is perfectly concentric and ordered] (13). Despite the restrictive path it implies, the descriptions of the work in the novel acknowledge its vibrant, colourful beauty that captivates the observer. The tapestry is described as 'una estructura convincente, placentera y dichosa' (21) [a convincing and pleasing structure, moreover a happy one] (15), suggesting that the images of the path it outlines trigger positive sensations in the observer, and, by extension, insinuate that following the path it outlines may lead to 'good' feelings, to a 'good' life. 'Captivating' is indeed an appropriate word with which to describe the work; it holds the observer's attention, but also draws him/her/them into its vision of the world.

In the same section of the text, impersonal verb forms and the first-person plural have the effect of universalising one subjective reaction to the tapestry. For example, the narrator states: 'En telas así sería posible vivir toda la vida, en medio de un discurso perfectamente inteligible, de cuyo sentido no se podría dudar porque es una metáfora donde todo el universo está encerrado' (15.) [Immersed in such art one could live one's life, engaged in a perfectly rational discourse whose meaning cannot be questioned because it resides in an image containing the whole universe] (14). But to whom does the impersonal 'se' or 'one' refer? Who is it that flourishes in this intelligible, mapped, totalising vision of the universe?

The novel highlights the exclusions on which the supposedly happy world of the tapestry is based. While the narrator describes the comforting sense of oneness with other elements of the design that the observer is encouraged to feel, we do learn that it is a certain type of person (the reference to 'man' here is not incidental) who feels this sense of harmony when the narrator states that 'todo está dispuesto para que el hombre viva en [cuadros así] exonerado del resto del mundo' (20) [Art like this beckons man to live within its world, freed from the sins of the other one] (14). The implication is that the sinners of the other world are those who do not fit this model and who challenge the way of living in the divine design. The violence and exclusions of the world depicted in the tapestry are alluded to even more explicitly in a footnote to the description: 'cualquier armonía supone la destrucción de los elementos reales que se le oponen' (14) [such harmony assumes the destruction of those aspects of reality which oppose it] (13). Those who do not obey, those considered to be perverted, the deviant are excluded, so as not to jeopardise the happiness of the rest of society. We learn that 'Equis contempló el tapiz como una vieja leyenda cuyo ritmo nos fascina, pero que no provoca nostalgia' (13) [Ecks studied the tapestry as one might read an old legend whose rhythm fascinates, but which evokes no nostalgia] (13). Equis's lack of nostalgia in response to the beautiful tapestry that observers supposedly long to enter highlights the exclusivity of its appeal.

Peri Rossi suggests that the very insistence on happiness and joy can be what stifles certain groups. We learn that the tapestry depicts sea creatures who are described as 'maravillosos *monstruos* que según [marineros y capitanes] habitaban el fondo del mar. *Vistos sólo un minuto, a la luz fantasmagórica de un relámpago* o en el desdichado momento en que el mástil se quebraba' (114, my emphasis) [marvellous *monsters* who, according to sailors and captains, lived in the depths of the sea. They were *seen for just a minute in the phantasmagoric light of a flash of lightning* or in the cursed moment in which the mast was breaking] (114, my emphasis). The narrator's seemingly contradictory comment, following the description of the terror that the creatures and monsters prompted in sailors, is relevant to our consideration of happiness:

> Los monstruos marinos del tapiz no inspiran temor. Se integran *armoniosamente* al gran sistema de la creación, junto a las aves y a las plantas. Son criaturas *curiosas pero no terroríficas* [...] Se deslizan por las aguas *de una manera natural, sin aparentes deseos de sobresalir* y los peces que las rodean no experimentan ninguna sensación de competencia o de peligro. (114, my emphasis)

> [The sea monsters of the tapestry do not inspire fear. They join *harmoniously* in the great system of creation, together with the birds and plants. *Strange-looking creatures they are, but their extraordinary appearance does not terrify* [...] They seem to glide *naturally* through the waves *with no apparent desire of emerging or attacking,* and beside them, unthreatened, swim the smaller fishes.] (114–15, my emphasis)

In the sea, the creatures inspire terror; in the tapestry, they do not terrify. Despite their containment, these creatures are described as integrated, in tune with the wider system. The monsters are described in terms that resonate with discourses of the assimilation of immigrants in idealised multiculturalism in which many cultures may exist and may well be officially celebrated as co-existing, as long as the so-called minority cultures do not threaten the structures and norms of the purportedly dominant and often singular national culture. In the tapestry, the monsters are curious to just the right degree not to be threatening and apparently display no will to break free of their containment. The fact that the monsters appear beneath the Pantocrator highlights their suppression. Mora sees these monsters as evidence of a search for harmony that involves '[e]l deseo de hacer *naturales* tipos y actos transgresores' (1995: 163) [the desire to naturalise transgressive characteristics and behaviours]. In contrast, I read the presence of the monsters as a critique of the very notion of the 'natural' and a reminder that 'harmony' inherently involves the suppression of difference and the stamping out of transgressive acts.

Peri Rossi's description of the monstrous creatures in the tapestry brings to mind Ahmed's point that 'happiness is used to justify oppression' (2010: 2). Ahmed draws on De Beauvoir who states:

> there is no way to measure the happiness of others, and it is always easy to call a situation that one would like to impose on others happy: in particular, we declare happy those condemned to stagnation, under the pretext that happiness is immobility. ([1949] 2011: 37)

The monsters, who had once been both threatening and marvellous, are now neutralised in their stagnation. Peri Rossi thus signals that positive feelings may not be a sign of liberation but of succumbing to pernicious conformity. Those who are not able or willing to stay happily in place presumably populate the world of sins that does not appear in the tapestry, and from which those in the tapestry are saved.

The description of the sea segment is one of many points in the novel (starting, of course, with 'La nave' of the title) at which the sea is depicted as a place of inconformity and of imagination. It was a common medieval practice to separate unwanted people from the rest of the population, as Foucault has outlined in 'Stultifera Navis' in *Madness and Civilization*: 'these boats [...] conveyed their insane cargo from town to town. Madmen then led an easy wandering existence. The towns drove them outside their limits' ([1961] 2005: 6). Foucault draws in turn on the German humanist Sebastian Brant's *Das Narrenschiff* (1494), translated into Latin as *Stultifera Navis* (1497), and Hieronymus Bosch's *Ship of Fools* (1490–1500). In 'Stultifera Navis', Foucault describes the sea as 'the freest, the openest [*sic*] of routes' (2005: 9); here nomadism stretches beyond known and visible lands. The madman 'has his truth and his homeland only in that fruitless expanse between two countries that cannot belong to him' (ibid.). One key moment in the novel resonates with Foucault's reading of the paradoxical freedom in dispossession. When a little boy on a ship tells his dad he wants to go out onto the streets, Equis tells him that there is a city submerged in the sea. Equis says that 'hay que saber mirarla, porque está escondida' (18) [you have to know how to look, for it is well-hidden] (11), pointing to the need for imaginative vision to make a place for oneself beyond the limits of convention.

Those who require such an imaginative vision are those who, unlike the allegedly universal observer, might not take pleasure in the tapestry's ordered world vision, who might be excluded from it for being *too* monstrous, unlike the monsters in the tapestry. Ahmed gives us some clues as to who these people might be. In her engagement with Love's notion of 'compulsory happiness' as the idea of 'emotional conformism' in an era of increased queer rights and assimilation into mainstream culture (2008: 54), Ahmed notes that deviating from a conventional path is often viewed as a sacrifice of one's own and others' happiness and well-being. Indeed, Love's term 'compulsory happiness' recalls Rich's conceptualisation of 'compulsory heterosexuality' (1980). Ahmed calls for resistance to the obligatory nature of 'positive' feelings which serve to validate some lives and dismiss others. She states that 'rather than assuming happiness is simply found in 'happy persons', we can consider how claims to happiness might be how social norms make certain forms of personhood valuable' (2010: 11). Ahmed highlights figures of resistance to a form of happiness that sees the 'unhappy' as obstacles to society's well-being and progress. Specifically, she points to the unconventional ways of living of 'melancholic migrants', 'unhappy queers', and 'feminist killjoys' (2010). Characters that could be described as such appear in Peri Rossi's novel in the text between the tapestry descriptions.

The novel suggests that a pleasant feeling of happiness may quash dissent. While directing people's behaviour, happiness may lead them to believe that they are acting on their own desires. Therefore, the tapestry's happy containment of monstrous 'nomads' of the sea poses a challenge to Braidotti's association of feminist insurrection as 'joyful nomadism' in revealing how positive affect can coax subjects to conformity.

Unravelling Convention

The idea of happiness as a unidirectional ideological imperative that leads subjects to progress down a conventional path — Ahmed traces 'convention' back to its root, 'to convene', from the Latin *convenire* meaning 'to come together', 'to agree', or 'to fit' (2010: 64) — can be seen as having its narrative correlative in linear plots in which meaning appears to be mastered. The happy observer's experience of the tapestry reflects a teleological vision. The narrator remarks that the observer 'puede contemplar [el tapiz] en toda su extensión desplazando su mirada del costado izquierdo al derecho y de arriba a abajo' (20) [can see it fully extended, one's gaze travelling from left to right or from top downwards] (13), therefore enjoying a sense of control over space. That the tapestry can be conceived as a whole demonstrates that the path, as ordained by a divine being, is clear and pre-determined. It supports the statement in the New Testament that 'Strait is the gate, and narrow is the way, which leadeth unto life' (Matthew 7:14), the origin of the English phrase 'straight and narrow', which refers to the obedient following of the good path. Using the first-person plural again, the narrator states that '[l]o que amamos en toda estructura es una composición del mundo, un significado que ordene el caos devorador, una hipótesis comprensible y por ende reparadora. Repara nuestro sentimiento de la fuga y de la dispersión, nuestra desolada experiencia del desorden' (21) [what we love in any structure is a vision of the world that gives order to chaos, an hypothesis which is comprehensible and restores our faith, atoning for our having fled and scattered before life's brutal disorder] (14). The description of disorder and dispersion as 'desolada', in contrast with an ordered and comprehensible depiction of the world as comforting and restorative, reveals a preference in the implied observer for mastery of the universe.

Peri Rossi frustrates the desire for mastery, structure, and predictability through drawing attention to movement in the tapestry's seemingly fixed and ordered world. The narrator describes the space between the central circle and the borders depicting activities that take place each month:

> todo indica movimiento: la expulsión del aire, los pellejos repletos, la cuidadosa disposición de los miembros del cuerpo de los ángeles, como si fueran a caballo. Bordeando el círculo de la Creación, al lado del Pantocrátor, esta inclusión de los vientos, en los cuatro costados, sugiere que en el universo, todo es movimiento, nada está quieto. (162)

> [Everything here indicates movement: the air escaping, the full leather bags, the studied position of the limbs of the angels as if they were riding. The inclusion of the winds, so close to the circle of Creation, at the side of the Creator Himself, suggests that all is moving; nothing in the Universe remains still.] (165)

The four winds, not actually present in the Genesis story, and, in fact, most iconically associated in the Bible with the Apocalypse, occupy most of the in-between space. They are unusually large for a medieval depiction of the winds (Calzada i Oliveras 1980: 187). The wind is also depicted as blowing in all directions from two of the figures. Therefore, even in what is physically present in the tapestry there is the hint of disruption to a static vision of the world, or, perhaps, the acknowledgement that there is inevitably drift and/or death within apparent stasis.

Aside from the disruption to stability in what remains of the tapestry, the narrator makes multiple references to its incompleteness. For example, he/she/they state(s) that '[e]l desgaste del tiempo (épocas enteras sublevadas) ha hecho desaparecer casi la mitad' (21) [the passage of time — whole epochs in revolt — has destroyed almost half of it] (14). Indeed, the final words of the novel refer to its missing parts: 'Faltan enero, noviembre, diciembre y, por lo menos, dos ríos del Paraíso' (198) [The tapestry is missing January, November, December and at least two of the rivers of Paradise] (205). Its incompleteness is symbolic of the unknown, unpredictable, messiness of life that Peri Rossi explores in the other parts of the novel, which perhaps offer some clues as to the nature of alternative routes to 'Paradise', routes cleared by 'epochs in revolt'.

Like Sappho's fragments, the tapestry remains in a process of 'becoming' and, indeed, unbecoming. It has undergone a number of restoration efforts, the first on record being in 1884, one hundred years prior to the publication of the novel. Interestingly, in that process, some of the fragments in the currently incomplete right-hand border were actually attached to the bottom of the tapestry by the French nuns who are believed to have carried out the work. They were moved in a later restoration in 1952 (Calzada i Oliveras 1980: 196). Some historians believe the months of the year on the right are not in their original order (Calzada i Oliveras 1980: 195–96). In 1975, more fragments of the tapestry were found, and the tapestry underwent a further process of restoration (Calzada i Oliveras 1980: 193). As such, the tapestry has been stitched together and unstitched, woven and unwoven, embroidered and unpicked, throughout its history.

In another point of confluence in Peri Rossi's and Ahmed's texts (and 'text' derives, fittingly, from the Latin verb *texere*, to weave), Ahmed describes her project through textile metaphors: 'My aim is to follow the weave of unhappiness, as a kind of unravelling of happiness, and the threads of its appeal' (2010: 18). Peri Rossi pulls into tatters the already disintegrating tapestry through scattering descriptions of it throughout the novel. So, contrary to the mastery of the universe that the material tapestry as a whole might have represented, its eroded state and textual scattering represent the undoing of the binds of 'religion', often said to be from the Latin *religare*, 'to bind', and the unravelling of the Catholic narrative — with Catholic stemming from the Greek *katholikos*, meaning 'universal' or 'relating to the whole' — as well as the unpicking of the threads of the appeal of happiness. Giorgio Agamben would disagree with this common etymological reading of religion, highlighting a Ciceronian reading of religion as coming from 'relegere', 'to go through again' (2007: 74–75). These two possible etymologies highlight an issue with the unravelling tapestry, which observers may endeavour to bind back together and/or to go over again in their imaginations.

The narrator states, using the universalising first-person plural:

> Lo que admiramos en la obra, además de su fina elaboración, de su bello entramado y *la armonía* de sus colores, *es una estructura; una estructura tan perfecta*

y geométrica, tan verificable que aún habiendo desaparecido casi su mitad, es posible reconstruir el todo, si no en el muro del catedral, sí en el bastidor de la mente. (21, my emphasis)

[What one admires in the work, besides the fine execution, handsome texture and *harmony* of colours, *is this structure — a structure so symmetrical, so dependable* that even when complete, it is possible to recreate the whole, if not on the cathedral wall, then within the framework of our imagination.] (14, my emphasis)

The fact that the narrator alleges that the tapestry can be recreated even though parts are missing is a nod to its predictability — emphasised through the repetition of 'estructura' — and, perhaps, its continuing appeal. On the other hand, even in this comment on predictability and ordered form, the narrator refers to a restoration of the work in 'el bastidor de la mente'. Invernizzi Santa Cruz emphasises the restoration of the tapestry, considering the novel to be a 'reconstrucción de la parte faltante del tapiz' (1995: 142) [reconstruction of the missing part of the tapestry], which she argues is the expulsion from Paradise and nostalgic search to return to it. I argue, in contrast, that the novel reveals that the tapestry cannot be reconstructed, not even in the mind, and the novel and its characters question the desirability of this alleged paradise rather than seeking to return to it.

Any reconstruction of the tapestry is certainly not verifiable ('verificable') with the information about it that we currently have. There are vastly differing hypotheses about what the tapestry as a whole might have looked like (see De Palol 1986: 74–76) and it has even been argued that the segments that depict the Legend of the True Cross might be from an entirely different work (Calzada i Oliveras 1980: 197). The tapestry's fraying, its incomplete state, and the mystery surrounding it point to the possibility of imaginative wandering, of alternative visions offered by the lives of those not depicted in and, in fact, excluded from the legible universe of the tapestry. Therefore, the narrator's restorative or redemptive hypothesis — that 'es posible reconstruir el todo' (21) [it is possible to recreate the whole] (14) — contrasts with the novel's creative hypothesis in which the holes in the tapestry's vision of the world point to an opening up to the unexpected, the unmastered, and the unmasterable.

The holes in the tapestry, its successive phases of piecing together and taking apart, as well as Peri Rossi's further scattering of it amongst the stories of itinerant characters recall Michel de Certeau's concept of a 'sieve-order'. In the *Practice of Everyday Life,* published the same year as *La nave,* De Certeau states that stories about places:

are composed with the world's *debris* [...] furnished by the *leftovers* from nominations, taxonomies, heroic or comic predicates, etc., that is, by *fragments* of scattered semantic places. [...] Things *extra* and other (details and *excesses* coming from elsewhere) insert themselves into the accepted framework, the imposed order. One thus has the very relationship between spatial practices and the constructed order. The surface of this order is everywhere *punched and torn open* by ellipses, drifts, and *leaks of meaning:* it is a sieve-order. (1984: 107, my emphasis)

The apparent order and symmetry of the tapestry, which contains a depiction of the entire universe and is described by Kaminsky as 'a sort of map that makes order out of chaos' (1993: 48), contrasts with the expansive, spontaneous, and unmappable journeys of the nomadic Equis, the '*extra* and other', the '*excess*' of De Certeau's sieve-order. The narrator states that 'es casi imposible trazar un mapa de los viajes de Equis por el mundo' (37) [it is almost impossible to trace the stages of Ecks' journey on any map] (32–33). Equis reveals the places he travels through to be part of this 'sieve-order'.

Through depicting his travels, Peri Rossi seems to advocate a messier and more engaged experience of place; a queering of place. The 'sieve-order' is formed, as De Certeau argues, from leftovers, fragments, debris, leaks of meaning; in this regard it recalls Halberstam's 'scavenger methodology' (1998: 13), Foucault's description of genealogies of ruins explored in Chapter One, and flores's revaluation of detritus: 'En el detritus de cada disciplina, de cada práctica, de cada género, efectos de la descomposición y recomposición de coyunturas y campos de acción hay una fertilidad insospechada para la disidencia, para el placer de perturbar' (2013: 28) [in the detritus of every discipline, of every practice, of every genre, as a consequence of the decomposition and recomposition of overlaps and fields of action, there are unsuspectedly fertile grounds for dissidence, for the pleasure of disruption]. Where in the city does the dissidence and pleasurable disruption amongst detritus take place?

Heights of Power

The contrast between the desire for mastery that the totalising vision of the tapestry represents and the 'unmappability' of Equis's journey recalls the difference that De Certeau highlights between distant 'voyeurs' and pedestrians in the city. De Certeau comments on the experience of being lifted to the top of World Trade Centre in New York. The twin towers of the pre-11 September 2001 complex were, at the time of their completion, the tallest buildings in the world. He describes how, from such heights, the city becomes 'a text that lies before one's eyes. It allows one to read it, to be a solar Eye, looking down like a god' (1984: 92). Speaking of the voyeur's gaze from atop the towers, De Certeau asks, 'To what erotics of knowledge does the ecstasy of reading such a cosmos belong? Having taken a voluptuous pleasure in it, I wonder what is the source of this pleasure of "seeing the whole," of looking down on, totalizing the most immoderate of human texts' (1984: 92). The pleasure in control and mastery described by De Certeau is akin to that experienced by those who revel in the tapestry's worldview, who may see themselves as reflections of the Pantocrator in the centre of the tapestry with lines radiating from it, like the tapestry's solar eye, mirroring the image for Sunday or 'dies solis' in the tapestry, in which Christ appears as a sun, the 'Sol-Oriens', 'Orient constant', or 'Sol Invictus' (Calzada i Oliveras 1980: 200).

De Certeau contrasts the voyeur's gaze from on high with that of the walkers down below, who write the city's illegible tales:

> The voyeur-god created by this fiction [...] must disentangle himself from the murky intertwining daily behaviours and make himself alien to them. [...The walkers'] bodies follow the thicks and thins of an urban 'text' *they write without being able to read it.* [...] It is as though the practices organizing a bustling city were *characterized by their blindness.* The networks of these moving, intersecting writings compose a manifold *story that has neither author nor spectator.* (1984: 92–93, my emphasis)

In the tapestry, the 'voyeur-god' is in a separate circle to the ordered, legible world that he has created, a world that can be read by the observer with a dominating gaze. Equis's unmappable route evades this order. The comment that these itinerant practices are 'characterized by their blindness' and form a story without 'author nor spectator' is relevant to the challenges to authoritative authorial practices that will be my focus in Part II of the chapter.

In a journalistic piece written in 1982, Peri Rossi analyses the spatialisation of class in Barcelona. In her description, the rich inhabitants who remain hidden are akin to the 'voyeur-god':

> En la parte alta de la ciudad, sobre la montaña, viven los ricos: el aire, allí, no está contaminado [...] No es fácil llegar al barrio alto si no se tiene vehículo propio [...] Los ricos han sabido aislarse de la multitud [...] Pero también podría pensarse que los ricos no están — a tal punto las calles parecen vacías — a cualquier hora del día. Hasta comprender que están, pero muy ocultos detrás de los primorosos jardines [...] como en las obras de arte, el autor desaparece detrás de lo creado. (2005: 125–26)

> [The rich live in the high part of the city, on the mountain-side. The air there is not polluted. It isn't easy to reach the high neighbourhood without your own car [...] the rich have figured out how to isolate themselves from the masses [...] However, it would also be easy to believe that the rich are not there, given that the roads seem completely empty at all hours. Until you realise that they are there, but very hidden behind their exquisitely pruned gardens. As in works of art, the author disappears behind their creation.]

The powers moulding space in the city are often invisible. Her description of the other part of the city, the city of the masses, is very much in line with De Certeau's characterisation of 'blind' pedestrians with their illegible routes. For her, the centre of the city is filled with confusing twists and turns:

> es amplia y confusa. Sus calles (llenas de humo y de ruido [...]) se retuercen en múltiples vericuetos [...] La población de esta ciudad parece flotar: grandes masas (anónimas) se trasladan de un lugar a otro, como las olas, como las mareas, como los bancos de moluscos; no siempre se comprende bien el sentido de esos desplazamientos (si tiene alguno). (2005b: 126)

> [it is wide and muddled. Its streets (filled with smoke and noise [...]) twist and turn into multiple paths [...] The population of this city seems to float: large (anonymous) masses move from one place to another, like waves, like tides, like shellfish reefs; one cannot always understand the meaning of these movements (if, indeed, they have any).]

In a sense, the twists of the city centre make it a queer space. The movements of the masses — likened to the sea (a space of imagination in the novel) and to shellfish (recalling the marine monsters in the tapestry) — are not legible; they do not always have 'meaning' or value by the standards of neoliberal logic. Similarly, in the novel, Morris describes how he struggles to read the city centre with its '[e] dificios, apartamentos, unos sobre otros, en *insoportable promiscuidad*. Todos iguales, de modo que muy a menudo uno cree haber entrado a un lugar, y en realidad, ha entrado a otro' (117, my emphasis) [buildings, apartments, one on top of the other in *unbearable promiscuity*. They are all the same, which means that very often you think you have gone into a particular place, only to find that you are, in fact, somewhere else] (119, my emphasis). The mixing or promiscuity of this part of the city may make it difficult to navigate; it may cause confusion.

Equis's name posits him as an everyman figure, one of the masses, and his wandering is also illegible. Emphasising the role of chance, he notes that '[p]or circunstancias especiales, que tienen más que ver con la marcha del mundo que con mis propios deseos, desde hace años viajo de un lugar a otro, sin rumbo fijo' (78). In a journalistic piece titled 'La última peatona', Peri Rossi casts herself as a wandering Equis. She displays her pride in being one of the last remaining true pedestrian inhabitants of Barcelona, also emphasising chance, surprise, and unpredictability in the act of walking. She writes:

> caminar es vagar, es decir, desplazarse con las piernas y los pies sin rumbo fijo, perderse deliberadamente por las calles; caminar es divagar [...] Caminar es concederle una oportunidad al azar, a la sorpresa, en medio de nuestras vidas cada vez más articuladas, cada vez más rutinarias [...] es concederle tiempo a la imaginación, a la fantasía. (2005b: 141–42)

> [To walk is to roam, that is, to move around on foot without a fixed route, deliberately losing yourself in the streets; to walk is to wander [...] Walking means leaving room for chance, for surprise, in the midst of our increasingly scheduled and routine lives [...] it means leaving time for imagination.]

Peri Rossi's reference to chance or fate, 'el azar' in Spanish, can be linked etymologically with 'ha*zar*d', that is, with risk. In the happenings of the life of Peri Rossi's wandering protagonist, where imagination is celebrated, happiness is not guaranteed; for Peri Rossi, nomadism is not necessarily 'joyful'.

I disagree, therefore, with critics such as Mora who have argued that the novel seeks a sense of harmony in which chance and the unpredictable are erased. In Mora's words, 'En el equilibrio ideal que se añora en la novela, lo azaroso, lo imprevisto, es mortal enemigo de la armonía, que también es estabilidad' (1995: 167) [In the ideal equilibrium longed for in the novel, chance and the unexpected are mortal enemies of harmony, which is equated to stability]. She draws on Lucía's comment on getting pregnant, presumably due to a condom breaking. Lucía refers to being a 'víctima del azar, otra opresión' (176) [victim of chance, one more form of oppression] (180) and states that chance enters women's lives through men. However, given the structural oppression depicted in the novel, which certainly cannot be attributed to chance, I would not read this statement literally. While I agree that the observer of the tapestry may long for such a balance, I believe that Equis the everyman paradoxically counters what the narrator describes as a universal pleasure in harmony — the novel paints a much more complex picture, in which chance and the unpredictable are ultimately celebrated.

The celebration of chance chimes with flores's assertion that chance is vital to interruptions, and interruptions to social transformation. Morgan Ztardust writes in the prologue to flores's *interruqciones* that '[u]n pequeño corrimiento y una pequeña intervención en el momento indicado (es decir, en el más *azaroso* de todos) pueden movilizar grandes e impensadas transformaciones, siempre que queramos abrazar la formidable violencia de lo *aleatorio* e *inesperado*' (2013: 16–17, my emphasis) [a minor slip or intervention at a particular moment (that is, at the most *random* moment of all), can trigger large and unforeseen transformations, as long as we are willing to embrace the formidable violence of the *contingent* and *unexpected*] (my emphasis). The force of chance and the unexpected may seem 'violent' due to being different and unfamiliar, but it can bring about an opening to alternative ways of being. Disrupting the status quo is inherently violent; in Middle English, 'violent' simply described something that had a marked or powerful effect.

Like Peri Rossi's celebration of wandering in the city, Ahmed associates 'happiness' with its etymological root of 'hap' in the sense of a chance occurrence, the 'perhaps'. She refers to happiness as a possibility rather than an objective:

> A politics of the hap is about opening possibilities for being in other ways, of being perhaps. If opening up possibility causes unhappiness, then a politics of the hap will be thought of as unhappy. But it is not just that. A politics of the hap might embrace what happens, but it also works towards a world in which things can happen in alternative ways. (2010: 223)

So, whereas Braidotti calls for a 'joyful' approach as she believes that much critical theory practised by those she terms 'the melancholics' contains 'too much critique, not enough creativity' (2014), Ahmed believes that it is the very emphasis on the idea of 'flourishing', 'happiness', 'joy' etc., as *imperative* that actually shuts down creative possibilities for resistance through its exclusion of those who are portrayed as getting in the way of the path to happiness. In the novel, Equis's diasporic encounters with sadness, suffering, and discrimination contribute to his eventual enlightenment and challenging of privilege. Both Peri Rossi and Ahmed posit, then, that imperative joy, as a gesture of mastery, may ultimately uphold the status quo.

It is interesting in this regard that Peri Rossi chose to continue living in Barcelona despite not feeling comfortable there, and feeling like a perpetual outsider. In fact, she did not choose to stay *despite* these factors, but *because* of them. As I mentioned in the introduction, she points out that she needs to experience some level of discomfort in order to write (Pérez-Sánchez 2007: 118), to imagine alternative possibilities. Marçal made similar statements, describing how her writing is 'rooted', paradoxically, in precarity: 'l'escriptura, almenys per a mi, comporta o arrela en una mena d'inseguretat radical' (2014b: 79) [for me, writing entails, or is rooted in, a sort of radical insecurity]. Peri Rossi and Marçal's acceptance, even embrace, of some level of insecurity recalls Anzaldúa's declarations on the potentially formative nature of discomfort:

> Living on borders and in margins, keeping intact one's shifting and multiple identity and integrity, is like trying to swim in a new element, an 'alien' element. [...] the 'alien' element has become familiar — never comfortable, not with society's clamor to uphold the old, to rejoin the flock, to go with the herd. No, not comfortable, but home. ([1987] 2012: 19)

The wandering of Equis, the 'extranjero', and other 'aliens' in *La nave* reveals the malleability of space and of the sense of home, which may involve being at home in discomfort.

De Certeau's '"wandering of the semantic", produced by masses that make some parts of the city disappear and exaggerate others, distorting it, fragmenting it, and diverting it from its immobile order' (1984: 102) is reflected in the changing place names to which Equis refers in the novel (36, 119). In *La nave*, Peri Rossi emphasises the connections between space, mapping, and power, highlighting the possibilities for a queering of authoritarian cartographies. Equis likes looking at old maps. The narrator comments that:

> después de una larga dictadura, muerto el tirano o derrocado el régimen, de las ciudades desaparecen sus huellas más visibles (los nombres de las calles, los bustos y monumentos) y otros nombres, otros monumentos los sustituyen, en los diccionarios las palabras aparecen, otras envejecen y mueren, se agregan acepciones y los mapas se modifican. (36)

> [after a long tyranny, the tyrant once dead and his rule broken, all visible traces disappear from the cities (street names, busts, monuments) and other names, other monuments replace them, so in dictionaries new words appear as others vanish, new meanings flourish and the maps are changing.] (31)

The maps reveal that any apparent order in the city is far from immobile. Here, the link between naming and controlling space is linked with inscribing power, a point that the Uruguayan writer Eduardo Galeano also underlines. He writes that '[h]asta el mapa miente. Aprendemos la geografía del mundo en un mapa que no muestra el mundo tal cual es, sino tal como sus dueños mandan que sea' ([1987] 2006: 362) [even maps lie. We learn world geography from a map that doesn't show the world as it is, but rather as its owners would have it be]. I will return to mapping and power in the discussion of *El libro* in the second part of this chapter.

As Equis wanders round the city seemingly aimlessly but with the feeling that his steps will lead him *somewhere*, he muses about what maps were like in the past:

> Así se viajaba en la antigüedad: con mapas imprecisos, llenos de mares misteriosos y animales fantásticos, costas advenedizas e ínsulas supuestas, pero al cabo, la carta del almirante al rey revelaba que en tierras apartadas, adonde los había conducido la tormenta, crecían árboles gigantes, plantas de la salud y vivían hombres de otra raza. (189)

> [That's how they travelled in the old days: by inaccurate maps with mysterious seas and fantastic monsters, unknown shores and imaginary islands. But in the end the admiral's letter to the king revealed that, in the remote land to which the winds had blown his fleet, gigantic trees grew, as did medicinal herbs and men of another race.] (195)

Referring yet again to the mysterious potential of the sea, Equis's description of an imprecise map could be an interpretation of the tapestry. His 'mapa impreciso', like Sara T.'s 'l'esbós', leaves space for the imagination. It leaves room for chance and for getting lost. In this sense, it contrasts with Kaminsky's aforementioned reading of the tapestry as a 'map that makes order out of chaos' (1993: 48). Equis's description of ancient maps suggests that previously the map was imprecise and the act of writing in reporting back to the King was the ordering principle of colonial logic. In *La nave*, the reverse is true. The visual and the textile are depicted largely as ordering forces, and the textual is a place of dispersion and unravelling.

The map of 'la metrópoli' that Equis and Graciela produce for Morris is 'un plano minucioso, lleno de líneas y de claves, de referencias visuales para que Morris no se extravíe' (119) [a detailed plan full of arrows and points of reference for Morris to follow] (120). De Certeau suggests that maps have shifted from being stories about space to systems of geographical places: 'maps, constituted as proper places in which to exhibit the products of knowledge, form tables of legible results' (1984: 121). He discusses the history of the map, pointing out that the first medieval maps involved a 'rectilinear marking out of itineraries', i.e. tracing the routes people have taken. He goes on to say that while '[t]he tour to be made is predominant in them' the maps were also a log of events that happened on the journey — 'not a "geographical map" but "history book"' (120). The maps told stories.

As an aside, in the context of Southern Cone dictatorships, the vagueness of space and a sense of how to arrive at a place without necessarily knowing its precise location carries particular political weight. For example, in *El sótano de San Telmo: una barricada proletaria para el deseo lésbico en los '70* [The Basement in San Telmo: A Working-class Barricade for Lesbian Desire in the 70s], flores notes that some lesbian militants never learnt or remembered the exact address of their gathering place. Instead, they remembered the route to get there, for security reasons, i.e. so that if they were caught and tortured, they would not have this information to reveal (2015: 29). Also in the context of the Argentine dictatorship, in advance of an inspection by the Comisión Interamericana de Derechos Humanos [Interamerican Commission of Human Rights) in September 1979 at the Escuela Superior de Mecánica de la Armada (ESMA) in Buenos Aires, the military altered the 'Casino de Oficiales' building, where detainees were confined in very close proximity to the naval officers' quarters. The ESMA was a major site of torture and detention where some 5,000 people were held over the course of the dictatorship, most of whom were disappeared. Since 2004 it has been a Human Rights and Memorial Museum. The alterations to the building involved the military removing a lift and concealing stairs leading to the basement in order to delegitimise witness accounts of sounds that they had heard and details of how they had been moved through the building. In this way, when the Commission visited in 1979, the military was successful in concealing the function of the building (see Dema 2011; Poore n.d).

Returning to De Certeau, he outlines how in the fifteenth to seventeeth centuries maps became more autonomous and there was a tendency towards the 'erasure of itineraries', shifting from process to 'totalizing' product:

> The map, a totalizing stage on which elements of diverse origin are brought together to form the tableau of a 'state' of geographical knowledge, pushes away into its prehistory or into its posterity, as if into the wings, the operations of which it is the result or the necessary condition. It remains alone on the stage. The tour describers have disappeared. (121)

Again, in the Southern Cone context, the 'disappearance' of the 'tour describers' carries particularly brutal connotations. In De Certeau's more general history of cartography, the map has shifted from a descriptive to a prescriptive mode. I would argue, following Ahmed, that the same could be said of conventional visions of happiness. In contrast, in *La nave*, which Kelly Austin describes as a 'pastiche travel narrative' (2011: 790), Peri Rossi brings back the sense of travelling and of happiness as an unpredictable story, rather than the following of a prescribed route.

Wretched Wanderers

Ahmed points out that the adjective 'wretched' came from 'wretch', which was a reference to a 'stranger, exile or banished person' (2010: 17). Those who are rejected from a particular society, community, or nation are considered to be 'wretched'. The characters in *La nave* are wretched exiles, those who are cast out of the utopian religious worldview the narrator perceives in the tapestry. The exiles' perspectives lead us to question the implications of an increasingly normalised vision of happiness. Ahmed asks: 'Can we rewrite the history of happiness from the point of view of the wretch? [...] The sorrow of the stranger might give us a different angle on happiness not because it teaches us what it is like or must be like to be a stranger, but because it might estrange us from the very happiness of the familiar' (17). Rather than considering the universe from the point of view of the content observer implied in the tapestry descriptions or from the perspective of the centred Pantocrator, Peri Rossi draws our attention to the unhappy' perspective of the wretched.

One example in the novel of a figure who won't stay 'in place' is the biblical figure of Eve. In the biblical story, Eve does not follow the order not to eat the forbidden fruit (signalled by the words LIGNUM POMIFERUM in the tapestry), which leads to the expulsion of humanity from Paradise. At the start of the section of the novel entitled 'EVA', there is a fragment that is said to be from an unpublished book of Eve's confessions. It includes the following lines:

> El castigo, para la iniciada que huye, es el desprecio, la soledad, la locura o la muerte. Sólo resta permanecer en el templo, en la casa de los dioses severos, colaborar en la extensión de los mitos que sostienen la organización y el espíritu de la tribu, sus ideas dominantes y ocultar para siempre los conflictos que esta sujeción plantea. (153)

> [The woman who [escapes] is ostracized and dies alone or mad. One must stay inside the temple, the house of our relentless gods, and collaborate in perpetuating the myths which sustain the structure, ideology and spirit of the tribe. Any conflict arising from our forced condition must be hidden]. (158)

Eve's reference to being compelled to be passive and obedient, and therefore complicit in concealing oppression, echoes the apparent happiness of the monsters in the tapestry, who are allowed a place in that world provided that they are contained and harmonious, with no desire to break free of their assigned place. However, despite the threat of scorn and loneliness, Eve does not obey.

The 'EVA' section includes some responses to Graciela's survey of schoolchildren between seven and twelve in which she asked them to describe Adam and Eve in Paradise. In contrast with the many qualities ascribed to Adam, the only positive adjective used to describe Eve is 'bella' [beautiful]. One child describes Eve as 'curiosa, pero que no estaba seguro de que ésa fuera una virtud o un defecto' (160) [curious, but he wasn't sure whether this was a virtue or a defect] (164) and the rest of the children judged her to be 'excesivamente curiosa' (160) [excessively curious] (164). Ahmed notes that the 'association between imagination and trouble is powerful. It teaches us how the happiness duty for women is about the narrowing of horizons, about giving up an interest in what lies beyond the familiar' (2010: 61). According to this worldview, to be happy women must remain within the limits of the 'familiar' in both senses of the word — within the family and within societal convention.

We can see, then, that unhappiness and suffering may be, in themselves, forms of resistance that show the limitations and injustices of the status quo and the endorsed way of being of a particular community or ideology. For example, Chapter IX describes the experiences of a political exile from the same country as Equis who was held in a torture and detention centre for two years before being released. The exile, Vercingetórix, is haunted by the disappearances, torture, and death of many of his compatriots and, particularly, by the fact that life outside carried on more or less 'as normal' for many people (61). Once he has been released, he feels paralysed; going on 'happily' knowing that such places may still exist would, for him, be an unforgivable act of forgetting. As Ahmed states:

> [t]he demand that we be affirmative makes those histories [of injustice] disappear by reading them as a form of melancholia (as if you hold on to something that is already gone). These histories have not gone: we would be letting go of that which persists in the present. (2010: 217)

Equis's encounters demonstrate that ongoing imbalances in privilege have an effect on the ease with which characters may happily break free from the 'straight and narrow', in exile or otherwise. The sex worker he encounters has been beaten up and the women travelling to London to have abortions that are illegal in their own country are disempowered. Peri Rossi thus acknowledges the inevitability of feelings not traditionally regarded as positive in the process of developing more just communities that are not based on the exclusion of those who challenge the oppressive nature of societal norms or simply expose the privilege of those who make such norms seem 'normal'.

The acceptance of negative affect rather than its exclusion or pathologisation is summed up poignantly in a poem by another writer who, like Peri Rossi, moved to Barcelona from the Southern Cone. Neus Aguado writes:

> La misión del alma es la errancia
> y la del cuerpo equivocarse,
> doblemente desorientados buscamos la luz
> para encontrar, con suma frecuencia, un poco de noche;
> la noche precisa que lleva a la aurora. (2000: 40)

> [The mission of the soul is errancy
> and that of the body is to make mistakes,
> doubly disorientated we search for the light
> to find, very often, a sliver of night;
> the very night that leads to the dawn.]

As mentioned earlier, the novel begins with a dream, 'un poco de noche' [a sliver of night]. In the dream the Parable of the Wheat and the Weeds is rewritten. The parable is from the Gospel of Matthew (Matthew 13: 24–30), the first book of the New Testament; its rewriting mirrors Peri Rossi's unravelling of Genesis, the first book of Old Testament, through her treatment of the tapestry. The parable states that in the Final Judgement wheat will be gathered by angels and admitted to heaven and the weeds, children of evil sown by the devil, will be burnt.

In Peri Rossi's reworking of the biblical version, Equis is separating wheat and chaff when a woman appears and encourages him to mix first a weed, then a stone and a mouse with the wheat. She then disappears. Equis says, 'Cuando se fue, quedé confuso. La paja me parecía más bella y los granos, torvos. La duda me ganó. [...] Bajo el cielo gris el horizonte es una mancha, y la voz ya no responde' (9) [When she had gone, I was confused. The straw seemed more beautiful and the grain, unyielding. Doubt overwhelmed me. [...] Under the gray sky the horizon is a smudge, and no voice answers] (1). The woman in the opening sequence sets the tone for the other encounters Equis has on his journey of feminist enlightenment. Counter to the pleasure in harmony the narrator emphasises in many of the tapestry descriptions, the dream scene suggests that there is beauty in disrupting order and neat categorisations, and questioning widely held beliefs and assumptions, even though this may involve moments of bleakness ('the gray sky'), uncertainty ('doubt overwhelmed me'), and loneliness ('no voice answers').

Beyond the questioning of convention in general, the image of unseparated wheat brings to mind the symbol of the fasces or *fascio littorio* adopted by Mussolini's fascist movement. The fasces is a bundle of wooden twigs with a protruding axe, based on a Roman symbol of power over life of death. It is used in a number of national symbols, particularly to represent institutions relating to law and justice. Most relevant to my analysis are two emblems that would have been familiar to Peri Rossi in both Montevideo and Barcelona. The emblem of the Spanish national police, the *Guardia Civil*, enforcers of Franco's authoritarian rule, and the shield of the Uruguayan police, upholders of military rule in Uruguay, both include the fasces. The wood is often depicted as yellow, as in the emblem of the *Guardia Civil*, and therefore looks like wheat. The mixing of the wheat and chaff in the novel's opening could be read as a challenge to the ideals of purity, segregation, and order on which fascism is based.

El libro, which I analyse in Part II of this chapter, depicts the generational struggle between the older members of an aristocratic family in Uruguay and the dynamism of the younger generations associated with the guerrillas. In *El libro* harmony and happiness are associated with authoritarianism. There is an example of the fascist invocation of happiness in a speech by the Paraguayan dictator, Alfredo Stroessner: 'Nos interesa la felicidad de todos los hombres de la Tierra. Nos repugna a la conciencia y en el corazón agregar un átomo de rencor que se sume al ya existente y contribuya a dividir, a separar a los hombres, que Dios y el estado hizo [*sic*] hermanos' ([1969] 1989: 100) [What matters to us is the happiness of every man on earth. Our hearts and conscience are disgusted by the thought of adding a mere atom of malice to that which already exists that would contribute to dividing and separating men, whom God and the State united as brothers]. Stroessner invokes happiness and brotherhood to maintain the status quo, promote national and familial unity, and vilify dissent. The notion of happiness through unity is actually based on division and separation that Stroessner claims to oppose; it separates the 'happy' citizens who follow the rules of a normative society and pits them against those who dissent. If fascism aligns happiness with order, Peri Rossi's textual mixing of wheat (the tapestry) and chaff (the stories of the diasporic wanderers and exiles) undermines a vision of happiness based on an order synonymous with separation and exclusion.

Like the errant soul that Aguado evokes, Equis passes through darkness to reach the light. Critics have commented that the wandering Equis is, in some ways, a Christ-like figure, with his name (X), also being the symbol of the cross (Tierney-Tello 1996: 258; De Rodríguez 1989: 523). However, unlike Jesus's one way, one truth, one light, he is a figure who takes a meandering, surprising, path. The narrator describes the segment of the tapestry in which the Angel of Light appears: 'se trata de una figura peregrina, que camina hacia alguna parte. Los tonos de este segmento son más claros, más luminosos' (84) [An angel in pilgrim's dress walking somewhere. In this section the colours are brighter and more luminous] (83). In the segment, the letters 'LUX', Latin for 'light', appear. In some senses, this angel prefigures the appearance in the novel of Lucía, whose name derives from 'lux'. Lucía is the aptly named character who brings Equis to his feminist en-*light*-enment. She is one of the women he meets while working for a company who charged women to be taken to have abortions in London from a country where it was illegal. Significantly, Satan himself masquerades as an Angel of Light in 2 Corinthians 11:14, hence the name 'Lucifer'. Picking up on the ambivalence of light in the Bible, Lucía goes against what traditional religion would deem to be the 'natural order', first through abortion and then through the sex acts she performs on stage in a club that runs transvestite shows. She comes to represent both ambiguity and multiplicity; a plural subjectivity.

Equis sees her in the dressing room of the club towards the novel's close:

> era un hermoso efebo el que miraba a Equis y se sintió subyugado por la ambigüedad. Descubría y se desarrollaban para él, en todo su esplendor, dos mundos simultáneos, dos llamadas distintas, dos mensajes, dos indumentarias, dos percepciones, dos discursos [...] La revelación era casi insoportable. (195)

[Lucía presented the perfect androgynous image [...] he felt overpowered by that ambiguity. He saw the unfolding of two parallel worlds in all their splendour; two different calls, two messages, two appearances, two perceptions, two languages [...] He was aware that the beauty of one increased the beauty of the other, that two pairs of eyes looked at him, four lips whispered, two wonderful heads shone in their harmony. The revelation was unbearable.] (202–03)

It is at this 'unbearable' point that Equis realises the answer to the riddle that has been posed to him in his recurring dream by a king who is in love with his daughter and does not want to let her leave his control. The king asks all of his daughter's suitors the same question: ¿Cuál es el tributo mayor, el homenaje que un hombre puede hacer a la mujer que ama?' (195) [What is the greatest tribute and homage a man can give to the woman he loves?] (203). In Equis's dream the daughter is Lucía. He must answer the riddle in order to free her. Upon seeing Lucía dressed as a man in the club he realises that the answer to the riddle is 'su virilidad', particularly ambiguous due to the unspecificity of the Spanish possessive pronoun 'su' which could mean his, her, or their virility, as Tierney-Tello has eloquently argued (1996: 203). The dawn of La nave subsequently comes in its triumphant feminist ending that seems to signal the collapse of patriarchy, at least in the protagonist's mind. In the final lines of the novel, the king disappears: 'el reyecito se hunde en el barro, el reyecito, derrotado, desaparece. Gime antes de morir' (197) [he falls to the ground, blends with the mud; overcome, beaten, the poor little king disappears. He dies with a whimper] (204). The novel's ending advocates what Geoffrey Kantaris has described as the 'cutting of the cultural bond between authority, power and male sexuality' (1995: 262).

Equis's enlightenment takes place when he realises that there are multiple perspectives, multiple paths, multiple desires in one person. It is significant that in order to reach this moment he literally passes through a dark basement before reencountering Lucía, through Aguado's 'night' to reach the 'dawn'. Whereas in the opening dream, ambiguity left Equis feeling bleak and lonely, in the final dream, he is enlightened by it. It is not incidental that Saint Lucy is the Patron Saint of the Blind, representing both what we see and know, and what we do not or cannot see or know, recalling Marçal and Vivien's Venus of the Blind. While Sara T. grapples with not being able to gain, picture, or evoke a complete image of Vivien, long dead, Equis's struggle is with a living person in front of him. Equis's transformation is ultimately an acceptance of the impossibility of fully knowing another being, which resonates with the epigraph to this part of the chapter: Equis's 'enlightenment' is an ambiguous revelation and a revelation of ambiguity. This is in keeping with the Latin roots of 'revelation' in which the re- in re-velare, can be read as signalling repetition or reversal of the act of veiling. To reveal: to unobscure or to obscure *again*?

In *Strange Encounters*, Ahmed is critical of discourses of multiculturalism in which, she argues, a dominant culture remains dominant. She is also critical of an ethics of 'yes-saying to the stranger', which she believes to be inadequate as it assumes that the stranger can be known. She states that 'there is never simply an encounter between self and self, or between self and other. There is always more than one *and* more than two in any encounter' (2000: 141). Equis's encounter with Lucía in all her ambiguity and multiplicity emphasises that there are aspects of others that we cannot know and access, just as the universe is not legible to us in its entirety. Sometimes accepting the obscurity of others is more ethical than a claim to have understood, or unobscured, another.

In the spirit of the impossibility of mastering the universe, others, and ourselves, the scattering of the tapestry descriptions amongst the tales of the exiles' nomadic wandering, fragmenting the novel's already fragmented form, can be considered in the light of Derrida's thoughts on dissemination, which can be linked etymologically with 'diaspora', from the Greek for 'dispersion', 'to sow', 'to scatter'. In the note to her translation of Derrida's *Dissemination* (1971), Barbara Johnson states:

> The Book, the Preface, and the Encyclopedia are all structures of unification and totalization. Dissemination, on the other hand, is what subverts all such recuperative gestures of mastery. It is what foils the attempt to progress in an orderly way toward meaning or knowledge, what breaks the circuit of intentions or expectations through some ungovernable excess or loss. (1981: xxxii)

The protagonists' diasporic wandering in the novel amongst 'things extra and other' of De Certeau's 'sieve-order' (1984: 107) leads us to question attempts to master the universe and others in it and to challenge prejudices, be these the cause of hostility towards individuals or groups or a premature acceptance, both of which are based on an assumption of knowing what or whom cannot yet, or perhaps ever, be known. Peri Rossi's disruption of conventional narrative through textual fragmentation and multiple narrative digressions can therefore be seen as a formal counterpart to her thematic questioning of disciplinary happiness, which is equated with ideological mastery over the universe and its inhabitants.

Privilege and Homogenising Home

As I sail towards some conclusions, I wish to tug at a key thread of the argument, in the spirit of Braidotti's nomadic consciousness as thought that resists settling. So far my analysis of the novel has taken me from Braidotti's 'joyful nomadism' to the novel's 'wretched wanderers' unravelling convention, but the emphasis on 'nomadism' has remained. In this section, I will suggest that while Peri Rossi's novel celebrates the potential in exilic and diasporic nomadism, it also demonstrates a wariness of new hegemonies and new exclusions.

Braidotti states of her own life that it is 'based on the permanence of temporary arrangements and the comfort of contingent foundations' (1994: 11), with the use of the word 'comfort' hinting at the privilege of her nomadic position. Indeed, it is on the basis of this *grounded* privilege that Braidotti's theory has been criticised by critics such as Dick Pels (1999). For many, including some of the women Equis meets in the novel and, to give an example from our contemporary reality, refugees currently trying to enter Europe, 'contingent' situations could not be considered to be 'foundations', and there is certainly little 'comfort' in their state of forced nomadism. In the chapter that shares the novel's title 'El viaje, VIII: La nave de los locos' [The Journey, VIII: The Ship of Fools], we read of a hauntingly resonant scene in which a boat of 'madmen' is abandoned to its fate at sea as the crew disembarks. In these inhumane times, it does not require much imagination to draw a connection between the eponymous 'Ship of Fools' and the boats carrying refugees on treacherous journeys to European shores that, in many cases, they never reach.

In the novel a number of the characters who have been forced into exile long to return home. Averis recognises that 'the freedom enabled by mobility must be considered alongside that of the freedom to stay at home' (2014: 30). Equis, for example, tries to establish some sense of continuity through surrounding himself with familiar objects: 'los libros que suele comprar, no bien llega y se instala en una ciudad, son casi siempre los mismos' (36) [The books which Ecks buys as soon as he arrives and settles in a new place are almost always the same] (31). He finds some consolation in places not changing: 'Cuando Equis regresó a la ciudad, buscó el bar y lo encontró. Se sintió reconfortado: le hacía daño volver a una ciudad y descubrir que en su ausencia, muchas cosas se habían modificado' (45) [When Ecks came back to the city, he looked for the bar and it was there. That comforted him: it hurt him to return to places and discover that so much had changed] (41). The sex worker whom Equis meets who has visible signs of violence on her body longs for a sense of home: the radio '[e]ra el único adorno de la habitación y demostraba que la dueña le tenía especial afecto. Una pasión quizá no controlada' (187) [was the only object which could be said to decorate the room; it showed that the owner was particularly fond of it, nurtured an uncontrollable passion for it] (193). These characters' longing for a sense of home suggests that celebrating nomadism is often only possible from the privileged perspective of those who have previously had or still have the comfort of stability against which to rebel. Similarly, an awareness of the privilege that is often a precursor to getting beyond identity recalls bell hooks's oft-quoted statement: 'It's easy to give up identity when you have one' (1990: 28). Perhaps it is also easy to give up home when you have one in the first place.

The novel's call to be mindful of privilege recalls Ahmed's wariness of the indiscriminate dismissal of family, home, and stability in some feminist thought. She draws on Lorde's association of 'freedom-from-family' with white feminist consciousness, suggesting that due to slavery and ongoing discrimination that has torn apart black families, black feminist consciousness may involve 'freedom-to-family' (2010: 86). In the introduction to this book, I mentioned the political importance of the biological family in the Southern Cone context. The 1976–83 Argentine military *junta* constituted an infamous attack on the 'freedom-to-family'. The dictatorship shattered families through disappearing citizens, often arbitrarily, in attempts to counter what they considered to be subversion.[4] Babies born to disappeared political prisoners were, in many cases, stolen and assigned new identities in right-wing military families. Under these circumstances, attempts by the mothers and grandmothers of the *Plaza de Mayo* in Argentina to reconstitute biological families were a politically defiant act against the 'official forgetting' imposed after the dictatorship through 'Amnesty laws' (see Amado and Domínguez 2004: 13–37).

Peri Rossi's novel, with its representation of imbalances in privilege in all of the places through which it takes the reader, suggests that celebrating the freedom afforded by exile or nomadism risks simplifying the complex realities of both the home country and country or countries to which the exile travels through. The romanticisation of exile may implicitly foster a reductionist vision of places where 'backward' or 'progressive' approaches to gender identities and roles prevail. While some critics such as Anzaldúa have problematised home, as mentioned in the introduction, Ahmed critiques the tendency to homogenise 'home' as a negative place in some writing about exile and migration in which the critic assumes that home is 'a purified space of belonging' or, indeed, a purified space of exclusion, that must be overcome. In *Strange Encounters*, Ahmed highlights the over-simplification inherent in this position, arguing that '[t]here is movement and dislocation within the very forming of homes as complex and contingent spaces of inhabitance' (2000: 88). We will see an example of this with the aristocratic house in *El libro* in Part II.

Ahmed's critique of the homogenisation of home also applies to those who celebrate the casting off by women of the gender binds they face in their home countries upon arriving in another country. Although family pressures might not be present as directly as in one's home country, in some cases, gender oppression is actually experienced more acutely in exile, especially where it is combined with classism, racism, and xenophobia. For Latin American women, especially those who challenged gender norms in the countries where they were born, their gender-bound experience might be exacerbated in Spain, for example, as they are faced with the triply marginalising force of being women, immigrants, and Latin American (see Benítez Burgos 2015). They are often domestic workers and they may well enjoy less cultural privilege than in their previous lives, if indeed they had such cultural capital before exile.

One example of Peri Rossi's reluctance to celebrate movement and 'activity' indiscriminately is her satirical depiction of a city referred to in the novel as 'la ciudad de B.' [the city of B], 'la metrópoli' [the metropolis], 'El Laberinto' [The Labyrinth], or 'el Gran Ombligo' [The Great Navel] (115–16), which bears great resemblance to Barcelona. Other authors, including those born in Catalonia, have used similar terms to mock what they perceive to be the city/region's navel-gazing. For example, Julià de Jòdar stated the following to *La Vanguardia* in 2010: 'Tenemos nuestras particularidades pero padecemos las cosas de una manera occidental de ver el mundo, nos consideramos el ombligo del mundo, como todo occidente' [We have our particularities but we suffer in a way that is due to our Western way of seeing the world, we think of ourselves as the centre of the world, like the rest of the West] (cited in Quelart 2019). Similarly, in Terenci Moix's novel *Siro o la increada consciència de la raça* [Siro or the Uncreated Conscience of the Race], the narrator describes Barcelona as suffering from 'el gran complex de ciutat-melic-del-món' (1972: 61) [the great complex of being the city at the centre of the world]. Morris spends some time in the apparently introspective city whose inhabitants are described as 'ombliguistas' [navel-gazers]. Equis warns him not to openly criticise the city and its inhabitants: 'Ten cuidado con lo que dices — le advierte Equis — . El Gran

Ombligo no perdona: persigue a los no afiliados' (119) ['Watch your words', Ecks warned. 'The Great Navel does not forgive; it persecutes dissidents.'] (120). Morris concludes:

> El movimiento del ombligo es polivalente y complicado, y estos espasmos suelen confundirse con la actividad, pero un análisis cuidadoso de tantas idas y venidas, de marchas y contramarchas permite asegurar que *no todo lo que se mueve avanza, ni todo lo que se agita progresa*. Lo que los ombliguistas llaman movimiento suele no ser más que convulsión. (123, emphasis mine)

> [A navel moves subtly in various directions. These spasmodic contractions can be taken for activity, but a careful analysis of the comings and goings, motions and commotions leads to the conclusion *that not all movement signifies change or progress*. What they describe as movement is in fact no more than convulsion.] (124, emphasis mine)

Through Morris, Peri Rossi offers a thinly veiled critique of what Pérez-Sánchez has described as the 'micro-nationalism' of the city (2007: 125), implying that exclusions can emerge in the most dynamic and apparently cosmopolitan and progressive places. However, rather than a critique of Catalan nationalism, the comments about the ciudad de B. in *La nave* could be read as a critique of an excessively urban focus and the way in which the peripheries, especially rural areas, are overlooked in considerations of Catalan identity, such as when Barcelona is seen as a synecdoche for the Catalan-speaking regions.

La nave suggests that the possibility for subjects to feel belonging in a state of unrootedness is deeply bound up with privilege and capital, be it financial or cultural. Ahmed's view that '[e]thics cannot be about moving beyond pain toward happiness or joy without imposing new forms of suffering on those who do not or cannot move in this way' (2010: 216) accords with the novel's suggestion that an indiscriminate celebration of a 'joyful nomadic force' is problematically exclusive and risks reinscribing the very hierarchies that feminism seeks to overcome. Nonetheless, Peri Rossi does seem to posit an exuberant nomadic opening up to chance, possibility, and the imagination. Hers, however, is a nomadism that may involve suffering and that may also, in some cases, lead to a state of homely settling or return, which, she suggests, is not necessarily incompatible with a transgressive mode of being. Traditionally nomadism is not, in fact, a lack of 'ground' or the shunning of settledness, but *seasonal* settling and movement, as Sophia McClennen has pointed out (2004: 48). Braidotti herself also notes that the word 'nomad' comes from 'noumos', meaning a plot of land. Originally a 'nomad' was a clan elder who supervised the allocation of land to the tribe (1994: 26). Therefore the criticism levelled against Braidotti's privileged position of stable intellectual 'nomadism' by critics such as Pels does, in some ways, hark back to the privilege and groundedness embedded within the term 'nomad', despite the fact that nomadic groups later came to experience great discrimination.

La nave's relentless challenge to binaries enables us to see within each of the two key positions in debates around affect and feminism discussed here (i.e. feminism as joy vs feminism as a challenge to compulsory happiness) the kernel of its own antithesis. After all, Ahmed does acknowledge that there can be a certain pleasure in resisting the happy settled life endorsed by societal convention: 'There is solidarity in recognizing our alienation from happiness [...] There can even be joy in killing joy' (2010: 87). Braidotti points to the nomad's ties to land and also acknowledges that her joyful perspective and that of the Derridean 'melancholics' are 'branches of the same family' (2014), so to speak. Read together, then, the three texts suggest that there can be settling within drift and drift within stasis, a certain happiness in 'melancholically' resisting a societally prescribed path to happiness *and* a melancholic entrapment in following these very same 'happy scripts' of convention.

As well as addressing societal norms and conventions and the forces behind them, Peri Rossi is aware of authorial practices and literary conventions and how these may be complicit with certain forms of authoritarian discourse in the home and nation. Art, authorship, and authority are key to *La nave*. Most relevant to this study is the *apparent* contrast between the Tapestry of Creation and the novel itself. I have shown that the tapestry depicts God's authorship of and authority over the universe that may be shared by the observer for whom seeing the tapestry induces a sense of harmony. In the novel, however, descriptions of the tapestry are scattered amongst a somewhat chaotic collation of documents and descriptions of the characters' travels, though its design was evidently deliberated by an author. The novel reveals Peri Rossi's suspicion of authoritarian discourse and her simultaneous awareness of its complexities, in which she is also implicated.

The *apparently* unpredictable wandering of Equis, along with the somewhat chaotic collation of documents in the novel (including a ship captain's log, poems, letters, interviews, and newspaper articles) give the impression of a text pieced together with no plan. The sense of disorientation to which this gives rise is exacerbated by the provision of partial information such as cities denoted by an initial (33, 115). Unlike the precise location of the tapestry in Girona Cathedral that is explicitly stated in the novel, the locations of most of the other places that the characters pass through are vague or unspecified. The narrator invites readers to guess where the cities denoted by an initial in the novel may be or to entertain the possibility that precise location does not matter, that the wandering, and not the destinations, is what is important: 'Equis omite deliberadamente el nombre de ésta y de otras ciudades, con el evidente propósito de no herir susceptibilidades [...] invito al lector a [...] averiguar el verdadero nombre de las ciudades evocadas en el libro en base a oportunas deducciones' (37) [Ecks deliberately avoids naming the city of A. and other cities, apparently to escape offending anybody's susceptibilities [...] the reader is invited to [...] guess the identity of those cities alluded to] (32). In this way, the narrator adopts a playful tone to mock the reader's desire to align the fictional work with 'reality' as they look to the narrator for clues.

As I write about *La nave* I find myself switching between passive verb constructions such as 'descriptions of the tapestry are interspersed throughout the text' to active constructions like 'Peri Rossi intersperses descriptions of the tapestry throughout the text'. Shifting between the passive and active voice led me to query the role of the author of a novel that criticises centralised authority. It is difficult to write about texts without suggesting that their effects are the consequence of authorial intent. Many phrases typical of literary criticism (and this chapter is no exception), such as 'Peri Rossi highlights...' and 'Peri Rossi invites us to...' imply the functioning of authorial agency.

Despite the novel being a chaotic text, we do finally have a book in our hands, and there are some hints that the seemingly chaotic novel is the result of a design process as rigorous as that of the tapestry itself. For example, the contents page calls into question the distinction between the apparent chaos of the text and order of the tapestry. On the contents page the chapters that describe Equis and others' wandering are largely numbered, whereas only the first tapestry description (of the twelve that appear in the novel) is listed. In this way our attention is drawn to the plan behind the seeming chaos, and the possibility that authority may function even when, or especially when, it is invisible. After all, there is a sense of narrative progression in the development of Equis's character as he becomes increasingly aware of the connections between gender and power. I also commented above on the changes in his attitude towards ambiguity, with which he becomes more comfortable as the novel progresses. Therefore, despite the textual fragmentation and multiple narrative digressions, there is some sense of progression in *La nave*.

It is important to ask to what extent a book can disperse authority. I commented on Johnson's remarks in the introduction to her translation of Derrida's *Dissemination* about the book being a structure of 'unification and totalization'. Johnson's words and Derrida's book lead me to consider the difficulty in representing the dissemination of authority in book form. It is therefore logical that an author who wants to challenge the concept of unified authority but also to make his/her/their readers think about alternative possibilities for the world that they live in (which is in itself a somewhat authoritative gesture, of course, 'to make readers...'), must grapple with fragmentation and totality.

Peri Rossi did not only come to grapple with these questions when she went into exile in Barcelona. She was already concerned with authority and narration in her first novel, *El libro*, originally published in Montevideo in 1969. In the 1989 Grijalbo edition, published in Barcelona, questions of authority and narration are evident even before we open the text. The blurb on the back cover makes the book an active subject and does not mention the author in the description of the novel. The description includes phrases such as '*El libro de mis primos* narra el derrumbamiento de una familia patricia [...] *Novela sobre* [...] es también *una obra sobre* [...] el punto de vista adulto [...] *se combina con* la fantasía poética' (my emphasis) [*The Book of my Cousins* narrates the downfall of an aristocratic family [...] *It is a novel about* [...] it is also *a work about* [...] the adult's point of view [...] *is combined* with poetic fantasy] (my emphasis), a manner of expression that downplays the author's craft, but also the presence of a writing subject, an 'agent'. Peri Rossi's biography appears below the novel description. While authorial authority is called into question through the impression that much of the text or documents in the novels are unmediated words from the minds or pens of the characters, I, as a reader-cum-author, a reader-writer, a critic, am aware that both *El libro* and *La nave* have obviously been carefully mapped by the author. It is to the figure of the author that I will now turn.

Part II: Property, (im)Propriety, and Posterity: The Figure of the Author in
El libro de mis primos **(1969) and** *Indicios pánicos* **(1970)**

> pienso en la sobrevida
> que me sobrevendrá
> en tu memoria
> [...]
> viviré más allá de mis años
> en tu memoria de mujer nocturna
> — PERI ROSSI (2014: 20)

> [I think about my survival
> that will survive me
> in your memory
> [...]
> I will live beyond my years
> in your memory, that of a nocturnal woman]

In this part of the chapter I explore how Peri Rossi's narrative works, specifically *El libro* (1969), *Indicios pánicos* (1970) [Panic Signs],[5] and *La nave,* analysed in Part I, engage with issues of authorship and authority in the run up to and during the 1973–85 military dictatorship in Uruguay. In 'What is an Author?', a lecture given in 1969, the year that *El libro* was first published, Foucault suggests that the figure of the author represents societal 'fear [of] the proliferation of meaning' (1984b: 119).[6] He highlights the authority readers tend to attribute to authors with regard to the meaning of their texts, a phenomenon with which Peri Rossi grapples. In particular, I am interested in the ways in which an author might deal with the risk of becoming a new site of hegemonic meaning in the process of challenging the discourse of totalitarian regimes. I also explore how Peri Rossi probes notions of authorship and ownership, disrupting the consideration of texts as the *property* of an author, thus complicating what Foucault has described as the 'circuits of ownership' (1984b: 108) of capitalism. These 'circuits' were highly relevant in the context of the increasingly corporativist Uruguayan State of the 1960s and 1970s.

I argue that in the texts analysed in this section, the apparent desire of Peri Rossi and of some of her diegetic authors for legacy and longevity through their works manifests itself through a disavowal of authorial authority rather than the violent imposition of authority that characterised the dictatorship. I demonstrate how Peri Rossi's deployment of the works of other authors in her own texts models collaborative, collective creation that ensures the posterity of earlier texts through intertextual engagement. In this way, Peri Rossi invites readers to engage actively with and appropriate her words also.

Authoring 1960s and 1970s Uruguay

The contexts in which Peri Rossi wrote these works offer some indication as to why her texts are concerned with questions of authorship and authority. *El libro* depicts scenes from the domestic life of a large wealthy Uruguayan family in what seems to be 1960s Montevideo (the one date that appears in the novel is 1966, the location is not explicitly stated). The chapters, most of which are written from the perspective of one of the eponymous cousins of the family, which consists of Abuela Clara, at least fifteen cousins, eight uncles, and ten aunts, provide the context for the subsequent downfall of the family.

The downfall is described from the point of view of three of the cousins in the novel's three endings. The 'Primer final', written in the voice of the young cousin, Oliverio, details a fantastical scene in which he destroys the family house and its older authoritarian inhabitants by throwing a stone during the cousins' game of 'guerrillas y soldados' [guerrillas and soldiers]. The 'Segundo final' is written in a fearful tone from the perspective of Oliverio's brother, Óscar, inheritor of the ideas of their once authoritarian but now decrepit father. Óscar laments his uncles' inaction and denial in the face of an impending attack by guerrillas. The final chapter of the novel is titled 'Federico' after the older cousin who has run away to join a guerrilla group. Federico describes the return of the guerrillas to the city after some time hiding in the countryside and implies that they are about to commit violent acts on private property.

For the purposes of this chapter, the most relevant characters are Oliverio and Federico as they are the novel's diegetic writers. Once Federico leaves the family home to join the guerrilla, Oliverio inherits his words and works and vows to continue them. The relationship between the two cousins symbolises the political inheritance of the guerrillas. The older family members are aware of Oliverio's allegiance to his cousin, emphasising the need to 'encauzarlo' (179) [direct him], reeducating him to adhere to the right-wing family principles, as his brother Óscar does. Questions of cultural and political inheritance are key to the text which was written in the midst of the generational conflict in 1960s Uruguay.

The climactic clash between the young cousins and the older aunts, uncles, and matriarchal grandmother can be taken as an allegory for the political rupture between the increasingly authoritarian Uruguayan State of the 1960s and the students, workers, and others who protested against it. Many left-wing movements in Latin America were galvanised by the Cuban Revolution of 1959. The clash of ideologies between the old guard and the energy of those wanting change is deftly summed up in Jordana Blejmar's analysis (2012) of generational rupture that reached a head in neighbouring Argentina in 1969 as evidenced by the student and worker uprisings and strikes that later came to be known as the 'Cordobazo'. In Uruguay the clash of ideologies led President Jorge Pacheco Areco to decree 'medidas prontas de seguridad' [emergency decrees] in June 1968. The measures permitted the temporary suspension of certain constitutional guarantees and civilian protections with the alleged objective of protecting national security against an 'ataque exterior o conmoción interior' (Article 168, Constitución de Uruguay). [attack from outside the nation or a domestic threat to peace] ('Constitución de la República' n. d.).[7]

Police repression of student organisation and protest as part of these measures involved violent encounters between the police and students, which reached a head in August and September 1968 with the deaths of left-wing student activists: the fittingly-named Líber Arce (in Spanish, 'liberarse' means 'to free oneself'), Susana Pintos, and Hugo de los Santos. In 1968, the measures were allegedly introduced to combat 'subversion' and, in particular, to eradicate the *Movimiento de Liberación Nacional-Tupamaros* (MLN-T) [Tupamaros National Liberation Movement], the main urban guerrilla movement in Uruguay. The MLN-T was formally created in 1965 (although members of the group had robbed banks as early as 1963) and their main phase of armed struggle took place from 1968–72. Their activities were guided by their Marxist principles: in particular, they were against private property, capitalism, and foreign ownership of national resources. Both the government and the MLN-T accused the other of submitting to foreign influences.

The tensions between Marxist internationalism and a sort of nativism or nationalism amongst the MLN-T is interesting. Hernández Arregui describes Octavio Getino and Fernando Solanas's revolutionary Argentine film *La hora de los hornos* (1968) [The Hour of the Furnaces] as 'cine universal por nacional, y en su raíz, negador del cosmopolitismo ficticio y caligráfico de las minorías intelectuales segregadas del país real' (cited in Aguilar 2009: 95) [cinema that is universal because it is national, and, at its root, denies the fictitious and writerly cosmopolitanism of an intellectual minority who are disconnected from the country's reality]. The 'fictitious cosmopolitanism' that he critiques in his praise for Getino and Solanas is aligned with writers; it is *calligraphic*. In contrast, Gonzalo Aguilar critiques the championing of the national, arguing that 'inadvertidamente *La hora de los hornos* se encuentra reciclando motivos conservadores que tradicionalmente pertenecían a la derecha' (2009: 105) [*The Hour of the Furnaces* inadvertently finds itself recycling conservative arguments that traditionally belonged in a right-wing domain]. He draws on a comment made by Edgardo Cozarinsky in 1969 on the recent ideological twist in political cinema. Cozarinsky notes that, in its concern for a purity from what it saw as foreign influences, the left had adopted a traditionally right-wing rhetoric. He describes the 'reivindicación por la izquierda de los mitos tradicionales de la derecha (la raza, la sangre, la tradición, el culto del líder y el pavor ante lo foráneo: en resumen, el irracionalismo)' (cited in Aguilar 2009: 20) [leftist vindication of the traditional myths of the right (race, blood, tradition, the cult of the leader, fear of the foreign, in summary, irrationalism)]. Cozarinsky reminds us of how both the left and the right can slip into an authoritarian concern for purity.

Indicios pánicos warns of the Uruguayan government's shift towards fascism in the 1960s through scenes that highlight State repression of left-wing movements, education, and culture in the run-up to the military *coup d'état* of 1973. Indeed, many consider the 1960s effectively to have been part of the dictatorship, though it did not *technically* break with the Constitution. The Museo de la Memoria in Montevideo opened in 2008. In the information leaflet handed to visitors when I visited in 2016 contained a message from the museum director Elbio Ferrario:

'Cuando hablamos de la dictadura también hablamos de la década del '60' [When we speak of the dictatorship, we are also referring to the '60s]. Juan Rial states that the Uruguayan government was only 'quasi-constitutional' from 1968 onwards (cited in McClennen 2004: 100); it effectively lacked an 'authoritative' governing text due to the aforementioned 'medidas prontas de seguridad' and the subsequent suspension of constitutional guarantees. *Indicios pánicos* is a collection of short texts, poems, short stories, and dialogues depicting scenes that have come to be seen as a premonition for the terror of the military dictatorship that would grip the country three years after the stories were published. Peri Rossi's conceptualisation of the roles of the author and reader in the text illuminates this chapter's analysis of the relationship between the figure of the author, reading practices, authority, and authoritarianism.

Language, literature, and culture were issues that concerned Uruguay's authoritarian government. Rúben Yañez describes how State violence was particularly targeted at culture and politics (1993: 133). One of the epigraphs to *Indicios pánicos* is an extract from a speech by the Italian dictator Benito Mussolini. The speech reflects the fascist State's fear of culture and education: 'Señores: Es tiempo de decir que el hombre, antes de recibir los beneficios de la cultura, debe recibir los beneficios del orden. En cierto sentido se puede decir que el policía ha precedido, en la historia, al profesor' ([1970] 1981: 5) [Gentlemen: It is time to say that man, before receiving the benefits of culture, should receive the benefits of order. In a certain sense, it can be said that, historically, the policeman has taken precedence over the teacher] (i). Peri Rossi specifically links the subordination of culture to discipline in Latin America in a footnote by the author (a 'nota del autor', which is evidently a device that permits the author to highlight one particular interpretation of the text, despite its lack of explicit locational and chronological specificity): 'Después de Mussolini, muchos pensadores en América Latina han sostenido la misma tesis, aunque llevándola a la práctica quizás con más esmero aún [...] La teoría ha sido especialmente bien recibida por los generales' (5) [After Mussolini, many Latin American thinkers have not only supported the same thesis, but have put it into practice, with perhaps even greater pains [...] The theory has been especially well-received by the generals] (i). The military State aimed to shape public perception of reality through the control of language; they wanted to ensure that their version of events prevailed.

A particularly pertinent portrayal of the State's efforts to control language can be seen in Costa-Gavras's film *État de siège* (1972). Shot in Chile during Salvador Allende's presidency, but about the guerrilla movement in Uruguay, the film is based on the Tupamaro's 1970 kidnapping and execution of Dan Mitrione, a US government adviser on torture for the CIA in Latin America. The following scene (00:26:20) depicts the tension between journalists and State agents:

Foreign journalist: Después de su comunicado parece que los Tupamaros —
Minister: Esa palabra la prohibe la ley. Nuestro país les ofrece hospitalidad. Respeten sus leyes.
Uruguayan journalist: Les llamamos los innombrables.
Minister: Son terroristas.

[*Foreign journalist:*   After their annoucement it seems that the Tupamaros —
Minister: That word is prohibited by law. Our country is offering
    you hospitality. Respect its laws.
Uruguayan journalist: We call them the unnameables.
Minister: They are terrorists.]

Alongside the torture, killing, and disappearance of the guerrillas and others, language was a key battleground in the depiction and manipulation of reality. The government hoped that by forbidding the use of the MLN-T's name here, indeed, erasing it, they could delegitimise it. It is in the context of this clash of ideology and manipulation of language that Peri Rossi writes *El libro* and *Indicios pánicos*.

The title of Foucault's aforementioned lecture 'What is an Author?' dialogues with Sartre's *What is Literature?* (1948) in which Sartre dwells on the role and responsibility of the artist in post-war Europe, clearly preoccupied by the spectre of war. Sartre believes it to be a mistake to divorce literature from the author, including the material historical circumstances of its creation. His notion of committed writing influenced Latin American revolutionaries such as Fidel Castro and Ernesto 'Che' Guevara. Sartre writes of the limitations of writing:

> The art of prose is bound up with the only regime in which prose has meaning: democracy. When one is threatened the other is too. And it is not enough to defend them with the pen. A day comes when the pen is forced to stop, and the writer must then take up arms. (1949: 65)

In *What is Literature?*, Jean-Paul Sartre argues that despite the limitations of all writing, prose, unlike poetry, is a politically committed form. Peri Rossi's writing, like Marçal's and Company's, does not lend itself to such a clear distinction between the genres. For Sartre, it is prose's greater transparency that lends itself to politically committed writing. However, Peri Rossi plays with the political power of the opacity of prose. Peri Rossi's works suggest that in a context in which an authoritarian regime is striving to mould reality to its words and to its version of events, ambiguity and opacity are political in themselves.

However, Sartre also points to the collaboration between reader and writer, as expressed in his oft-quoted line, '[t]here is no art except for and by others' (1949: 43). I would argue that Peri Rossi's 'art' clearly ascribes to this dictate. However, her approach is not wholly in line with Sartre's perspective that a writer writes for his contemporaries, for his time and place. Peri Rossi's texts engage with both the particular and the universal in her use of allegory; with her time and place, and with others, a sentiment expressed in the lines cited in the epigraph to this part of the chapter — 'viviré más allá de mis años' (2014: 20). However, Peri Rossi's literary techniques and the statements made by Federico when he joins a guerrilla group do chime with Sartre's emphasis on the committed writer who compels the reader to be committed in their reading practice: 'the author's whole art is bent upon obliging me to *create* what he *discloses* therefore to compromise myself — so both of us bear the responsibility for the universe' (1949: 61). I would argue that the reader-writer has to create what is not wholly disclosed too, especially when the disclosure cannot be transparent. In any case, the reader must read *passionately*: 'what the writer requires of the reader is not the application of an abstract freedom but the gift of his whole person, with his passions, his prepossessions, his sympathies, his sexual temperament, and his scale of values' (1949: 51).

There is, therefore, a tension here between freedom in creating one's own reading, on the one hand, and, on the other hand, the demands of committed reading in 'creating' meaning already 'disclosed' to reveal some truth. Peri Rossi struggles also with this tension, evident in her concern not to be perceived as a postmodernist writer, when *La nave*, for example, is clearly a postmodern text in its form. Pérez-Sánchez writes eloquently of the tension between clear political meaning and a troubling of Manichean messages in Peri Rossi's philosophy of writing and her works (2007: 119–42). Pérez-Sánchez concludes that Peri Rossi 'wants to keep her persona of engaged modern intellectual while she actively participates in the Spanish postmodern environment of the 1970s and 1980s' (125). I will return to the writer-reader inheritance in my reading of the transmission of political ideals in *El libro*.

We have seen why the tensions around writing and authorial authority may have been particularly pressing for Peri Rossi in the context of authoritarian regimes that attempted to control language, reality, and history. I will now go on to consider the author's conundrum in opposing authoritarian discourse while being aware of his/her/their own possible complicity with a different didactic discourse that could emerge in its place, especially if that is what the reader expects and desires.

Harmony and Alienation: Readerly Expectations

Peri Rossi's grappling with the authority that the reader tends to attribute to the figure of the author recalls Foucault's observations in 'What is an Author?'. Foucault states that the point of writing has become 'a question of creating a space into which the writing subject constantly disappears' (1984b: 102), but he also highlights the contradictory preservation of and fixation with the concept of the author: 'It would seem that the author's name, unlike other proper names, does not pass from the interior of a discourse to the real and exterior individual who produced it; instead, the name seems always to be present, marking off the edges of the text, revealing, or at least characterising, its mode of being' (107). Contemporary literary criticism (indeed this very chapter in a book structured by author is a case in point) tends to treat authors as 'the principle of a certain unity of writing' (111). As mentioned above, for Foucault, the emphasis on attribution of literary works derives from fear of not being able to pinpoint the message of a text:

> the author [...] is a certain functional principle by which, in our culture, one limits, excludes, and chooses; in short, by which one impedes the free circulation, the free manipulations, the free composition, decomposition, and recomposition of fiction [...] The author is therefore the ideological figure by which one marks the manner in which we fear the proliferation of meaning.
> (118–19)

Similarly, a fear of multiple meanings existed amongst the authoritarian state, as highlighted in the scene from *État de siège* detailed above. I will return to the 'free circulation' of fiction in the section titled 'Collective Creations' below. For now, I will focus on this fear of not being able to control how language might be interpreted.

In 'Diálogo con el escritor' [Dialogue with the Writer] in *Indicios pánico*, a generic reader asks an unnamed writer to define and delimit the meaning of his book. The conversation, part of which I reproduce here, is revealing of the readerly attitude observed by Foucault that Peri Rossi's work challenges:

> — He leído su libro.
> — ¿Qué piensa de él?
> — Es algo confuso.
> (En cambio, su alma, señora, es clara.)
> — Lo siento mucho.
> — Usted, quizás, pudiera explicarme qué quiso decir en él.
> — No puedo contestarle. Si lo supiera, no lo hubiera escrito.
> — Entonces, las letras, ¿son todas tinieblas?
> — No sé qué decirle. En esa misma época, mucha gente moría en las calles. Usted todavía podrá apreciar la cantidad enorme de lisiados, de baldados que recorren la avenida, o piden limosna, o esperan de la caridad pública un poco de piedad.
> — Pero usted, en tanto, lo escribía.
> — No señora: lo soñaba.
> — Los sueños no siempre son fáciles de entender.
> — Yo escribo, señora, como sueño.
> — ¿No cree que podría tener un poco más de respeto por el lector?
> — Lo respeto tanto, señora mía, que no quisiera nunca tocar el sueño, tocar el libro, traicionar la magnífica alienación de la metáfora. (40)

> ['I read your book.'
> 'What do you think of it?'
> 'It's a bit confusing.'
> (On the other hand, your soul is clear, señora.)
> 'I'm very sorry.'
> 'Maybe you could explain to me what you meant in it.'
> 'I can't answer you. If I knew, I wouldn't have written it.'
> 'So the words are all darkness?'
> 'I don't know what to tell you. At that very time, a lot of people were dying in the streets. You can still see the large number of wounded and crippled that roam the street, or beg for alms, or hope for a bit of compassion and public charity.'
> 'But meanwhile, you were writing it.'
> 'No, señora: I was dreaming it.'
> 'Dreams are not always easy to understand.'
> 'I write the way I dream, señora.'
> 'Don't you think you could respect the reader a bit more?'
> 'I respect the reader so much, señora, that I would never want to touch the dream, nor the book, nor betray the magnificent alienation of metaphor.']
> (24)

Clarity, understood here as the act of limiting multiple interpretations to one meaning, is seen by the writer as a betrayal of the 'alienation' caused by meta-phor. The writer evidently values the 'magnificent alienation' prompted by reading 'confusing' texts, associating alienation with respect. The experience of the disconcerted reader in this scene contrasts with the contentedness in order experienced by the observer of the Catholic tapestry in *La nave* in which everything is in harmony. For the writer in this scene inducing a feeling of harmony through clarity in the text would be to disrespect the reader. Alienation is respectful in the sense that it respects readerly autonomy through prompting readers to have their own thoughts, which may remain other or alien to the writer's thoughts.

Readerly alienation in the process of interpretation is also evident in the dream scene that opens *La nave* that I analysed in Part I of the chapter. The dream begins with a voice ordering Equis to describe the city in which he arrives. Equis responds, '"¿Cómo debo distinguir lo significante de lo insignificante?"' (9) [How shall I know what is meaningful from what is not?] (1). In this way, the dream positions Equis as reader and writer of the city. As mentioned above, Equis mixes the wheat and the chaff, which initially leads to bleakness. He is confused and alienated. In antiquity, alienation referred to a state of ecstasy (from the Greek *ekstasis* 'standing outside oneself' via late Latin) and the word comes from the Latin *alienus*, meaning 'of another place or person'. With this in mind, the alienation that the reader experiences could be seen as a feeling that leads him/her/them to question the status quo, considering other perspectives and alternative political possibilities. Indeed, Equis's despondent alienation in the first dream gives way to a state of almost ecstatic alienation in his feminist enlightenment when faced with the ambiguity of the aptly named Lucía, as we saw in Part I.

Indicios pánicos and *La nave,* then, present a vision of literature in which the reader has to confront the ambiguity and alienation of the text in order to know what is meaningful. While the author may have some control over the effect their words have on the reader, the writer's comments in the dialogue above (that he did not know what message he was trying to communicate and that he writes how he dreams) draw attention to the role of the subconscious in the creative process. Therefore, it is not simply that the writer has authority over the text and intends to share that authority with an active, critical reader, but that language precedes and exceeds the writer. Derrida describes the text as a network: 'a "text" is henceforth no longer a finished corpus of writing, some content enclosed in a book or its margins, but a differential network, a fabric of traces referring endlessly to something other than itself' ([1977] 1979: 84). The text goes 'más allá' [beyond], in Peri Rossi's words, beyond itself, to another time, to another place — I will return to this below.

The uncontrollable text recalls Nietzsche's analysis of the tendency to over-emphasise the volitional first-person subject in the act of deliberation, when, as we saw in Chapter One, he argues that our thoughts are perhaps not as autonomous and willed as we would like to think. The author never has complete authority over their texts; even their thoughts exceed them. In the prologue to *Indicios pánicos*, Peri Rossi refers to her inability to control her mind and thoughts through an anecdote about counting jumping sheep in an attempt to get to sleep:

la primera oveja del grupo se niega a saltar. No camina, no se mueve, *no obedece* mis órdenes. *Permanece ajena* a cualquier esfuerzo por imponerle una voluntad [...] me parece la evidencia de que aun en las fantasías más inofensivas, en apariencia, se manifiestan las *relaciones de poder*. En un sentido muy claro, *no soy la dueña de la oveja que convoco con mi imaginación* [...] (12–13, my emphasis)

[the first sheep in the flock refuses to jump. The sheep doesn't walk, doesn't move, *doesn't follow* my orders. *It remains indifferent* to any effort to impose my will on it [...] it seems to me that even in the most inoffensive of fantasies, *power relations* are apparent. In a very clear sense, *I don't own the sheep that I summon in my imagination* [...]] (3, my emphasis)

The sheep can be summoned, but not controlled; like a spectre, it haunts the writer. The 'oveja rebelde' [rebel sheep] also appears in a short story of the same name by Peri Rossi in which the narrator hits the sheep repeatedly in order to get to sleep, and ends up killing it. The writer can only attempt to control the scenes she imagines through an act of symbolic violence.

As I have shown in this section, the author's conundrum in striving to deconstruct the official story without replacing it with another is challenging, especially if readers might be looking to her as the person who holds the key to the meaning of her novel and to society itself and its unofficial — supposedly true(r) — stories. However, as we saw in the violence of the narrator in 'La oveja rebelde' and will consider in more depth below, it is not just the reader who looks to the author for a clear worldview; the author herself may also have to confront a desire within herself to portray a clear message, with authority, especially if such a message is politically urgent. In the following section I will consider how the form of Peri Rossi's novels could be seen to embody the author's dilemma, reflecting the tension in the text between what Foucault describes as 'a space into which the writing subject constantly disappears' (1984b: 102) and a space where new authorities emerge.

Problematising Authorial Authority: Fragmentation and Totality

In this section I will explore how Peri Rossi confronts the author's dilemma outlined above; the challenge of offering alternative readings of reality without becoming a figure of absolute authority. Despite her apparent awareness of the impossibility of controlling language and interpretations of a text, Peri Rossi describes her desire to control her texts, to depict an ordered vision of the world. She therefore seems to pivot between contradictory positions regarding authorial authority. In the prologue to *Indicios pánicos* she states that '[o]rganizar la dispersión y la disparidad de pistas y de pautas es nuestra tarea, y también, específicamente, la tarea del escritor' (9) [Our duty is to put some order into these scattered and disparate clues, and such ordering is the specific duty of the writer] (1). However, she goes on to produce this very dispersion in *La nave*. The tension between order and dispersion is an example of Peri Rossi's aforementioned self-definition as a modernist writer whilst producing a postmodern text (Pérez-Sánchez 2007: 125).

These fragmented texts encourage multiple creative readings, while at once recognising the appeal of the 'complete' or 'absolute' work. In order to explore the tension between fragmentation and totality, between multiplicity and unity, I will consider Oliverio's desire in *El libro* to create 'una obra tan vasta (todo debía entrar en ella como en una arca prodigiosa y contemporánea)' (40) [a work so vast (everything must fit within in it as in a prodigious and contemporary ark)]. I will analyse the ways in which Peri Rossi challenges authorial authority while demonstrating an awareness of its ineluctable seduction.

As we saw in Part I, in *La nave*, Peri Rossi's challenge to authority, teleology, and mastery of time and space is evident in the contrast between the worldview of the tapestry that Equis sees in Girona Cathedral, and Peri Rossi's treatment of it in the novel. As we saw earlier, in one of the tapestry descriptions, the narrator highlights the redemptive quality of the religious artefact in the face of 'nuestra desolada experiencia del desorden' (21) [life's brutal disorder] (14). Here, chaos, disorder, and dispersion are associated with a feeling of 'desolation', similar to the readerly alienation espoused by the aforementioned diegetic writer in *Indicios pánicos*. It is this very sense of dispersion that appears to characterise the novel. The scattering of centralised authority is emphasised through the text's depiction of the diasporic wandering of a political exile, Equis, and others.

El libro challenges authorial control over the narrative through the novel's multiple endings which frustrate a simple closure of the plot. The novel ends — or, rather, complicates the possibility of a conclusion — through the three aforementioned endings that describe the family's downfall. However, the first two of the three endings are numbered; a principle of numerical order still obtains. Having said that, the ending with which the book actually closes, titled 'Federico', finishes with the words 'HEMOS LLEGADO' (218) [WE HAVE ARRIVED]. In this way, the ending is a beginning, an arrival, and it gives the impression that the text ends in the middle of the action. We saw above that in *La nave*, the final lines of the novel highlight the rivers to Paradise that are missing in the tapestry. Therefore, neither of the novels leave us feeling that we know the full story. Seen from another perspective, while the multiplicity of endings in *El libro* seems to deny the closure of the text, at least in any singular sense, one might say the very opposite: that Peri Rossi prolifically affirms closure by offering many endings.

The majority of the chapters of *El libro* are written from the perspective of a family member and, in general, the chapter titles include the name of the character in whose voice they are written. Through the multiplicity of perspectives, Peri Rossi repeatedly calls into question the authority of a single narrative voice in the text. Carlos Raúl Narváez describes the rejection of an omniscient narrator as a rejection of 'the vision of a "God" controlling everything that surrounds him' (1983: 26), which we can link back to Part I's Pantocrator in the tapestry and De Certeau's 'solar Eye' or 'voyeur-god'. However, the text hints at a more complex reading. An omniscient god might be able to offer or feign multiple perspectives. Indeed, there are hints at the possibility that Oliverio has written the whole work, adopting the (imagined) voices of his relatives. Despite apparently being written from the perspective of different characters, the style of almost all of the chapters is very similar. The title of the book also reflects the ambiguity surrounding the diegetic author of the text. The preposition 'de' [of] in *El libro de mis primos* may refer to the fact that the book belongs to the narrator's cousins, was written by them, or is merely about them.

We could consider the fading away of an omniscient narrator into multiple voices in the light of the 'oracle effect' as conceptualised by Pierre Bourdieu. It is an effect by which the absence of an identifiable individual author may increase their authority. Bourdieu states:

> It is when I become Nothing — and because I am capable of becoming Nothing, of abolishing myself, of forgetting myself, of sacrificing myself, of dedicating myself — that I become Everything. I am nothing but the delegate of God or the People, but that in whose name I speak is everything, and on this account I am everything. ([1982] 1991: 211)

Paradoxically, then, what we might be seeing here, and in the apparently chaotic proliferation of documents in *La nave*, is the diegetic or the extradiegetic author exercising more authority through their apparent absence, in a god-like manner. The phenomenon of the authority of anonymity or of the multitude is also evident in a dictatorship without a single dictator, as Peri Rossi observes. She describes the Uruguayan military dictatorship 'que ni siquiera tenía un dictador con nombre propio, como Pinochet o Videla (las dictaduras sin nombre son las peores: se convierten en metafísicas)' (2005a: 15) [which didn't even have a named dictator like Pinochet or Videla (dictatorships without a name are the worst: they become metaphysical)]. We can also observe the phenomenon in the norms of literary criticism when critics express their opinions in the first person plural, as indeed I have done in this sentence and in many in this book. For example, phrases such as 'we observe', 'we feel', 'we think' abound. Universalising a reaction to a text, which is inevitably a subjective reaction, is a way of imposing one's authority.

In Chapter V, 'La obra', Oliverio expresses a unified totalising notion of art and authority. He describes his desire to produce a total work:

> Fuera lo que fuera — sinfonía, estatua, mármol, celuloide, color, planos, dimensión, imagen, símbolo, arquitectura, puente, prosa, tiempo, poesía — , ella resultaría muy importante, como que sería la suma de *todas* las cosas que yo encontraba dispersas, sueltas por el mundo. Mi obra debía encerrar, pues, a *todo* el mundo, *todo* lo conocido: bastaba con que yo encontrara el medio adecuado para expresarlo. En mi obra, debía aparecer *todo* lo que yo conocía, *todo* lo que imaginaba, lo que había podido ver y lo que no. (40, my emphasis)

> [Whatever it ended up being — symphony, statue, marble, celluloid, colour, shots, dimension, image, symbol, architecture, bridge, prose, time, poetry — it would be very important, it would be the sum of *all* the things I found loose and dispersed around the world. My work had to encompass, then, the *whole* world, *everything* known: I just needed to find the appropriate means to express it. In my work, *everything* I knew had to appear, *everything* I imagined, all I had been able to see and even what I had not.] (my emphasis)

His reference to gathering together dispersed things is similar to the reference in *La nave* to structures as artefacts that heal 'nuestro sentimiento de fuga y de la dispersión' (21) [our having fled and scattered] (14). Morris, in his visit to the Editorial Albión in *La nave*, also struggles to define and delimit his work: 'Mi obra trata del *todo*. Del enorme *todo* y sus diversas partes. O sea: del *todo* minimizado' (128, my emphasis) [The work deals with *everything*. Of the *whole* in its multiple aspects. That is, of the *whole* in its infinitesimal particles] (129, my emphasis). The reference to capturing the 'whole' recalls the draft letter in the Marçal archives in which Sara T. describes Vivien as a fragment that has the illusion of being a 'whole': the 'impossible synecdoche' discussed in Chapter One. In all three cases — *La passió, La nave, El libro* — the use of the word 'todo' or 'tot' highlights the characters' obsession with the total artwork; they want to be omniscient 'voyeur-gods'.

Oliverio's vision of the work contrasts with the fragmented text we are holding, which might be the very work of which he speaks. Indeed, his very name underlines the tension between fragmentation and harmonious totality in the work. There is a stark contrast between the two main etymological roots of his name. It derives from the Latin *Olivarius*, related to the olive tree, and thus associated with peace. However, it is also associated with Germanic names related to armies and warriors. The incongruous roots of the name point to the contrast between his creative desire to form a harmonious whole through his creation of a *complete* work of art, on the one hand, and, on the other hand, his destruction of the family house and creation of a fragmented text.

In the context of growing authoritarianism in the Southern Cone, a quest for complete knowledge and control has sinister undertones. Peri Rossi describes her own attempts to create encyclopaedic records of films and books in Montevideo, noting that '[a]quellos humildes pero completísimos ficheros caseros fueron el antecedente no reconocido de las computadoras y de internet' (2005b: 24) [those humble but totally complete home-made index cards were the unrecognised antecedent to computers and the internet]. While this may have been a throw-away remark, her use of the loaded word, 'fichero', brings to mind the military dictatorship's records on political prisoners and surveillance of the general population. That she sees these 'ficheros' as a precedent for the internet and virtual databases points to developments in more recent government surveillance of political activities.

The contrast between wholeness and fragmentation could be seen as an example of the tension described by McClennen in her study of works by Ariel Dorfman, Juan Goytisolo, and Peri Rossi. She highlights the seemingly contradictory desires to narrate alternative (and, at times, apparently 'totalising') stories and a suspicion of truth which lead to a 'crisis of representation' and fragmentation:

> through the representation of the gaps between the communicability of language and the experience of exile and alienation the narrative effectively presents the crisis as a problem which escapes facile resolution. this can be noted by the untotalizable narratives of these writers, which at the same time display totalizing impulses. (2004: 162)

McClennen also describes Peri Rossi as 'the author of texts that struggle with [...] the author's role in subverting the authoritarian's desire to control the bond between signifier and signified' (146). In addition to presenting the authorial battle between fragmentation and totality, another key literary device for challenging the bond between signifier and signified is allegory, a device that is characteristic of much of Peri Rossi's oeuvre. However, is allegory totalising or does it multiply the meaning of a text?

Allegory: Deferring Meaning 'Elsewhere' in Time and Space

In an interview with Parizad Tamara Dejbord, Peri Rossi speaks of her desire for her texts to be relevant beyond a particular time and place:

> Creo que el sueño de cualquier escritor es ser leído en cualquier época y por cualquier lector. Creo que todos los escritores nos alegramos cuando nos traducen [...] Por lo tanto, las coordenadas espaciales y temporales son irrelevantes a la hora de escribir. (1998: 230)

> [I think that the dream of all writers is to be read in any time period and by any reader. I think that all writers are happy when their works are translated [...] It follows, then, that spatial and temporal coordinates are irrelevant when one starts to write.]

Her comment ties in with critical debates on the particularity and universality of her literature, a debate clearly outlined by Claire Lindsay (2003: 19–46). Peri Rossi refers also to translation, literally a 'carrying across' to other contexts. The blurb on the back of *Indicios pánicos* points to the text's lack of specificity as a way of bridging the particular and the universal. The text is described as lacking 'precisiones geográficas, con alusiones simbólicas que le dan — por lo tanto — significado universal' [geographical precision, with symbolic allusions that, therefore, imbue it with universal significance]. Given the text's vague location, contextually rooted sociopolitical readings could be seen as possible interpretations that do not limit other readings based in different contexts. In this section we will see how allegory can be a way of writing a text that bridges the particular and the universal, lending itself to transnational readings.

Allegory, as a way of constantly deferring meaning and truth elsewhere in space and time, offers us a possible authorial attitude to posterity that does not involve freezing a specific moment in time. Winterson writes: '[t]he best texts are time machines; they are of their moment [...] But they are something more too — they live on into the future because they were never strapped into time' (2007: xiii). Peri Rossi's concern for posterity, her reference to travelling 'más allá' in time (2014: 20), like a time machine, might have a connection with a 'más allá' in space, including the space beyond that of the text, i.e. moving beyond the text as text to readings that engage with society and politics.

The question of wanting to persist in time but not be 'strapped into time' is an especially pressing question in the context of authoritarian regimes that want to freeze history in the moment of their absolute power. Peri Rossi's desire to be remembered may seem at first to be incompatible with her suspicious attitude towards the idea of a singular authority behind a text. However, I will argue that her emphasis on the reader and their interpretation of 'other stories' in an attempt to disperse centralised authority does not contradict, limit, or hinder her desire for posterity; quite the reverse — it seems *vital* to the project of ensuring her legacy. Derrida, in a comment that resonates with Winterson's remarks, describes writing as a machine that will function beyond his death: '[t]o write is to produce a mark that will constitute a sort of machine which is productive in turn, and which my future disappearance will not, in principle, hinder in its functioning' ([1972] 1988: 8). The machine may continue to function, but it does not have a controller — it never has done.

In *El libro*, the children's 'guerrillas y soldados' game in which they eventually destroy the house and its older inhabitants lends itself to allegorical readings of the political situation in Uruguay in the 1960s and early 1970s. The date that appears in one of the chapters, 1966, written from the point of view of the guerrilla Alina, stands out amidst the novel's lack of chronological and locational specificity. The older inhabitants' attitude to change can be read as an allegory for the authoritarian state, which wishes to crush elements of resistance to its house of power. The destruction of the house, described with varying degrees of fantasy and imagination by different characters in the novel's three endings, hints at the eventual triumph of the Tupamaros against the authoritarian state.[8]

Critics are divided over whether allegory is inherently a reactionary or a progressive literary device. Of course, the nature of allegory has changed over time and its use in fables, for example, tended to be more didactic. Partly influenced by this use of allegory, some critics state that it cannot be used as a tool for contesting authoritarian discourse's control of reality because allegorical texts themselves require complicity between reader and writer to be read as allegorical in the first place. For example, in 'The Will to Allegory in Postmodernism' (1982), Paul Smith refers to the 'ideological compliance' that allegory demands of the reader (115). While it may be true that the criticism implied through an allegorical reading requires some degree of complicity of thought, the very manner of transmitting this message through allegory permits the author to overcome the conundrum of not wanting to impose a single reading of reality. Although on one level it may conjure a particular reality (the confrontation between the state and the Tupamaros, in this case), allegory simultaneously questions the status of truth and reflects on the production of meaning.

Tierney-Tello argues against critics who claim that allegory is reactionary. She notes that 'allegory' comes from the Greek word *allegoria* which in turn comes from *allos*, meaning 'other', and *agoria*, meaning 'speaking'. Tierney-Tello thus points to the deferral of meaning 'elsewhere', that encourages the reader to have an eye to multiple other stories and voices. She describes allegory's metaliterary nature as it presents a different perspective whilst simultaneously revealing its own mediation of meaning:

> while allegory certainly involves setting forth its own particular reading of the world, its own interpretation of what is true, this contradictory trope makes no claim to unmediated access to meaning and, indeed, shows its own meaning to be ultimately constructed and produced [...] it tells one thing to say another, continually deferring its meaning as other and elsewhere. (1996: 21)

Tierney-Tello's approach to allegory is similar to that of Benjamin in *The Origin of German Tragic Drama* (1927). For Benjamin, allegory, in its very form, reflects the inaccessibility of truth. Bainard Cowan expresses Benjamin's conceptualisation of truth particularly eloquently:

> Truth does not consist of a content to be possessed after digesting away the linguistic form of a philosophical inquiry; rather, as Benjamin insists, the truth is the form. Representation is thus not to be viewed for its end product but for its process. The activity of representation is the dwelling place of truth, the only 'place' where truth is truly present. (1981: 114)

In an approach that finds truth *in* representation, the writer always defers meaning, which therefore exists in posterity. Besides a reading of the novel that interprets truth as a comment on a particular sociohistorical situation, there are other stories, other truths in the narrative. In the case of *El libro*, for example, the narrative can be read as a broader comment on inheritance, posterity, and the relationships between generations.

The older generation of the family, especially Abuela Clara and the uncles, defend the sacred space of the house from nature's intrusions. They fear that the trees around the house will engulf it, which is perhaps symbolic of their fear of uncontrollable posterity:

> la madeja de las ramas se tejía tan velozmente, que aunque mi tío les diera orden de apurar, de acelerar la excavación, cada día, al despertarnos, veíamos menos la luz de afuera, el follaje nos aislaba más del exterior, ciñéndonos al interior de nuestra casa, como a un museo [...] Yo pensaba que al último momento, si los carpinteros no le ganaban a los árboles, él incendiaría el jardín, para salvarnos. (47–48)

> [The web of branches was weaving itself together so quickly that even though my uncle was ordering them to hurry up, to speed up the excavation, each day, upon waking we saw less light outside, the foliage was isolating us more from the outside world, confining us to the inside of our house, as in a museum [...] I thought that if the carpenters were not able to beat the trees, he would set the garden alight in order to save us.]

The uncles strive to repress the processes of nature to ensure that the house remains constant in form but ever-*present*, rather than becoming a 'relic' or a 'museum', cut off from the world. In *La nave*, Equis refers to museums as places where time is fixed: 'Los simétricos museos, donde el tiempo no transcurre. En los museos está excluido el azar' (175) [Symmetrical museums where time stands still. In these museums chance [...] is shut out] (180). In *El libro* the older generations want to minimise chance and unpredictability to remain *present* but unchanging.

Paradoxically, in resisting the changes in nature, Abuela Clara and the uncles seal the family's fate; robbed of youthful vitality, it will indeed be consigned to the past. Abuela Clara's attitude is similar to that of the uncles. In the 'Segundo final', Óscar, Oliverio's brother, describes his grandmother's attitude when she was faced with the possibility of the end of the world. While neighbours panicked and first inundated, then raided the church, she did not let anyone from the family leave the house:

atrancó todas las puertas, cerró las ventanas y se dispuso a esperar el fin del mundo haciendo labores, *como siempre*: exigió que cada uno de la casa tomara posición en el lugar que *le correspondía*, que *le estaba asignado* [...] Lo tenía todo dispuesto, *todo previsto*; afrontaría el Juicio Final con entera dignidad, sin un solo estremecimiento, dentro de la casa, como había vivido; de su casa, que fuera la casa de sus padres y de sus abuelos, la casa de sus hijos y de sus nietos; la casa que guardó, como una virgen consagrada al culto, el himen de los nuestros, jamás hollado, la rosa de los vientos aparcelada pero intacta. (213–14, my emphasis)

[she bolted all of the doors, shut all of the windows, and prepared to wait for the end of the world doing household chores, *as always*: she demanded that each member of the household took up their *rightful* role, the role that was *assigned* to them [...] She had everything ready, *everything foreseen*; she would face the Final Judgement with complete dignity, without a single tremor inside the house, just as she had lived. Inside her house, which was the house of her parents and grandparents, of her children and grandchildren; the house that held, as if it were a consecrated Virgin, the unbroken hymen of our lineage, a compass rose — in segments, but intact.] (my emphasis)

Abuela Clara would prefer to die with her status intact and family standing unchanged — everything is as it always was, as corresponds, as assigned, as foreseen — than to leave the house or fight for the future. Here, the idea of a pure inheritance, emphasised by the continuous family line from great grandparents to grandchildren and the sense of direction implied by the compass, is prioritised over an uncontrollable posterity. Abuela Clara strives to keep said family line, represented by house and hymen, untainted by intruders. However, she does not consider that the intrusion that she so fears may come from within the house itself, through incest, which could even be considered to be the logical consequence of her isolationism.

In contrast with Abuela Clara and the authoritarian state who strive to freeze a moment in time, Peri Rossi, through her use of allegory, embraces the notion of representation as process, not as product, not as a freezing, *prise*, or capture. She wants to live on *through* multiple versions, *through* multiple interpretations of history, *through* the proliferation of meaning. Peri Rossi has frequently voiced her desire to be remembered and to leave a legacy. For example, in the prologue to her *Poesía reunida* she remarks that even as a girl she was concerned with posterity: 'Deducción que hice a los trece años: hay que pensar siempre en la posteridad. Ni una frase, ni un verso superficiales o superfluos' (2005a: 9) [A conclusion I reached, aged thirteen: one should always think about posterity. Not a single sentence or line should be superficial or superfluous]. For her, the aforementioned 'ungovernable excess' (Johnson 1981: xxxii) of a multiplicity of textual interpretations is not superfluous, but the key to her existence in posterity.

Correspondingly, positing a particular reality as definitive and eternally unchanging robs the future of its vitality. Peri Rossi reflects on the interplay of spatiality and temporality under dictatorships in a 1985 newspaper article:

el aislamiento en el espacio que provocan [las dictaduras] tiene como función destruir el elemento dialéctico del tiempo. Las dictaduras pretenden eternizarse,

crean una noción arbitraria pero ilusoria del tiempo: antes de ellas, nada;
después, nada [...] la historia se convierte en un cuadro fijo, colgado de la
pared: un presente eterno que es fundamentalmente un pasado muy remoto.
(2005b: 45)

[the spatial isolation that dictatorships cultivate serves to destroy the dialectics
of time. Dictatorships strive to make themselves eternal, to create an arbitrary
but illusory notion of time: before them, nothing; after them, nothing [...]
history is converted into a fixed painting, hung on the wall: an eternal present
that is, fundamentally, a very remote past.]

The reference to the 'cuadro fijo', a fixed, even untouchable representation, recalls
the house as museum mentioned above. The picture is also a fetishistic protection of
the art object as a thing of value; we will return to the concept of art and ownership
in the next section. The picture also brings to mind the map hung on Oliverio's
wall in *El libro*.

Oliverio misses Federico and has gathered from older members in the family that
his cousin has gone to 'las guerrillas'. He slips into speaking about 'las guerrillas'
as a place (172) and is not able to glean any further information about it from his
elders who, as in the scene from *État de siège*, seem not to want to speak explicitly
about the guerrilla groups as a way of eradicating them. Frustrated at not being able
to determine Federico's whereabouts, Oliverio draws on the map that his teacher
wants him to memorise:

no he podido ubicar muy bien ese lugar de las guerrillas, pese a que lo he
buscado prolijamente en el mapa. En el mapa que tiene a todo el mundo. Ese
mapa que está colgado en mi cuarto, que allí lo puso el maestro para que yo
de noche me fijara en los nombres y los aprendiera; pero a mí de noche no se
me daba por mirar el mapa, sino por pensar en otras cosas, y nunca lo miraba;
a veces, de la rabia que le tenía, le hacía marcas falsas con los lápices de colores;
marcas de ríos falsos y de carreteras inventadas, para divertirme, así no sería fácil
hallar el camino de los nombres y los nombres de las ciudades y las montañas
por donde suben las calles y los arroyos que cruzan las montañas. (172–73)

[I have never been able to locate with any precision that place, 'The Guerrillas',
despite having searched for it at great length on the map. The map that contains
everyone. The map that is hung in my room where the teacher put it so that
at night I would study the names and learn them. At night I didn't feel like
looking at the map, I preferred to think about other things and I never looked
at it. Sometimes, because of how angry I was with the map, I added false lines
to it with colouring pencils, marks for false rivers and invented roads, to amuse
myself. That way it would not be easy to find where the names went and the
names of cities and the mountains where the roads rise up and the streams that
cut through the mountains.]

In Part I, I mentioned Galeano's comment about maps often being determined by
the conception of space held by the most powerful in the world. Oliverio, inheritor
of the guerrillas' ideas, refuses to learn in that manner. He rejects the version of
reality and space that his teacher — a representative of authority — presents him.
He chooses to alter the map, adding new roads and rivers, creating a muddled
map, like the seemingly inaccurate medieval maps in *La nave* that Equis so loves.

In response to Oliverio's questioning about the whereabouts of 'las guerrillas', his mother previously responded that it is in the mountains and streams. Perhaps in altering the map, adding false rivers and invented roads, he is symbolically helping Federico and his fellow guerrillas to hide, or multiplying their presence.

Oliverio is a creator; he will not passively receive cultural artefacts, concepts, or language. One particularly poetic example of his attitude to new concepts takes place in the doctor's surgery where his family have taken him due to his long crying episodes. His response to being diagnosed with anxiety is revealing:

> AN — GUS — TIA — ANG — Ang — ANG — ANGGGG — UUTIA
> — USTED — GUSTIA — GUUU — GGGGUUUU — ANG — ANGGG
> — Me pareció una palabra muy nueva y llena de significados [...] Me gustaba acariciarle amorosamente los bordes, tocarla, pasarle la lengua por los costados, sorbérmela como si fuera de miel. (75)

> [ANG — ZEYE — ITTY — ANG — Ang — ANG — ANGGGG — ZEYYYYYE- IT — YOU — LIKE — IT — ZEYYYYYE — ZEYYYYYE — ANG — ANGGG — It seemed to me to be a very new word, full of different meanings [...] I liked to caress its borders lovingly, to touch it, run my tongue along its sides, suck it as if it were made of honey.]

Oliverio describes the pleasure he derives from savouring new words in his mouth as he imagines a multitude of possible meanings for them. In this case, anxiety is transformed into pleasure as Oliverio defamiliarises the word. In *Kafka: Toward a Minor Literature* (1975) Deleuze and Guattari write about language as 'a deterritorialization of the mouth, the tongue, and the teeth' (1986: 19) from their first territory of food. They argue that language is a compensation by the mouth, tongue, and teeth for their initial deterritorialisation. For them, there follows a compensating 'reterritorialization in sense' (20) in which the mouth shifts from the senses of taste and touch to sense as meaning and representation. However, the mouth may be deterritorialised once more through 'nonsignifying' (13), 'sonorous material' (6), evading the signifying order — 'a sonority that ruptures in order to break away from a chain that is still all too signifying' (6) — enabling new 'becomings' (22), new possibilities.

Sounds that rupture and fragment words, like Oliverio's stuttering and stammering, are part of a process of becoming a foreigner in one's own language (Deleuze and Guattari 1986: 19). Feeling a sense of alienation in language prompts Oliverio to reexamine and question the familiar; both that to which he has grown accustomed, and the sphere in which the process of familiarisation took place: the family. At the end of the second chapter in the novel, 'Oliverio: Los sueños' [Oliverio: Dreams], Oliverio describes dreams as sites for deconstructing meaning inherited during what he describes as the 'time of obedience' of childhood that becomes, for him, a time of disobedience:

> La estación de los sueños bajaba a mí cada mañana, dejándome su carga, de la cual yo extraía [...] grupos de sílabas que me entretenía en descomponer, aspirando a combinaciones nuevas. Así supe que el sonido es una geometría que podemos componer, y el significado, apenas una referencia ostensible a las cosas que aprendimos a nombrar de niños, en el tiempo de la obediencia. (19)

> [the season of dreams descended on me every morning depositing its load, from which I extracted [...] groups of syllables. I entertained myself pulling them apart, aspiring to create new combinations. That is how I discovered that sound is geometry that we can design, and meaning, just a possible reference to things we learnt how to name when we were children, in the time of obedience.]

Deleuze and Guattari write that '[c]hildren are well skilled in the exercise of repeating a word, the sense of which is only vaguely felt, in order to make it vibrate around itself' (1986: 21). Oliverio exemplifies the vibrating defamiliarisation of language through breaking words down into 'nonsignifying' parts. He is thus able to imagine futures that are different to the status quo that his elders enjoin him to uphold.

Aware of Oliverio's loyalty to Federico, one of his aunts says to Oliverio's mother 'Ema, este chico te ha salido igual que Federico. Si no lo encauzas a tiempo, buenos problemas tendremos con él' (179) [Ema, that boy has turned out just like Federico. If you don't rein him in in time, we'll have real trouble with him]. For the older members of the family, education, true to its root (the Latin *educere*, to lead out) involves 'channelling' ('encauzar' means to direct or to channel). The novel suggests that whatever happens with the guerrilla movement, the poetic Federico will live on through Oliverio. It is important to remember that conditioning, the impact of the past on the present, could come from the family, through political affiliation, or both, and through many other channels. It is also not exclusive to left- or right-leaning figures or institutions. A concern with wanting to ensure that one's worldview persists into the future spans the spectrum of political ideologies.

Peri Rossi's texts suggest that for a truly radical politics, one should accept the inability to control the future; one's words might be used with very different meanings and in different contexts to those in which one intended them to be used. The short story 'El prócer' [The Hero] in *Indicios pánicos* represents the difficulty of accepting the unexpected deployment of one's words. In the story, a statue of General Artigas (evidently in Plaza de la Independencia in Montevideo, though the location is not explicitly specified), considered the father of the Uruguayan nation, comes to life and descends from his horse. He is fed up with the twisting of his words by generals and politicians, who give ceremonial speeches in front of the statue but then punish students who cite Artigas in support of their protests:

> algo había pasado con su frase, que ahora no gustaba; durante años la había oído repetir como un sonsonete en todas las ceremonias oficiales que tenían lugar frente a su monumento, pero ahora se veía que había caído en desuso, en sospecha o algo así. (178)

> [something had happened with his slogan, it was no longer popular; for years he'd heard it monotonously chanted in all the official ceremonies that took place in front of the monument, but it had obviously become obsolete, or suspect, or something.] (110)

He is relieved when he speaks to a young man who is a former political prisoner who intends to keep fighting against the authoritarian government. In the final line of the story, we learn that having spoken to the left-wing man, Artigas '[a]hora estaba seguro de que había dejado descendientes' (183) [was now sure he had descendants there] (112).

Through the statue of Artigas, we observe the persistence of the desire to leave a clear and authoritative legacy, even when one is fighting for freedom. Returning again to the sociopolitical context of creation of the novel, in his account of his time of imprisonment under the military dictatorship, Mauricio Rosencof (a former Tupamaro leader) reflects on posterity and the inheritance of political ideals: 'defeat — and, of course, victory — are indeed illusions [...] We are only truly defeated when we, our children, or our children's children relinquish our most cherished ideals' (1993: 132). There is a certain contradiction in a fight for freedom that desires a legacy in which the ideals of future generations match one's own. Perhaps this dilemma is analogous to the author's dilemma that we have been considering: does one have to accept, as the price of freedom, one's words being used for causes for which they were not written? The possibility of ideals changing through the generations is an integral part of freedom. In that way, ideals, like texts, stay alive. One might or might not approve of the ways in which one's words are deployed.

Collective Creations: Literature, Property, Capitalism

I have addressed Peri Rossi's use of allegory to defer the meaning of a text elsewhere in time and space. The author may live for posterity through multiple interpretations of their works. How do the works of Peri Rossi and those of her diegetic reader-writers stage this process in their dialogues with other texts? I will now explore what the reader-writer's intertextual entanglements might suggest about authorship and the 'circuits of ownership' (1984b: 108) described by Foucault.

Foucault notes that prior to the seventeenth or eighteenth century, literary works were often anonymous. However, the identity of authors of scientific works was very prominent and their theories or discoveries were often designated by their names (e.g. the Hippocratic Oath, Newton's law of universal gravitation). According to Foucault, there was later a reversal in these trends which saw scientific writing become more 'anonymous' while the identities of the authors of literary works was considered to be of utmost importance. He notes that initially the concern with knowing the author of a work was the result of authors being subject to punishment for being transgressive, rather than due to texts being products or goods caught up in 'circuits of ownership', as they are now.

The history of authorship, impropriety, and property is interesting for the case of Peri Rossi and other exiled writers whose books were banned in Uruguay under the military dictatorship. In interviews and essays Peri Rossi has lamented the commercialisation of literature, striving to restore its transgressive potential outside the 'circuits of ownership' of capitalism. Foucault connects the figure of the author, individualism, and capitalism. However, he remains optimistic about possibilities for the future of fiction as an 'experience'. It is worth quoting him at length here:

> since the eighteenth century, the author has played the role of the regulator of the fictive, a role quite characteristic of our era of industrial and bourgeois

society, of individualism and private property, still, given the historical modifications that are taking place, it does not seem necessary that the author function remain constant in form, complexity, and even in existence. I think that, as our society changes, at the very moment when it is in the process of changing, the author function will disappear, and in such a manner that fiction and its polysemous texts will once again function according to another mode, but still with a system of constraint — one which will no longer be the author, but which will have to be determined or, perhaps, experienced. (1984b: 119)

Peri Rossi's narrative offers an example of what this 'experience' might look like. Her works seem to return to the concept of literature as trangression rather than as a commercial product. However, the trangressor is no longer the author as individual, but reader-writers and their collaborative creative practice. *El libro* prompts what may be an example of the sort of experience to which Foucault refers; an experience not fully regulated by the author in which the system of constraint may simply be the limits of the reader's own imagination.

flores, for example, seems to encourage such an experience. She writes that she refuses to capitalise her name as a mark of giving way to collective meaning-making. Giving up the proper name is to give up the notion of the text as her property:

> una estrategia de minorización del nombre propio, de problematización de las convenciones gramaticales, de dislocar la jerarquía de las letras, una apuesta al texto antes que a la firma de la autora, percibir el propio nombre como un espasmo de una ficción llamada 'yo', un yo deslenguado que funciona como eco de muchas otras voces, que reviste un tono singular en las ondulaciones del texto en el que no cesa de latir ese murmullo colectivo. (2013: 4)

> [a strategy of diminishing the proper name, problematising grammatical convention, dislocating the hierarchies of literature, investing hope in the text rather than in the signature of the author, perceiving the proper name as a spasm of a fiction known as 'I', a loose-tongued [or 'without a tongue' i.e. des-lenguado] I that functions as the echo of many other voices, that provides a singular tone amongst the ondulations of a text in which a collective murmur does not cease to throb.]

Her reference to a 'yo deslenguado' resonates with Vivien's 'glotis paralitzada' [paralysed glottis/vocal cords] of Chapter One; in both instances we hear of individuals in which many perspectives converge. While flores's reflections that the text should form part of a collective process are relevant to the act of reading and writing in general, they carry particular weight in our considerations of the context of growing authoritarianism in the clash of capitalism and socialism in the 1960s and 1970s Southern Cone. Though, of course, such contextualisation also delimits the texts; it also has authoritative functions. In any case, the cousins Oliverio, Federico, and Alejandra offer examples of the textual experience advocated by flores towards which Foucault was perhaps gesturing.

As I mentioned earlier, Oliverio is the inheritor of his cousin Federico the guerrilla's words and work. He is responsible for the survival of Federico's philosophy. Federico shows Oliverio texts he is writing and says to Oliverio that Oliverio must continue writing these works when Federico is not able to: 'A veces él me dejaba entrar al cuarto y revisar sus cuadernos, su memorial, un libro que iba escribiendo con los sucesos de todos los días. "Cuando a mí se me acabe, lo seguirás tu", me decía Federico' (163) [Sometimes he let me go into his room and look at his notebooks, his memoir, a book that he was writing as everyday events unfolded. 'When I stop writing, you will continue it', Federico used to say to me.] The scene supports the hypothesis that the book we have in our hands, including a chapter titled 'Páginas del Diario de Federico' [Pages of Federico's Diary] could be the work that Federico started and Oliverio continued. Oliverio recalls that Federico was aware of the transience of his existence: 'me recuerdo ahora de Federico de su manera de hablarme de su suavidad y de su andar por la casa como si no estuviera, como si nada fuera suyo' (175) [I recall Federico now, the way he spoke to me, his gentleness, the way he walked around the house as if he were not really there, as if nothing belonged to him]. His attitude to worldly objects in some ways recalls that of Peri Rossi who, commenting on her own nomadism, writes: 'No tengo, sino usufructo' (2005b: 48) [I do not own, but borrow], as mentioned in Part I. Perhaps Oliverio, therefore, adopts Federico's words, as Federico did with the words of others.

In the spirit of the words that compose a creation not belonging to the author, Peri Rossi composes parts of the novel with lines from other writers pulled together, as Marçal did in the 'Monòdia final' at the end of *La passió*. In *El libro*, Chapter VIII, 'Federico: Alejandra', contains a poetic description of Alejandra, one of Federico's cousins and lovers, the book's most explicit example of incest. The chapter also includes speeches that seem to have been made by Tupamaro guerrillas jumbled together with fragments from Troubadour songs in Provençal, lines from thirteenth century Italian poets, and part of General Stroessner's aforementioned speech. In Chapter XI, 'Federico: El incesto', Federico and his cousin and lover, Aurelia, rewrite old texts. They inherit the language of the past and, with it, create new meaning:

> nos gusta jugar con los versos, quiero decir, cambiarlos de lugar, mezclarlos, reelaborar poemas, volverlos a estructurar; así, hemos llegado a veces a composiciones como ésta [...]
>> el sol, el mar seguro azul lejano,
>> (*caían desplomados como pájaros ilusos*)
>> [...]
> ★ Los versos que aparecen en bastardilla corresponden a los siguientes poetas. Heberto Padilla, Ernesto Cardenal, Salvador Puig, Vicente Huidobro, Juan Gelman, Sarandy Cabrera, César Vallejo, Gonzalo Rojas, Pablo Neruda y Manuel Scorza. Asimismo, se han empleado dos poemas del escritor Jorge Arias, titulados *Música* y *Palabra natural*. (150–51)

> [we like playing with the lines, I mean, swapping them around, mixing them up, rewriting poems, restructuring them; in this way we have ended up with compositions like this one [...]
>> the sun, the safe blue distant sea,
>> (they collapsed like gullible birds)
>> [...]
> ★ The lines in italics correspond to the following poets. Heberto Padilla, Ernesto Cardenal, Salvador Puig, Vicente Huidobro, Juan Gelman, Sarandy Cabrera,

César Vallejo, Gonzalo Rojas, Pablo Neruda y Manuel Scorza. Similarly, two
poems by Jorge Arias were used, titled *Music* and *Natural Word*.]

Just like *La nave*'s creative hypothesis in which the tapestry is not restored, but
textually scattered and the holes in it filled with tales of the diasporic wandering
of Equis and others, Federico and his cousins pull together disparate texts to create
new meanings. Both of these sections appear in the chapters that depict Federico's
incestuous relationships with his cousins thereby signalling a connection between
impropriety, the challenge to language as property, and how from *within* the
same text, new works can emerge. Incest is a form of endogamy, a perpetuation,
from within, of the family. However, in this case, it is not a perpetuation of the
conservatism of the older generations, but of the new visions of the younger
generations.

In the first edition of the text published in Montevideo in 1969 there is a
footnote, cited above, listing the names of the authors whose works Peri Rossi has
used (almost all Latin American, many communist). In contrast, in the 1976 Plaza
y Janés edition published in Barcelona, there is no attribution (Narváez: 6). The
lack of attribution could be a sign of Peri Rossi's increasing reluctance to consider
words the property of individual authors. Narváez describes this approach to
intertextuality effectively when he states that the literary and political intertexts in
El libro 'function as a means of invalidating the notion of the work (and of literary
production in general) as the creation of a single individual' (110). Intertextuality is
a network or web; it is relational. Peri Rossi the writer shows herself to be, above
all, an avid reader, through composing parts of the novel from fragments of texts
she has read. In this way, she demonstrates her belief, akin to Marçal's, that the
reader is also a creator. Therefore, the author figure she espouses does not impede
the 'free circulation, the free manipulations, the free composition, decomposition,
and recomposition of fiction' (1984b: 118–19), the obstruction of which Foucault
mourns in 'What is an Author?'.

As a parallel to the ownership of words, the description of the killing of
guerrillas in the novel, presumably by state forces, contains references to the air
and wind being owned by foreign (particularly USA-based) government agencies
or corporations:

> sus manos crispadas sacudiendo el aire propiedad de la U.E. gas Co. [...] sus
> pies hinchados recogiendo entre los dedos separados, como puertas abiertas con
> machetes, las escorias que el viento domesticado por los agentes del Pentágono
> y la CIA ha diseminado en su camino. (97–98)

> [their contorted hands were sending vibrations through the air, which was
> the property of U.E. Gas Company [...] between their splayed toes, like doors
> forced open with machetes, their swollen feet clung on to the dregs scattered by
> the wind domesticated by agents of the CIA and the Pentagon.]

In contrast to state capitalism and the commercialisation of nature, the text
emphasises the collective ownership of culture and language. Federico represents
the figure of the writer for whom language is a key site of the struggle against the
authoritarian state. His attitude contrasts with that of some of his comrades who are

suspicious of culture, such as Alina: 'No necesitamos poetas, sino combatientes' (189) [We don't need poets, we need fighters], she affirms. Alina reports conversations she has had with Federico (note that he is given the name of a fallen comrade, Pablo, another symbol of political inheritance) and Rafael, the group leader:

> ¿Cuántos podrían apreciar, captar el sentido de ese arte? 'Para eso mismo estamos haciendo la revolución. Para que todos tengan los medios para entender y para apreciar', dijo [...] Le he dicho a Rafael que no creo que la poesía de Pablo sea realmente revolucionaria. El hombre común no la entendería, y el otro, el que ya está iniciado, no necesita versos para descubrir dónde está la verdad. 'No esquematices — me ha respondido Rafael — . Seguramente, con el tiempo, será más fácil entender la poesía, y al mismo tiempo, habrá muchos más poetas, pero se habrán borrado casi las diferencias entre el poeta y el que no lo es.' (192)

> [How many people can appreciate and understand the meaning of that art? 'That is the very reason we are bringing about a revolution. So that everyone might have the means to understand and appreciate it', he said. I've told Rafael that I don't think that Pablo's poetry is really revolutionary. The common man wouldn't understand it, and others, who have already been taught how to understand it, do not need poetry to discover where truth lies. 'Don't schematise people', responded Rafael. 'Surely, with time, it will be easier to understand poetry and, at the same time, there will be many more poets, but the differences between the poet and the person who is not a poet will have been all but erased.']

Federico and Rafael's references to bringing education, understanding, and creativity to the masses, rendering redundant the category of 'poet', hint at the role that Peri Rossi envisions for the reader, who may be a poet too. The vision of the reader or 'hombre común' as poet has some resonances with the Gramscian idea of the intellectual in *The Prison Notebooks* (1971).

Antonio Gramsci writes that '[a]ll men are intellectuals [...] but not all men have in society the function of intellectuals' (1992: 9). Gramsci considered structural change and ideological change as part of the same struggle. He saw the intellectual as necessary for changing popular consensus in civil society, for shifting mass consciousness to create a counter hegemony. Writing of the 'traditional intelligentsia' (1992: 9), such as the clergy, men of letters, and professors, he considered the view that intellectuals are a separate category independent of class to be a myth. He believed that intellectuals develop alongside the ruling class and usually function for that class's benefit. He denoted as 'organic intellectuals' (4) those who grow 'organically' with the dominant social group. Gramsci thought that for revolutionary change to occur, the traditional intellectuals needed to shift their allegiances to the revolutionary cause, but that, in addition, the working class movement needed to produce its own intellectuals. For him, intellectual thought could not be imposed on people by the elite but must be grounded in their everyday lives. He believed all people to have the capacity and capability to think, given that everyone 'carries on some form of intellectual activity' (9) and 'participates in a particular conception of the world' (ibid.). Rather than simply implanting ideas into the minds of others, 'intellectuals' must persuade others to act and think for themselves, thus deploying their own intellectual capacities.

I have argued that Peri Rossi overcomes the author's dilemma of disavowing authority by enacting a reading/writing strategy that treats the written text as material to be deconstructed and reconstructed in new collaborative creations. The collaborative creation in Peri Rossi recalls my analysis of the implicated reading of the implicit text in Marçal's *La passió*. For Peri Rossi and Marçal, then, authors are remembered for posterity not merely through the preservation of their work, but through its creative reformulations, which perhaps constitute the new 'experience' of the text to which Foucault refers in 'What is an Author?'. Peri Rossi's utopian vision of collaborative creation not only goes hand in hand with her idea of legacy as a writer but is also a response to particular socio-historical situation. Through the techniques she deploys in her writing — fragmentation, allegory, ambiguity, and alienation — she straddles the particular/local/temporal and the general/universal/atemporal in her 'time machine' texts.

Another sort of time travel and collaborative creation takes place in epistolary exchanges. Travelling forward again to 1980s Barcelona, Company's first novel, *Querida Nélida*, considers the temporal twists of the epistolary form with a particular focus on obsession, understood as a form of haunting. Whereas Peri Rossi shuttles constantly between text and sociopolitical context, in Company's novel the world beyond the text is effectively bracketed. However, this in itself is a comment on the social context of the text's publication in 1980s Barcelona, not long after the decriminalisation of homosexuality in Spain in 1979. In that context, those in gay and lesbian relationships often had to exist in a separate world in order to survive, plagued by the very recent past of Francoism and its enduring social impact. The issues at play in the text also resonate with the intellectual context of late 1970s and early 1980s lesbian feminism (important to the genealogy *of* the queer), such as the works of Luce Irigaray, which evoke a specular or dyadic closure (between two women or within one woman) in which the world beyond is set aside.

Notes to Chapter 2

1. *La nave de los locos* was translated into English as *The Ship of Fools* by Psiche Hughes in 1989. I have used her translations in this book.
2. Fons Capítol Catedral de Girona, Autor CRBMC. All rights reserved.
3. Hughes frequently translates the Spanish word 'extranjero' and derivatives as 'stranger'. In Spanish, the word is usually used to mean 'foreigner' (with 'desconocido' used more commonly to mean stranger) and I would argue that her translations make more sense if we read 'stranger' as 'foreigner'. I have altered her translations accordingly.
4. The number of citizens disappeared is disputed, but some human rights activist groups, such as 'Proyecto Desaparecidos' claim that the figure may be as high as 30,000 or more ('Desaparecidos' n.d.)
5. Translations from the 2002 translation *Panic Signs*, trans. by Angelo A. Borrás and Mercedes Rowinsky-Geurts (Waterloo: Wilfrid Laurier University Press).
6. This was also two years after the publication of Barthes' aforementioned 1967 essay 'The Death of the Author' in which he rallied against readings that rely on considerations of authorial intent and the sociopolitical context of the text's creation. As is evident from the 'context' section below, I believe contextualised reading offers important interpretations of the text, especially of socially-engaged works that confront extreme political situations such as dictatorships. However, I believe that such interpretations are just some amongst many other possible interpretations.

7. President Jorge Pacheco Areco repeatedly used the 'medidas prontas de seguridad' (Article 168) during his presidency (1968–1972), as did President Juan María Bordaberry (1972–1973).

8. In some ways, the coming into power of the Frente Amplio coalition in 2005 represents the eventual 'victory' of the Tupamaros' values. The coalition was formed in 1971, a couple of years before the dictatorship. At that point the Tupamaros were not part of the coalition; they joined in 1989. The former president, José 'Pepe' Mujica, who was in office from March 2010–March 2015, was previously a Tupamaro.

CHAPTER 3

Queer Temporalities in Flavia Company

Per tu retorno d'un exili vell
com si tornés d'enlloc. I alhora et sé
terra natal, antiga claror meva,
i l'indret on la culpa es feia carn.

Retorno en tu, per tu, a l'espai cec
d'on vaig fugir sense poder oblidar;
desig sense remei, ferida arrel
arrapada, clavada cos endins.

— MARÇAL ([1989] 2017: 455)

[For you I return from an old exile
as if I were coming back from nowhere. Meanwhile I recognise you as
my homeland, ancient light of mine,
the place where guilt became flesh.

I return in you, for you, to the blind space
from which I fled without being able to forget;
unquenchable desire, damaged root
clinging, nailed within my body.]

Part I: Obsession: Sitting Opposite Lovers Past in *Querida Nélida* (1988)

My reading of Company's first published work, the epistolary novel *Querida Nélida* (1988), focusses on the temporality of obsession, conventionally understood in terms of ideational fixation and compulsive repetition. The most common contemporary usage of obsession to refer to a psychological state, as in 'to be obsessed *with* something or someone' (i.e. thinking of it constantly or doing it compulsively), arose in the late nineteenth century. However, in late Middle English, to 'obsess' meant to 'haunt' or to 'possess', referring to an evil spirit. The word obsession comes from the Latin *obsidere* that meant 'to besiege' or, literally, 'to sit opposite' (a compound of *ob* 'opposite' + *sedere* 'sit').

The root of obsession thus has temporal and spatial associations, signalling both an obstacle to physical movement and an inability to get on with one's life. It has, in this regard, some similarities with melancholia, often understood in psychoanalysis as a pathological inability to get over the loss of a loved person or thing. I posit that contrary to the usual associations of obsession and melancholia with individuals who are seen as being stuck in the past, unable to let go, to move with the times, to move on, obsession in the novel is *vitally* future-oriented. However, the novel's obsessive future orientation takes place in what might be called a 'queer time' (Freccero 2006: 5; Halberstam 2005: 1), which is out of sync with conventional notions of progress and development.

The novel depicts an erotic relationship between two women, Celia and the eponymous Nélida. The driving force behind the women's exchange of letters is a trip. Nélida has only known Celia for a few days when she asks her to sign a contract committing to travel with Nélida for two years, visiting at least seventeen countries. Celia refuses to sign the contract, but the trip remains present as a prospect over a number of years as the women's relationship unfolds through their letters and encounters in Barcelona. We learn in the letter that forms the prologue that when Celia stops responding to Nélida's letters, the latter pursues her: 'Aunque te ocultes bajo otro nombre, tras el buzón de otra casa, en una calle cualquiera de Barcelona, o de cualquier otro lugar del mundo... voy a encontrarte' (11) [Even if you hide under another name, behind the letterbox of another house, in any old street in Barcelona, or anywhere else in the world... I will find you]. From the outset we see that Nélida haunts Celia, she obsesses and is obsessed by her.

Obsession is mentioned repeatedly in the novel, appearing in noun, verb, or adjective form at least ten times in the fifty pages that make up the main body of the text (19, 30, 41, 43, 45, 48, 52, 60, 61, 63). It is usually Nélida who is described as being obsessed with Celia — 'Todo me remitía a su recuerdo. Celia me obsesionaba' (63) [Everything made me think of her. Celia obsessed me] — and with the idea of the trip that overwhelms her — 'la obsesión del viaje, iba más allá de mis deseos' (43) [my obsession with the trip went beyond my own desires]. However, when Nélida takes longer to respond to her when she is on an extended trip, Celia, who generally displays calm reserve and self-control, describes analysing Nélida's opinions 'a veces casi de forma obsesiva' (45) [sometimes in an almost obsessive manner]. Throughout the novel we observe the shifting temporality of obsession, from Nélida's fixation on a past 'recuerdo' to her compulsive planning of the potential future trip.

The unsigned contract propels the narrative but does not appear in it; it is a vital text *in absentia*, like Sara T.'s script in *La passió*. The contract is rejected in favour of an exchange of texts. A single binding document in which devotion, dedication, and commitment are regulated and reified is thereby substituted with an endless proliferation of letters in which the women's desire remains in flux, oriented towards future modes and forms of relationality. The epistolary form is an apt medium with which to explore the slippery temporality of obsession. As a number of critics have noted (Ohi 2015; MacArthur 1990; Kauffman 1992; Epps 1999), epistolary fiction itself is frequently considered to be a relic that peaked in the eighteenth century and has no place in the modern age. However, literature has proved otherwise. Indeed, as mentioned in Chapter One, Riera's 'Te deix', takes the form of a letter. Not only is the form not dead but, as Elizabeth MacArthur argues, it is characterised by resistance to closure, as is the case in *Querida Nélida*, a text that keeps coming back to life.

Company returned to her novel, bringing it back to life, when she wrote a further letter from Nélida to Celia, dated 21 November 2001, exactly twenty years after the prologue letter. That letter appeared in *M'escriuràs una carta?* [Will you write me a letter?], an exhibition at the Museu d'Art de Girona in 2000, and was published in a book of the same title that commemorated the exhibition. It appears as the epilogue to the second edition of the novel, published in 2016. The letter implies that the characters have remained in touch and confirms that the trip never happened. Celia has settled down with someone — 'Querías seguridad, y la tienes' (2000: 205) [You wanted security, and you have it] — and Nélida is still travelling: 'sigo moviéndome sin parar. No encuentro motivos para quedarme quieta' (205) [I keep moving ceaselessly. I see no reason to stay still]. In addition, the novel itself, a collation of the women's letters, brings the women's exchange back to life. The whole novel could be a response from Celia, who is described as a 'mujer de letras' (35) [woman of letters], to Nélida's 1981 letter that forms the prologue. The novel's title, *Querida Nélida,* reads as the opening of a letter and the final line of the novel is 'CELIA', a sign off.

Company thus deploys a form, the epistolary form, that can be revived to evoke a queer mode of desire that 'exists always on the horizon' (Muñoz 2009: 11), just like the trip. Eva Gutiérrez Pardina attributes the unrealisation of the trip to Nélida's cowardice and lies. In contrast, I argue that Nélida always intended the trip to remain a potentiality always in process, even if not in progress. I read the unrealisation of the trip as a result not of Nélida's cowardice, but of her bravery in the face of the compelling, even compulsive, lure of societal convention to progress, to develop, to move beyond allegedly adolescent games and fantasies. Halberstam has called for recognition of a queer challenge to an adolescent/adulthood binary in 'the stretched out adolescences of queer culture makers that disrupt conventional accounts of subculture, youth culture, adulthood, and maturity' (2005: 153), especially given that many queers 'refuse and resist the heteronormative imperative of home and family' (161). In a sense, Nélida resists what Muñoz and others have described as 'straight time' (2015: 461).

My analysis of the novel begins with an exploration of how the women are haunted both by convention and by their fantasies. I go on to consider how and why the epistolary form is particularly suited to evoking a spectral shift between temporalities. I suggest that, contrary to its pathologisation, melancholia can be associated with positive affect, as in the conclusion to my analysis of *La nave* in which I argue that there can be a sort of happiness in rejecting societally prescribed happy scripts. I end by proposing that the trip-not-taken is associated with a utopian vitality that thrives on what remains *potential* in the texts and in the women's relationship.

Spectres of Convention

As she awaits a response from Nélida, who has delayed her return from Argentina (46), Celia describes being besieged — or perhaps 'obsessed' — by phantoms: 'Estoy aterrada. [...] Los fantasmas me invaden, me aterrorizan, me torturan' (52) [I am terrified [...] Phantoms invade, terrorise, and torture me]. Whereas previously Celia felt *settled* in the material world, her use of the adjective 'aterrada', with its roots in 'terror' and 'tierra', connects her groundedness with fear. Celia is petrified without Nélida's words and presence, and the absent presence her words signify. But who or what are the spectres that obsess her? They seem to be the uncanny spectres of the strangely familiar or the familiar estranged. Contrary to the more common notion of strangeness referring to something new or unfamiliar, Epps, writing on Riera's *Questiö d'amor propi* [A Question of Self-Love], describes strangeness as a 'refusal or inability to let go of norms and conventions' (1999: 108) and as 'the turn to, or return of, the familiar' (ibid.). In many ways, Celia is haunted, and taunted, by her own conformity to societal convention, by a familiar reality that invades her when she cannot seek refuge in her shared fantasies with Nélida.

In the novel the women are presented, superficially at least, as polar opposites: Celia is associated with settling, security, and convention and Nélida with drift, risk, and unconventionality. The novel's epigraph, from Deuteronomy 13:6, reinforces a binary reading of the characters' personalities through the implication that Nélida is encouraging Celia to stray from the straight and narrow:

> Si el amigo a quien más amas, como a tu misma alma, quiere persuadirte y te dijere en secreto: Vamos y sirvamos a los dioses ajenos, no conocidos ni de ti ni de tus padres, dioses de las naciones que te rodean, vecinas o lejanas, de un cabo del mundo al otro, no condesciendas con él, ni le oigas, ni la compasión te mueva a tenerle lástima y a encubrirlo; sino que al punto lo matarás. (1988: 10)
>
> [If [...] your friend who is as your own soul entices you secretly, saying, 'Let us go and serve other gods,' which neither you nor your fathers have known, some of the gods of the peoples who are around you, whether near you or far off from you, from the one end of the earth to the other, you shall not yield to him or listen to him, nor shall your eye pity him, nor shall you spare him, nor shall you conceal him. But you shall kill him.] (English Standard version of the Bible)

In warning of the wayward lure of foreign lands, nations, and gods, the novel seems to pit the heavenly obedient Celia (whose name stems from the Latin *caelum*, meaning 'heaven') against the rebellious Nélida, who challenges the well-worn paths of tradition, habit, and religious obedience. However, are Nélida and Celia as diametrically different as they first seem? Do the specular connotations of Celia loving Nélida as she loves herself point to similarities between the women? Are Celia's skies the placid skies of the heavens or does she, like Nélida, have her head up in the clouds of daydreams? The changeability of the weather, the other sense of 'tiempo' in Spanish, resonates with the 'aparición intempestiva' [unruly apparition] of which Saraceni writes in relation to anachronous spectres, as mentioned in the introduction. Is Nélida as autonomous and bold as she makes out? I suggest that she is not as unbound as her penchant for travel might suggest; indeed, the epistolary form is a relational mode rife with expectations, directions, and destinations.

Among the reasons that Celia gives for not wanting to go on the trip is '[el] apego que [tiene] por las cosas' (42) [how attached she feels to her things]. She aligns the loss of her material possessions with psychological dispossession, a loss of her sense of self: 'eso significa *desprenderme* de todo. [...] No me esperarán las cosas, ni las personas queridas. [...] Ni siquiera yo, que *me perdería por ti*, para *viajarte*' (42, my emphasis) [that would mean *letting go* of everything [...] neither my things nor my loved ones will wait for me [...] not even I will wait for me, *I would lose myself for you, to travel you*] (my emphasis). Celia tellingly opts for the erotically charged 'viajarte' [to travel you] rather than 'viajar contigo' [to travel with you] in her refusal to sign the contract, seeing the trip as a journey to and through, as well as with, Nélida. Celia's use of the less common transitive form of the verb, which usually refers to a mercantile traveller or, indeed, a trafficker, points to a transactional relationship between the women. Celia explicitly holds her belongings to be more valuable than travelling with, or submitting herself to, Nélida. She is perturbed by Nélida's attempts to control her: 'si renuncio a mis cosas, será para *someterme* a otra realidad *dominante*: tú y tus ideas' (43) [if I give up my things, it would be to *submit* to another *dominant* reality: you and your ideas] (my emphasis). She believes that her 'dispossession' from the world would be to give into Nélida's obsession, that is to say, to be besieged and *possessed* by Nélida. The women's references to possessions, possessing, and being possessed emphasises the transactional nature of their vision of the trip.

Nélida sees Celia's attachment to her material possessions as a mark of her existing dispossession and alienation from herself: 'Tus cosas no te pertenecen. Eres tú quien pertenece a ellas. Ellas te hacen rechazarte a ti misma para optar por servirlas' (42–43) [Your things don't belong to you. It's you who belongs to them. They make you reject yourself in order to serve them]. Irigaray describes alienation amongst lesbian women as a result of trying to conform to heteronormativity: 'you attempt to conform to an order which is alien to you. Exiled from yourself, you fuse with everything that you encounter' ([1976] 1980: 73). As Nélida criticises Celia's bonds (or fusion) to the world, she overstates her own freedom, referring to her freedom in terms that style it as entrepreneurial: 'A ti te ciñen las estructuras, te preceden y te limitan. Yo las construyo para hacerlas mías, las invento y las aplico' (43) [Structures constrict you, they precede and limit you. I construct them to make them mine, I invent them and apply them]. It is paradoxical that Nélida berates Celia for not *submitting* to her plan given her claim to value autonomy. In a letter, she cites a passage from one of her notebooks in which she is writing plans for the trip: '*Hay dos caminos de que disponer. El primero es el de proyectar nuestra violencia sobre las cosas para implantarles de forma total nuestra percepción. El segundo camino es dejarnos violentar por las cosas y a partir de ahí caminar hacia una forma de percepción determinada*' (44, italics in original to signal that it is a citation from her notebook) [There are two possible ways of proceeding. The first is to project our violence onto things to shape them fully in line with our way of seeing the world. The second way is to let things exert their violence on us and, from there, to proceed towards a set way of seeing the world]. In outlining the two opposing options of submitting to structures or moulding them to one's ideals, Nélida makes no reference to the often invisible entanglement of these options or to the difficulties of negotiating them separately.

Celia challenges Nélida's hypocritical assertion of her own boldness and troubles her binary vision: '¿Acaso la cobardía no será *tuya*, tú que *huyes* cada dos semanas a una ciudad diferente para *replantearlo todo*?' (45, my emphasis) [Maybe *you* are the cowardly one, *fleeing* every two weeks to a different city to *rethink everything*?] (my emphasis). Celia suggests that when Nélida cannot mould the structures around her, she runs away from them, leaving them intact, which is precisely what Nélida accuses Celia of doing. In highlighting Nélida's *evasion* of these structures and the women's creation of a separate fantasy realm, Celia reveals that perhaps the women are not as different to each other as they first seem and, indeed, that they are bound together in a complex economy of exchange.

When Celia finally agrees to the trip during an uncharacteristic moment of desperation prompted by one of Nélida's long silences, Nélida does not agree to go on the trip for which she has supposedly been longing. Nélida's unwillingness to go ahead with the trip could be read, as Gutiérrez Pardina has read it, as a mark of her own fear of going beyond convention, of her own bonds to the world that she knows. Indeed, in her first notebook, she writes: 'nada puedo aún realizar porque estoy atada a la tierra de pies y manos' (31) [I can't put anything into practice because I am tied to the earth by my hands and feet]. Ironically, in order to go on the journey that she posits as a sign of her autonomy, she requires not simply a travel companion, but a contractually-bound travel companion. It appears, in short, that Nélida is not as autonomous as she would like to believe, and as she would like Celia and the reader to believe. It appears that Celia's refusal to go on the trip has allowed Nélida to use Celia as a scapegoat for her own ties to convention.

In drawing up a contract, Nélida reveals her desire to be in control, to have the security of an *obligation*, etymologically linked with a bond or a tie, for her travelling companion. She also seems to see herself as doing a favour for Celia in freeing her from her attachments to her possessions. Indeed, in a number of languages, obligation is related to gratitude, as in the English 'much obliged' and the Portuguese 'obrigado/a', said to express thanks. Nélida's meticulous planning of the trip may thus be read as an attempt to minimise unpredictability, to ensure that she always arrives at her destination. In the notebooks that she shares with Celia, Nélida writes her plans for the trip, including the places they must reach (not disclosed to the reader) and the times at which they must arrive at each. She states in her notebook that they must stick to the predetermined schedule at all costs: '*El viajero debe tener en cuenta la necesidad de conservar el orden prefijado sin abandonarlo nunca por ningún motivo, en ninguna ocasión*' (24) [The traveller must bear in mind the need to stick to the prefixed order without ever abandoning it for any motive, on any occasion]. Her notebook 'trataba la *perentoria* necesidad de conservar *tal y como* se había trazado, la guía de horarios *pertinente* a cada momento del viaje' (24, my emphasis) [outlined the *urgent* need to keep to the timetable that *fits with each moment* of the trip, in *exactly* the way it had been drawn up] (my emphasis). There is, in her imperative tone, the spectre of the law. She goes on to say that they must arrive at the scheduled times even if their transport is delayed, by using blackmail or other threats as required, '*ya que de otra forma no podría recobrar en ningún momento el orden necesario*' (24) [otherwise the necessary order will never be restored].

The schedule could be seen as a parallel to the expectations of 'straight time', the aforementioned obligatory milestones and so-called achievements that mark a 'happy' and conventionally successful life, as outlined by Ahmed (2010): marriage (preferably heterosexual), property ownership, and procreation. Nélida's journey to freedom that supposedly goes beyond the structures of the world thus seems to rehearse the disciplinary fixed time of convention, of what is proper and pertinent, of what belongs to a particular place and time. So configured, Nélida's projected, desired journey betrays a concern for a predetermined *order*, be it of her own creation or not. Autonomy and freedom seem to be hers to create, but both she and Celia must agree to obey Nélida's rules. Therefore, she too follows, insists on following, plans on following, a predetermined script.

However, there are some clues that what is at play is more complex than a mere fear of the unknown and a penchant for order. Nélida's notebooks tellingly contain 'las instrucciones para realizar los planes *perfectos* para lanzarse a la aventura del viaje' (25, emphasis mine) [the instructions to bring to fruition the *perfect* plans by which to throw oneself into the adventure of the trip] (my emphasis). The trip aspires to *perfection* — from the Latin *perfectus* meaning 'completed', 'fully made' — in its planning and execution. The astute Celia asks, '¿Crees que un viaje podría de verdad llevarte más allá que esta *formalización* del mismo?' (31, emphasis mine) [Do you think that a trip really could take you beyond the *formalisation* of the trip itself?] (my emphasis). It is significant, therefore, that Nélida does not actually want to undertake the trip when Celia finally agrees to it. She is reluctant to *formalise* their desire, to give it a set *form*, to adhere to the perfect plans.

In this vein, Celia's choice of words when she eventually agrees to the trip are telling: 'estoy dispuesta a realizar contigo el viaje *de los sueños*' (49, emphasis mine) [I am willing to go on the *dream* trip with you] (my emphasis). She believes that it is a 'dream trip' for Nélida, in the sense of it being a perfect trip but also in the sense of it being an unrealisable trip, that is, there is a utopian/dystopian sense to the trip. Nélida's response is equally revealing: 'jamás imaginé — *aunque sí soñé* — , que la decisión fuese el viaje' (50, emphasis mine) [I never imagined, though *I did dream*, that she would opt for the trip] (my emphasis). For Nélida, who seems to be aware of the insidious draw of convention even for the most overtly unconventional subject, like herself, the long-planned trip was to remain a trip of dreams, formless, out of reach.

Noemí Acedo Alonso comments on letters, desire, and dreams in the novel: 'Las cartas siempre me han parecido puentes entre lugares imaginarios [...entre] el lugar del deseo, el deseo de decir' (2008a: 81) [Letters have always seemed to me to be bridges between imaginary places [...] between the place of desire, the desire to speak]. Perhaps Nélida does not want their boundless imaginings to become the reified desire of a disciplined, contract-bound, normativised reality after all. Nélida hints that she only suggested the trip as part of a game: 'Yo sólo jugaba. Ella sabía perfectamente que una de mis ocupaciones preferidas era inventar preocupaciones, motivos de neurosis, motivos obsesivos de desesperación' (52) [I was just playing. She knew perfectly well that one of my favourite pastimes was to invent worries, reasons for neurosis, obsessive reasons for despair]. Maintaining the trip *as possibility* keeps her imaginative exchange with Celia, their games and dreams, alive. To *undertake* the utopian trip, to *complete* it, to give it concrete *form*, to *perfect* it, would be to betray it, inevitably.

In Nélida's view, Celia has broken one of the unsaid rules of their relationship. Indeed, the double meaning of 'cartas', as letters and cards, as in a card game, is at play here; card games have rules. Celia was not supposed to agree to play Nélida's games: 'Jamás aceptó los propuestos por mí. Si ella hubiera aceptado, yo hubiese sido la que negara. Eran locuras peligrosas en las que la victoria significaba la vida y la derrota, necesariamente, la muerte' (60) [She never accepted the games I proposed. If she had accepted, I would have been the one to say no. They were dangerous mad ideas in which victory meant life and defeat, necessarily, meant death]. Nélida's suggestions are too risky; card games often involve gambling. Nélida aligns the undertaking of the trip, for example, with an end that is rife with death: 'La única forma de encontrar un sentido al viaje es, pues, disponerlo de modo que el final signifique exactamente eso' (35) [The only way of finding meaning in the trip is to arrange it so that the end would really mean the end]. The reading of the trip as death is reinforced when she describes the possibility of the trip helping her to reach 'la sensación de *infinitud* y *desarraigo* que produciría en mí el *exilio eterno* del mundo' (31, my emphasis) [a feeling of *infinity* and *uprootedness* that *eternal exile* from the world would produce in me] (my emphasis). The sense of a definitive end that is also one of infinity, uprootedness, and eternal exile is only possible in death.

However, death could also be an afterlife, beyond death; someone else, or other, can, of course, read the letters beyond or beside the couple named as protagonists. In any case, for Nélida and Celia, the trip is utopian, a trip to no-place. As such, the planned perfection must remain in planning phase. As Celia states, there is no such thing as a perfect crime: 'El único crimen perfecto, aunque resulte paradójico, es aquél que no se comete' (37) [Though it may seem paradoxical, the only perfect crime is the crime that is not committed]. Similarly, the only perfect utopia, the only living, vital utopia, is, inherently, one that is not realised but that exists only as potential. The perfect trip is a trip to nowhere, which is, for this very reason, a trip to everywhere. The absolute autonomy that Nélida claims to have, her illusion of complete freedom from embedded structures of the world, could only be achieved in death, as Gutiérrez Pardina has emphasised (2003: 43). The notion of *complete* autonomy from embedded structures in life, as well as a sign of privilege, is an illusion. For those who are living, the closest to absolute autonomy and freedom from material structures is through fantasy, as Nélida well knows.

Phantasmal Fantasies

Nélida's implicit equation of the signing of the contract and the actualisation of the trip with death frames her exchange of letters with Celia in which they discuss but always *defer* the trip as a mark of vitality. Over the course of their textual exchange and their physical encounters, the women imagine and create new games and new worlds. Nélida describes how games unsettle her articulation of word and world: 'en mí lo lúdico llega a convertirse en una especie de secuencia continua que desordena incluso mis palabras jugándolas al escrabel' (29) [in me the ludic ends up becoming a sort of continuous sequence that disorders even my words, playing scrabble with them]. The continual disordering of language is characteristic of the spaces the women create and share.

One game, invented by Celia, involved writing the same word over and over again as many times as possible for as long as possible: 'Era obsesivo. Tardamos más de tres días en dormirnos. Quedábamos exhaustas' (60) [It was obsessive. We went for three days without sleeping. We were exhausted]. Writing words again and again in a compulsive manner recalls comments by scholars of trauma on melancholia and repetition. Judith Butler writes of the melancholy of (sexual) identity, arguing that the normative script must be rehearsed again and again because it is at once powerful and fragile, insistent and prone to interruption (1990). Margo Natalie Crawford comments on language in the extremely different context of the traumatic legacy of slavery. Despite the difference in context, it is nonetheless illuminating to consider Nélida and Celia's fixation on words in the light of her analysis. Crawford argues that 'people stuck on a word or a sentence are still in the process of writing' (2016: 70). Nélida and Celia, knowing that their relationship does not quite *fit* with the world around them, write the same words over and over again in an effort to change their meaning so that they describe an imaginary world in which they can live out their desires. Their repetition of words recalls Oliverio's stammering over the word 'angustia' mentioned in Chapter Two. Nélida writes: 'Por medio del juego hacíamos nuestras las palabras, hacíamos nuestras las formas, los colores, nos hacíamos nuestras...' (61) [Through the game we appropriated words, structures, colours, we made them ours]. Nélida only gives the example of the first word with which they played the game: 'geométrica', originally from the Greek *gē* 'earth' and *metrēs* 'measurer'. Resonating with Oliverio, who ponders what he describes as the 'geometry' of sounds, the women literally get stuck on and, consequently, 'make theirs' the shape and space of words and the world, while repossessing themselves.

Nélida and Celia's game-playing is evidently not simply light-hearted amusement, but a desperate attempt to imagine alternative worlds. Nélida goes on to comment that their 'afán por los juegos fue neurótico, hasta el punto de llegar a competir por la creación de nuevos juegos. La ganadora era la que creaba el más original' (60–61) [their thirst for games was neurotic, they even went as far as competing to invent new games. The winner was the one who created the most original game]. It is the process of inventing new games and creating new worlds that drives the women; they want to live *differently*. Nélida says of the games: 'Todos nuestros juegos eran interiores, mentales. Eran íntimos. El reto era privado. Jugar no era deleitable o divertido. Era *obsesivo*, impresionante. *Nos evadíamos* de todo. *Olvidábamos* todo aquello que formaba parte de *lo cotidiano*' (61, emphasis mine) [All of our games were internal, psychological. They were intimate. The challenge was private. Playing wasn't fun or enjoyable. It was *obsessive*, impressive. We *evaded* everything. We *forgot* everything that was part of the *everyday*] (my emphasis). The women's obsessive playing evokes a queer detachment or suspension from the 'straight time' of the world to live temporarily in another time and place.

The characters' distance from the rhythms of daily life is also evident in their limited engagement with specific places in the novels. For example, Nélida's lack of rootedness is reflected in the superficial and almost superfluous references she makes to Barcelona and Buenos Aires. Although both Celia and Nélida live in Barcelona and although Nélida occasionally visits Buenos Aires, place is in fact incidental, a mere backdrop to the relationship. The centrality of the incidental has become characteristic of the queer. The apparent insignificance of place in the novel perhaps also points to the women's lack of a place beyond their private exchanges in which they can express and live out their desires. They exist out of sync with 'straight time', out of step with 'straight place'.

Existing out of sync with the conventional time of daily life is characteristic of fantasy, and also of phantoms. The women's 'evasion' of 'lo cotidiano' causes them to fear that the other might be a spectre that does not exist outside of their fantasy world. Nélida plays to Celia's fear that she is a figment of Celia's imagination: '¿No tienes miedo de estar escribiendo a nadie? ¿De estarte inventando a alguien y creyéndotelo? ¿Y si no existo? ¿Y si sólo parezco?' (51) [Do you not fear that you might be writing to no one? That this person might be an invention of yours in which you have come to believe? What if I don't exist? What if I just seem to exist?]. When Nélida is away, Celia describes her obsession with her intangible memory of Nélida, which she finds unsatisfactory:

> Porque estarás conmigo en que el recuerdo es una forma de existir, a veces más obsesiva que la presencia, ¿no? Si pervives en el recuerdo, ¿pervives realmente? No me atrae esa forma de pervivencia, tan sutil. Y digo sutil por lo imperceptible de su forma. (48)

> [Because you will agree with me that memory is a way of existing, sometimes more obsessive than actual presence, right? And if you endure in my memory, do you really endure? I'm not drawn by this subtle form of survival. I say subtle because it has no perceptible form.]

We are brought once more to form and formlessness, which at heart is a question of visibility and recognisability. For Celia, formlessness, or the lack of a *recognisable* form, runs the risk of irreality. The symbolic power of convention may have the effect of giving those who do not share or subscribe to convention the sense of being unreal.

Similarly, in one of the letters at the end of the novel where it is unclear who is writing to whom, the writer questions her own existence beyond the reflection of herself in the recipient: '¿Y has creído que existo fuera de ti? ¿Por qué? Y los ojos en los ojos, y las manos en las manos. Y esas palabras...' (67) [And do you think that I exist outside you? Why? And my eyes in your eyes, and my hands in your hands. And those words...]. It is the obsession, the 'sitting opposite' her lover of the past with 'los ojos en los ojos, y las manos en las manos', in reality or otherwise, that enables the writer to imagine her future. Rodríguez describes fantasy as a way of 'forming a vision of the world and of ourselves that *exceeds the present*. Through its relation to imagination, fantasy urges us to suppose the *potentialities beyond* and before the now, to *step across* the borders of the possible' (27, my emphasis). Both Nélida and Celia depend on being haunted or possessed by the other to sustain their own existence, dreams, and imagination. The slippage between temporal and physical crossings in Rodríguez's words resonates with Celia and Nélida needing to think and be in another time and another place.

The difference between the women is that Celia wants the perceived security of a formalised relationship — 'Te has comprado un palacio de excelente cemento y compartes la mesa con alguien que jamás va a abandonarte' (2000: 205) [You've bought a solidly built palace and you share meals with someone who is never going to abandon you]. Through the reference to concrete structures, physical and psychological security are conflated. In contrast, Nélida, although tempted by order, sees formalisation as a threat to the vitality of the women's desire. The prologue letter reveals Nélida's desire for affirmation that Celia exists beyond her fantasies, if only to return, yet again, *to* fantasy:

> ¿Cuándo por fin te atreverás a escribirme, a revelarme que estás ahí, que no es sólo una fantasía mía — que yo sé que no es? [...] ¿Cuándo volveremos a los *juegos de palabras*, a las cartas, a los viajes *fantásticos* que *jamás han existido* más que en una o dos habitaciones de esta Barcelona terrible?' (11–12, emphasis mine).

> [When will you dare to write to me, finally, to reveal that you are there, that you are not just a fantasy of mine (which I know you are not)? [...] When will we return to our *word games*, to the letters, to those *fantastic* trips that *have never existed* anywhere but in one or two rooms in this terrible city of Barcelona?] (my emphasis)

For Nélida, imagination, phantoms, and fantasy are, in their formlessness, more vital than *straightforward* visibility.

Epps sums up the tension between the virtual and the real in his work on Riera's 'Te deix' and 'Jo pos per testimoni les gavines'. Drawing on Wittig and Meese, he writes of the importance of imagination as part of the 'real', describing a 'productive virtuality':

> This productive virtuality, capable of generating a body from a footprint, love from a lost letter, or writing from silence and erasure, is not without its obstacles [...]; but it does signify a process of cultural signification in which *the imagination is itself a crucial aspect of the real*. Thus, even as I read Riera's text against the specter of a dismissive, or negative, virtuality, I also bear witness to the productivity of another virtuality which, like some rich and resistant reserve of meaning, realizes itself in writing. (1995: 323)

Nélida, convinced of the power of virtuality, wants to keep the textual exchange alive. Celia may seek a life and loves more concrete, less 'sutil', but she also keeps writing to Nélida, and it is probably she who has compiled the letters, which are, without a doubt, a 'rich and resistant reserve of meaning'.

Castle writes that '[o]nce the lesbian has been defined as ghostly — the better to drain her of any sensual or moral authority — she can then be exorcized' (7). However, rather than the spectral as a disempowered form, Nélida's haunting presence and the repeated coming to life of the text in *Querida Nélida* emphasises the power of an insistent, if not eternal, return. As Castle herself remarks, '[o]nly something very palpable — at a deeper level — has the capacity to "haunt" us so thoroughly' (7). A similar sentiment is expressed in Company's novel when Nélida comments on Celia's denial of the existence of their desire and her running away from Nélida as: 'una forma de querer demostrarte que no existo, que jamás he existido en otro lugar que no sea tu imaginación. Pero *el hecho mismo de la huida demuestra que existe aquello que no queremos*' (11, my emphasis) [a way of wanting to show you that I don't exist, that I have never existed anywhere outside your imagination. But *the very fact of your fleeing proves the existence of that which we wish did not exist*] (my emphasis). Spectres, partial presences, present-absences, can repeatedly return; only the reified can be consigned to the past.

In this regard, obsession in the novel can be considered in the light of Freccero's 'ethics of haunting' in which she valorises 'queer spectrality' as 'ghostly returns suffused with affective materiality' (2007: 488). Haunting is vitality, living on. As the protagonist of *Melalcor* states, '[p]robablement l'únic món que no caduca és el que s'imagina' (41) [the imagined world is probably the only world that does not become obsolete]. Fantasy and phantasmal worlds permit the women to imagine future horizons.

Epistolarity: Spectral Futurity

It is significant that Company chooses the epistolary form as the *medium* through which to tell the story of Nélida and Celia's obsessive relationship. I use the word 'medium' deliberately and with an eye to its polysemic implications as not merely a means of doing something but also as a mode of spectral communication between different temporalities, consistent with the obsessive use of the word 'obsession' and its variants in Company's text. Franz Kafka describes the phantasmal quality of letter writing as 'communication with spectres, not only with the spectre of the addressee but also with one's own phantom, which evolves underneath one's own hand' (cited in Altman 1982: 2), pointing to engagements with selves and others who change through time. The writer's words, once written, are already words from the past that will reach a recipient, or indeed the writer themselves, in a different time and place.

As with a number of the traits of epistolary writing, Kafka's comment could be extended to apply to all literature. Ohi reminds us that the writer, described by Samuel Johnson as 'someone who has already disappeared' (2015: 13), can haunt us in her ongoing presence through her works. Whereas Dinshaw's 'touching across time', which I mentioned in Chapter One, refers principally to a *comforting* identification between readers and writers of different times through text, being haunted may not be so comforting. The prologue letter and the front cover of the first edition of *Querida Nélida*, published by Montesinos, highlight the power of letters and literature to move the reader/recipient, but in a less reassuring way; they can startle, challenge, possess, and cause discomfort to the reader/recipient from afar.

The front cover of the Montesinos edition features a Robert G. Harris painting of a woman sitting in an upholstered floral armchair reading a letter. Celia's desire for a well-to-do domestic life is reinforced by the image that was apparently used as an illustration for *Good Housekeeping* magazine. The woman seems overcome by shock and fear as she holds one page of a letter in her hand, gripping another page between her teeth. The brightness of the white paper compared to the darkness of the rest of the room highlights the power of the written word to move and to stun and also evokes a ghost, like Sappho's full blank page in Wittig and Zeig's *Lesbian Peoples*, mentioned in Chapter One. The woman in the painting, who is drawing herself away from the page that she is reading into the protective floral upholstery of the chair, looks as though she has seen a spectre.

Upon opening the novel, the first letter that the reader encounters is, as noted, the prologue letter, evidently written after the letters that it precedes in the novel. Time thus appears disordered from the outset. In the prologue letter, Nélida conjures the erotic scene of Celia naked in front of a mirror reading the letter from Nélida that 'cruza un océano de tiempo para descubrirte a solas, desnuda ante el espejo, con las manos tocándote el cabello... y las cosas rozándote de a poco las pupilas; algún arañazo, algún objeto tenía que poder' (12) [crosses an ocean of time to find you alone, naked in front of the mirror, your hands caressing your hair... and the things graze your pupils slowly; some sort of scratch, some sort of object was bound to be able to do so]. The (specular) 'touching' of textual and carnal body is a prelude to an erotic relationship that is largely experienced (and that the reader only accesses) textually. Nélida mentions the materiality of her words that, in letter form, touch Celia psychologically and physically, across space and time. Nélida imagines the letter as reminding Celia that their relationship is 'un arañazo'; not a touch but rather a scratch, a presence that is incisive, irritating, intrusive, and even painful i.e. the letter or word made flesh or inscribed in the flesh.[1] 'Las cosas', presumably in the letter, tellingly brush her pupils, disrupting her sight literally and metaphorically, troubling her complacent perspective on the world. As in Freccero's queer haunting, the 'commingling of times [is an] affective and erotic experience' (489).

The persistent interruption and disruption of Nélida in Celia's life contrasts with traditional narrative. MacArthur draws on Sartre to conclude that '[t]he insistence on closure in both the novelistic and the critical traditions might represent [...] an attempt to preserve the moral and social order, which would be threatened by *endlessly erring narratives*' (MacArthur: 16, my emphasis). In one of the letters at the end of the novel in which it is unclear whether Celia or Nélida is writing, the sender states: '¿Quieres decir que no es tu locura de mí en ti la que te hace *errar* así? ¿No sientes en tu cuerpo el agotamiento de la *fantasía*?' (66, my emphasis) [Do you mean to say that it is not your madness at having me within you that makes you *err* like this? Don't you feel the exhaustion of *fantasy* in your body?] (my emphasis). The Spanish verb 'errar' can, of course, relate to being mistaken and to wandering, as with 'to err', both of which come from the Latin *errare*, 'to stray'. The writer's association of erring texts and erring bodies with fantasy concords with Sartre's analysis of narrative closure as tending to preserve the status quo. In my analysis of the Tapestry of Creation in Peri Rossi's *La nave*, I considered the common association of sin with the act of straying from the straight and narrow. Similarly, while 'to err' literally means 'to wander' or 'to go astray', it can also mean 'to sin'. In the light of such a worldview, narratives that twist and turn, stop and start, encourage, it would appear, a 'sinful' disorder. Nélida endlessly errs both in her relentless movement and unwillingness to *settle*, and in her repeated revival of her textual exchange with the grounded Celia.

Linda Kauffman describes the epistolary form's 'Janus-like ability to look backward and forward, as remembrance and prophecy' (1992: xiv). In these temporal acrobatics, we experience the spectral quality of letters. Spectres are often seen as figures returning from the dead due to some unfinished business in the world, to influence the *future*. Similarly, MacArthur describes epistolary literature as inherently open-ended, perpetually unfinished and relentlessly forward-looking: it 'drives forward to an open future instead of looking back over a completed past' (1990: 32), a description that recalls Foucault's aforementioned assertion that genealogy 'does not pretend to go back in time to restore an unbroken continuity that operates beyond the dispersion of forgotten things' (1984a: 81). Spectres, as conceived of by Derrida, rather than simply a reminder of things long gone, are an ongoing *presence*, a figure of something that will not completely disappear, and can therefore represent an anachronous vitality. The endlessly erring, open narrative of the epistolary form readily evokes the queer temporalities of a haunted future.

'Feliz melancolía': Pleasures Against Progress

> Dolor de ser tan diferent de tu
> Dolor d'una semblança sense termes...
> Dolor de ser i no ser tu: desig.
>
> — MARÇAL ([1989] 2017: 434)
>
> [The pain of being so different to you
> The pain of a likeness without limits...
> The pain of being and not being you: desire.]

The ambivalent temporalities and affective force of spectres and of the epistolary form continue in the merging of the women's letters at the end of the novel. The final four letters (66–67) are addressed to 'Querida mía', 'Mi querida' [My dear], or 'Querida' [Dear], and are not signed off with a name, simply 'Tuya' [Yours] or 'Siempre tuya' [Always yours]; the women's identities are thus confused, the personas masked. The first letter in which it is unclear which of the women is the recipient and which the sender contains the following lines: 'He estado dando vueltas a la frase *guardar las apariencias*. ¿Te das cuenta? ¿Qué apariencias podemos guardar tú y yo? La apariencia de las palabras, que desaparece tras el anonimato infligido por nuestros *espíritus equivocados*. ¡Equivocarse así! Te confundo' (66, my emphasis) [I have been going over the phrase '*to keep up appearances*'. Do you realise? What appearances could the two of us keep up? The appearance of words, which disappears behind the anonymity inflicted by our *mixed-up spirits*. To be mistaken in this way! I confuse you] (my emphasis). Company plays with the shared root of 'apariencias' and 'aparición', i.e. a spectre or spirit. The women are 'keeping up appearances', in the sense of keeping their relationship secret, of *apparently* adhering to societal convention in public, 'masquerading', as Joan Riviere (1929) would have it, as 'normal women', but also stubbornly sustaining the haunting apparitions of their alternative worlds through their words and letters.

'Equivocarse', another provocative word in the letter, literally means 'to be called the same name'. It connotes confusion and being fooled by appearances, but also a troubling of the pertinence and propriety of the proper name. It is more commonly used, of course, to mean 'to be wrong'. The word prompts a number of differing readings of the novel's close. The textual merging could suggest the women's ecstatic fusion, but it could also refer to their loss of identity in a sort of paralysing melancholia. The final line of the novel reinforces the novel's ambivalence: 'De pronto me di cuenta de que ya nada tenía sentido' (68) [Suddenly I realised that nothing made sense any more]. What is it that does not make sense to the narrator? Her relationship to another woman? The society in which the women live — together and apart? The trip? Their wish for the letters to have 'sentido', in the sense of their effects being *felt* in the real world beyond the imaginary worlds created through and in the text?

It is not just the reader who is confused about who has written what; the women themselves cannot tell whether their words are their own. Celia writes the following in the final letter that is signed off with a name:

> Te recuerdo, sencillamente toda. No podría olvidar nada. Es como sentirte en mí como a mí misma... ¿Has dicho esto ya? ¿Lo has dicho tú antes? Releo tu última carta y me doy cuenta de que sí. [...] Tus ojos brillan en mis ojos cada vez que miro al espejo; y me parezco tú, aparecida tras la cortina helada de la propia identidad. (65)

> [I remember you, simply all of you. I couldn't forget anything. It is like feeling you within me like I feel myself... Have you already said that? Did you say that before? I reread your last letter and realise that you did. [...] Your eyes shine in my eyes every time I look in the mirror, and I look like you, appearing behind the frozen curtain of my own identity.'

Celia's memory of Nélida whole within herself suggests a melancholic absorption. As well as Celia's (con)fusion or identification with Nélida, the complex final letter brings into play a number of issues that permeate the women's epistolary exchange: melancholia, death, and the erotic. Celia's mention in the same passage of a mirror and a curtain, drape, or screen, brings to mind the fact that in some traditions and religions, such as Judaism, mirrors are covered in a house of mourning to ward off the visitation of ghosts. Therefore, through the image of the mirror she evokes at once Nélida as her reflection, and Nélida as a spirit to be banished. There is also a hint of eroticism through the suggestive '[e]s como sentirte en mí' [it is like feeling you in me] and also through the mention of the curtain or drape, given that the distinction between eroticism and pornography classically relies on the presence or absence of such a covering.

Nélida also describes the uncanny feeling of reading one of Celia's letters: 'Sus palabras me resultaban extrañas. Era como si yo lo hubiese escrito. [...] La confusión se hacía desbordante' (62) [Her words seemed strange to me. It was as if I had written them. [...] The confusion was overwhelming]. Referring again to her (con)fusion with Celia, Nélida states that hearing Celia's dreams made her forget her own (58). She also describes experiencing time as limitless space:

> El tiempo se me había extendido todo él ante los ojos sin ofrecerme fronteras. [...] Más allá del plano, el plano posterior. Más allá del plano posterior, el plano. Y un punto, el punto, mi única línea. Yo el punto, yo la línea. No sé aún si Celia el plano. Uno y todo se unían. Posiblemente en nada, que es todo, y es una. (58–59)

> [Time in its entirety had extended in front of my eyes with no limit. [...] Beyond the first plane, the plane behind. Beyond the plane behind, the plane. And a dot, the dot, my only line. I am the dot, I am the line. I don't know yet if Celia is the plane. One and all were merging. Possibly into nothing, which is everything, and which is one.]

The description is rife with ambivalence and ambiguity; time-space is extensive and boundless but also flat (or plane), stratified and pointed, with one linear path or a single line. The passage could be read as a description of the two-dimensional space of the page, of writing vis-à-vis the real world, indeed of the characters themselves as lines on paper. Such a reading resonates with the 'ya nada tenía sentido' [nothing made sense any more] of the novel's close, if we read 'sentido' as 'sense' in terms of meaning *and* in terms of feeling or lived reality beyond the text. The reminder that the text is text, that the characters are being generated from words, draws the reader out of a figurative investment in Nélida and Celia as people.

The passage could also be read in the light of Irigaray's lesbian feminist texts, particularly those published in the late 1970s and early 1980s around the time that Company wrote the novel. In 'This Sex Which Is Not One' (1977) and 'When Our Lips Speak Together' (1976), Irigaray contrasts the 'one' of the penis, which she aligns with 'the individual [...] the proper name [...] proper meaning' ([1977] 1985: 26), with her (since much criticised for essentialising) description of women's genitals as being 'formed of two lips in continuous contact [...] that caress each other' (1985: 24). She writes of woman as multiple: 'in a culture claiming to count everything, to number everything by units, to inventory everything as individualities. *She is neither one nor two.* Rigorously speaking, she cannot be identified as one person, or as two' — the multiplicity to which Irigaray gestures in her texts is echoed in Company's 'Uno y todo se unían' [One and all were merging]. Irigaray also writes of women's pleasure as a 'sort of expanding universe to which no limits could be fixed' (1985: 31), much like the time and lines (and timeline) that Nélida describes. In her works Irigaray challenges a narrative driven logic of desire, emphasising what she characterises as the more diffuse and lingering eroticism of lesbian pleasure:

> You kiss me, and the world enlarges until the horizon vanishes. Are we unsatisfied? Yes, if that means that we are never finished. If our pleasure consists of moving and being moved by each other, endlessly. Always in movement, this openness is neither spent nor sated. ([1976] 1980: 73)

The women's epistolary exchange in *Querida Nélida* does hint at limitless time and space, at utopian potentiality, which I describe in the following section. However, Nélida's words are more equivocal than Irigaray's. They reveal her ambivalence between a nihilistic sense of nothingness and the plenitude of being seduced into and perhaps merged with Celia's time-space. Has she been besieged by Celia's settled dreams? Is the infinite but pointed stretching of time a rendition of the eternal romantic love of 'straight time' rather than the vanishing horizon of Irigaray's lesbian pleasure?

Nélida's listlessness and sense of being overcome by Celia mirrors the structure of melancholia. The Freudian notion of melancholia as incomplete, failed mourning involves the preservation of the beloved object 'through the medium of a hallucinatory wishful psychosis' ([1917] 1971: 244). In Sigmund Freud's analysis in 'Mourning and Melancholia' (1917), introjection led to the libido being 'withdrawn into the ego' (1971: 249), establishing a pathological 'narcissistic identification' (ibid.) with the abandoned object. The preservation of the other fantasmically within the self chimes with the blurring of the women's identities and their haunting of each other, offering another interpretation of the merging of one and all, described by Freud (1971: 59).

In the introduction to their edited collection of essays on melancholia, Martin Middeke and Christina Wald note the association of melancholia with loss or a sense of loss, which, they argue, inevitably situates it in the past: 'From a psychological or psychoanalytical perspective, a melancholic experience of time and temporality unveils itself as a *pathological* sadness, a *paralysing* anxiety and, particularly, as an agonizing (if sometimes comforting) *insistence on the past*' (2011: 4, my emphasis). Following Freud, they elaborate on what the pathological paralysis of melancholia means for the future:

> The insistence on the past entails the *loss of the future*; it creates the impression, as it were, of a *standstill* of time. Such a *deadlock* situation involves the impossibility of forgetting, a confounding self-punishment and a tantalizing sense of guilt, which makes it impossible for the melancholic mind to live *freely* with and *in time* or to strive confidently for the future. In the melancholic mind, the temporal limits of human life, the temporality of human existence, and the very consciousness of it determine a precarious experience of the present moment. (4–5, my emphasis)

Their reference to a 'standstill', to frozen time, recalls the structure of obsession. Melancholia entails an 'insistence', 'deadlock', and 'standstill' that interrupts the normative valorisation of progress, of 'freely' living and moving 'in time.' But 'in time' with what or with whom? What is the nature of the future lost? Is there a future gained in the process? Who defines the normal timeline?

As an aside, technically speaking, time was standardised and universalised in Greenwich Mean Time, which was internationally adopted in 1884 — the year of the Berlin Conference and the partitioning of Africa — at the International Meridian Conference in Washington D.C. Thus the latter years of the nineteenth century saw the normativisation, regularisation, and globalisation of time measured according to a clock (a machine) rather than the sun (a 'heavenly' body that we could associate with Celia in the novel); the former is invariable, the latter, variable as solar time varies throughout the year, which likewise varies. Sexology, with its own obsession with pathological categorisations and deviance arises concurrently. Richard von Krafft-Ebing's *Psychopathia Sexualis* was published in 1886. For Krafft-Ebing, any sexual activity that did not have procreation as its objective was a perversion. Foucault's writing on the history of sexuality refers to such ideas, demonstrating that the birth of the concept of homosexuality was part and parcel of the will to knowledge in the global order. In short, the 'normal timeline' is historically bound to power: that of rich, white, Western men, themselves bound to Empire.

Let us return to Wald and Middeke's remarks. Their bracketed reference to comfort (amidst agony) is important for it suggests a tension, in melancholia, between pain and pleasure, as well as, perhaps, the suspension of eroticism and its maintenance. Melancholia, as dissatisfaction with the present, does not mean that it is *necessarily* trapped in the past or in an eternal present. I propose that a 'precarious experience of the present moment', more than paralysis, standstill, and deadlock, suggests a restless uncertainty, a straining of time.

In other words, while the two women's melancholic merging may signal a past-bound paralysis, it may also suggest the coexistence of pain and pleasure, and, crucially, the impossibility of a full and final — or perfect — merging. The descriptions of their partial and temporary fusion, at once in and out of time, are, moreover, highly erotic. Eroticism, linked to lingering, to a refusal of climax, like Nélida's description of time stretching out endlessly cited above, resonates with Irigaray's distinction of female (lesbian) pleasure and erogenous zones beyond the normative genital locus of pleasure — '*woman has sex organs more or less everywhere. She finds pleasure almost anywhere*' (1985: 28) — which Irigaray contrasts with the master site and signifier of male phallic pleasure.

When Nélida sees Celia again after a long absence, she is gripped by fear, but it is a fear that oscillates between destruction and empowerment:

> Un miedo extraño se me apoderó de las manos, del ser. Notaba mi cuerpo como frontera y como principio. Celia me hacía darme cuenta de mi espacio. Tomé consciencia de mi forma y mi manera gracias a ella, o a pesar de ella, ya no sé... Una extraña incertidumbre que rociaba las palabras, las madrugadas de mis deseos, me reconstruían. Creo en realidad que me destruían reconstruyendo a Celia. (58)

> [A strange fear took over my hands and my being. I experienced my body as a limit and as a beginning. Celia made me register my space. I became conscious

of my form and ways thanks to her, or in spite of her, I don't know any more...
A strange uncertainty that fell upon my words, the dawn of my desires,
reconstructed me. I think that in reality they destroyed me by reconstructing
Celia.]

Celia at once helps Nélida to become aware of the limiting physicality of her
body, but also of her body as a site of potentiality. Laura Mulvey (1975) and many
other feminists saw the destruction of normative pleasure as necessary to other
pleasures.

Nélida describes stages of melancholia in the breakdown of her communication
with Celia (marking their loss of each other) and their subsequent absorption of
each other:

> Te impido comunicarte conmigo, te dejo sola. Pero a pesar de eso, ¿no estoy
> ya un poco dentro de ti como tú misma te estás ocupando? Sin violarte, entro
> dentro de tu persona haciéndola mía, que no es al fin y al cabo sino lo mismo
> que ser tuya. [...] No te duela esta irrupción de mí en ti, que no es otra que la
> de ti en mí. Los mismos límites se entrelazan, se miran, se miden, se recorren,
> se reconocen, se aman, se contaminan... (64)

> [I prevent you from communicating with me, I leave you alone. But despite
> that, am I not already somewhat inside you just as you live in yourself? Without
> violating you, I enter you making you mine, which is, at the end of the day, the
> same as being yours. [...] Don't be pained by this irruption of me in you, which
> is the same as the irruption of you in me. Our very limits intertwine, observe,
> measure, run along, recognise, love, and contaminate one another...]

Yet again, the absorption of one woman into the other is described as an erotic
process that is both pleasurable — '[l]os mismos límites [...] se aman' [our very
limits [...] love one another] — and potentially painful. Nélida's imperative 'no te
duela...' [don't be pained by...] suggests that the phantom of pain remains present.
The reference to the 'irrupción' of the women in each other resonates with the
queer interruptions of linear time and the breakdown of a coherent self-sufficient
subject as the women linger within each other. Unlike Wittig's aforementioned
split subject j/e, Irigaray's lesbian subject is a fused multiplicity: 'From your/my lips,
several ways of saying echo each other. For one is never separable from the other.
You/I are always several at the same time' (1980: 72).

In its ambivalence, the vision of melancholia in the novel chimes with Maria
Torok's 'lost idyll preserved', as described by Freeman (2010: 120). In Freeman's
reading, the past 'consists of latent excitations not yet traversed by the binary
between pain and pleasure, preserved and suspended in this very ambivalence and
capable of being released *as pleasure* rather than simply being repeated as incomplete
mastery over pain' (119). Nélida describes actively and willingly thinking back to the
trip never taken with the seemingly oxymoronic words 'Recuerdo, feliz melancolía'
(26) [I remember, happy melancholy]. Her obsession with the unrealised journey
and with the memory of Celia appears to exemplify the painful pleasure in haunting
and being haunted that Torok has theorised. The reference to a remembered, happy
melancholy appears in Nélida's sixth notebook, which is revealingly blank apart
from that phrase. Rather than a longing for the past, Nélida frames her (queer)

longing as a longing for things she has never had: 'Mi añoranza es tal... Añoranza de las cosas que jamás he poseído' (46) [My longing is like that... A longing for things that I have never possessed]. Nélida looks back over a relationship that, while involving an economy of desire, is not ultimately possessive in the sense of having ownership of or claim to each other, but possessive in the obsessive sense of haunting. Nélida emphasises the pleasure she takes in remembering her relationship regardless of the fact that, or rather *because* of the very fact that, it did not and does not progress or develop in the manner of conventional relationships.

A number of feminist, queer, and critical race studies scholars have critiqued and disrupted Freud's initial pathologisation of melancholia and the temporal logic that it entails (e.g. Butler 2003: 471; Schiesari 1992: 3). Freeman argues that melancholy refuses 'the progressive logic by which becoming ever more visible was correlated with achieving ever more freedom' (2010: 9). Nélida's 'feliz melancolía' is a sombre joy in the unrealisation of an erotic past because of the potential it contains for shaping a *different* reading of the past and a different future. Freeman describes Torok's reading of melancholic 'incorporation' as a pleasurable haunting that harbours 'residues of positive affect (idylls, utopias, memories of touch) [that] might be available for queer counter- (or para-) historiographies' (120). It can be a mode of imagining a different mode of existence. While the last letters in the novel point to some sort of letting go — 'Te he olvidado. Podemos empezar. Me he olvidado' (67) [I have forgotten you. We can begin. I have forgotten myself] — we know from the prologue letter that the women do stay in touch by way of letters, at least. Perhaps rather than forgetting and letting go, the women *need* to remember, to allow themselves to remember; perhaps it is the very insistence on moving beyond a pathologised melancholic state that in fact induces melancholia. Counterintuitively, then, melancholia *can* be future-oriented and sustaining; it might only seem paralysing to those who would discount or delegitimise alternative ways of being.

Utopian Potentiality

Nélida describes how her preparations for the trip involve a continual process of reading and rewriting, of returning to texts written previously:

> El viaje me ligaba a la lectura. Seguía preparándome incansablemente; perfeccionando el contrato, ultimando los detalles. Fue fácil descubrir que la finalidad no existe. Ni tan sólo la inmediata. Cuando una dice para, dice por. Toda finalidad es causal. Una causalidad no casual, sino perentoria. Una causalidad del deseo, que se extiende más allá del poder. Y ya querer no es poder, ni poder querer. (59)

> [The trip tied me to reading. I was still preparing myself tirelessly, perfecting the contract, finalising details. I soon discovered that finality does not exist. Not even momentary finality. Saying 'in order to', is also to say 'as a result of'. All sense of finality is the cause of something else. Causality is not down to chance, but necessity. A causality of desire, which extends beyond one's ability to desire. And so to want to desire does not mean that you will be able to do so, and being able to do so does not mean that you want to do so.]

That the trip ties Nélida to writing recalls the voyages and travels of texts in the intertextual webs of Equis's and others' journeys in *La nave*. The refusal of finality highlights how, for Nélida, her relationship with Celia is an incomplete process rather than a final destination. Her approach to the trip reveals an attitude similar to that which Muñoz signals in relation to queers: a belief in the possibility of a better time and place, even though — or perhaps, indeed, *because* — we do not think that we will ever reach it.

Nélida describes her desire as a desire for what is *beyond* her power and possibilities. The trip never taken and Nélida's happy melancholia resonate with what Muñoz presents, via Ernst Bloch, as a 'Not-Yet-Here'. Muñoz writes that '[q]ueerness as a utopian formation is a formation based on an economy of desire and desiring. This desire is always directed at that thing which is not yet here, objects and moments that burn with anticipation and promise' (2015: 457). In marked contrast to Edelman, on whose work he nonetheless draws, Muñoz associates queerness with hope and futurity (2009: 11). He does not, however, maintain that 'progress' is the only mode of futurity and instead argues that accepting disappointment, accepting incompleteness, and accepting failure permits one to commit to a better future (2009: 9).

During her preparations for the trip, Nélida sketches ideas for the trip in her notebooks: 'El primero [cuaderno] no era más que el esbozo de la idea' (19) [The first notebook was no more than a sketch of the idea]. As in *La passió* in which 'l'esbós' is a key trope associated with Catalan lesbian identity, linking the island of Lesbos with the fragmentary sketch, the word 'esbozo' is mentioned a number of times in *Querida Nélida*. Nélida explains that the third part of the fourth notebook 'esbozaba la idea del viaje de forma premonitoria' (24) [sketched out the idea of the trip in a foreboding manner]. Nélida writes that in the contract that she asks a solicitor friend to draw up, the trip '[q]uedó esbozado' (27) [was sketched out]. The sketch is an apt motif for potentiality, for existing in between lack and the urge towards wholeness, for being open to the unknown, multiple possibilities of the past, present, and future.

Nélida reads to Celia an extract from a book from a national library (39) that evokes Muñoz's 'anticipation and promise' (2015: 457). Tellingly, Nélida does not specify *which* national library the book is from (presumably that of Argentina, Spain, or Catalonia).[2] As in much of the novel, nation and place seem to be incidental, reflecting the fact that the women build their identities around their relationship with each other, around their desire. The extract states:

> Las palabras se unen en mí para formar un conjunto totalizador que universalice el acto del lenguaje de forma significativa. Ese conjunto, ajeno a la voluntad de los propios signos que lo forman, establece un sentido más allá de lo previsible, corrigiendo en vano las diversas interpretaciones a que puede estar sometido. De forma sorprendente, el significado aparece, emerge de la unión de partes, para formar un todo incompleto que mezcla en sí el para sí que constituye todo discurso coherente. (39–40)

> [Words come together in me to form a totalising whole that universalises the act of language in a meaningful way. That whole, beyond the will of the signs

of which it is composed, creates meaning beyond the predictable, correcting in vain the many interpretations to which it could be subjected. In a surprising way, meaning appears, it emerges from the joining together of parts to form an incomplete whole that mixes within itself the self-referentiality that constitutes all coherent discourse.]

The reference to an incomplete whole may be read as a sketch that is complete in its incompleteness; but it may also be read in relation to something that was once more complete, such as the damaged Tapestry of Creation. The incomplete whole may also describe a spectre, a remnant of something that was and/or something that is to come; haunting, persistent, obsessive.

The multiplicity of interpretations that cannot be contained, the turn to, and return of, each other and each other's texts marks Nélida and Celia's awareness of potentiality in writing of the past. Drawing on Agamben's idea of potentiality in 'Bartleby, or On Contingency', Ohi comments that writing represents both the coming into being of something or some things and the *not* coming into being of other things: 'On the writing tablet of the celestial scribe, the letter, the act of writing, marks the passage from potentiality to actuality, the occurrence of a contingency. But precisely for this reason, every letter also marks the non-occurrence of something' (2015: 27). Accordingly, the letter is not simply a remembrance of what was, but also a remembrance of what was *not*. Indeed, every letter exchanged by Nélida and Celia about the trip marks the non-occurrence of the trip. Returning to writing, then, is to return to a site of potentiality. As Ohi argues, '[i]f not always marked explicitly as such, potentiality is a recurrent topos in queer writing, [...] where imaginings of utopian sexual possibilities take shape in readings and rewritings of precursor texts' (2015: 29). Nélida and Celia's exchange as they cite and rewrite each other's words is akin to the process of queer transmission that Ohi describes.

Contrary to first impressions, *Querida Nélida* hints at queer futurity not *despite* its melancholic and obsessive tone or its epistolary form and spectral returns but *because* of these characteristics. The epistolary form's open-endedness, as MacArthur notes, lends itself to the depiction of a recurring past and an ever-signalled but never reached future. Celia's signature, which Nélida sought for the contract, finally appears at the end of the novel. The papers that she signs are not a binding contract, but a collation of the letters she has exchanged with Nélida, letters that sketch the constant deferral of the trip and allow it to remain a vital potentiality 'on the horizon' (Muñoz 2009: 11). Rather than symbolising a melancholic entrapment in the past or an evasion of reality, as it first seems, Nélida and Celia's obsessive relationship, their recurrent returns to the past, actually sustain queer possibilities in their *present* and future.

Muñoz states that to 'see queerness as horizon is to perceive it as a modality of ecstatic time in which the temporal stranglehold that I describe as straight time is interrupted or stepped out of' (2015: 461). Indeed, societal conventions that pull people in the same way are themselves obsessive inasmuch as they repeat, compulsively, a fixed path. The games that the women play, which they describe as a suspension or evasion of daily life, are a mark of Muñoz's 'stepping out' of time.

Nélida cannot resist straight time on her own. It is the very obsession with her past lover — real, imagined, or re-membered — that enables Nélida *not* to be pulled along unthinkingly by the hegemonic norm of progress or by Deuteronomy's call to sacrifice friendship to obedience to family, nation, and religion. In 'sitting opposite' Celia, Nélida experiences a sort of freedom. In the Girona letter, Nélida writes 'Y vuelvo a irme. Otra vez me alejo de ti para acercarme a Buenos Aires. Ella, tanto como tú, es la ciudad incomprensible *donde nací*' (2000: 205, my emphasis) [And I leave again. Once more I distance myself from you to get closer to Buenos Aires. She, like you, is the incomprehensible city *where I was born*] (my emphasis). The likening of Celia to Buenos Aires points to the (re)birth of Nélida's identity with and through Celia. The obsessive remembering of Celia is vital to her survival. For Nélida, the only essential journeys are those she makes to Celia — imaginary, a fantasy, a phantom, real — through her letters.

In this case, the worlds imagined by the women are, particularly for Nélida, a way of not conforming to a world in which she sees no place for herself. However, the separation from the world does little to challenge — at least directly — the norms and conventions of a society. Nélida and Celia's relationship was never public; they did not confront — again, directly — societal norms or the policing of sexuality and gender. Celia berates Nélida, whom she describes as the one who flees repeatedly, positing that Nélida's cowardice in running away is no more beyond reproach than what Nélida sees as Celia's cowardly conformity. Nélida writes of creating her own structural frameworks by which to live, but not of confronting the existing structures by which she considers Celia to be bound.

Straddling the conventional and the unconventional, the novel summons forth spectres of a sticky yet slippery terrain that has long concerned LBGTQ+ activists. In so doing, it implicitly grapples with the tensions between those who would maintain lesbian/queer exceptionality, subcultural or otherwise, and those who would engage in battles for *formal* legal recognition (the contract could be seen as representing marriage, for example) that have often gone hand in hand with the absorption of queer culture into the mainstream. The novel, in other words, represents the tension between time as regulated (Celia's groundedness, Nélida's meticulous plans for the trip, the contract) and queer time as out of sync (the women's games and letters). Often campaigns for visibility and access to societal privileges reinforce rather than contest the rationale of such privilege (Joseph 2002: 165). Increased visibility and tolerance have often resulted in an acceptance of certain *kinds* of queers, the *right* sort, those who are willing to be assimilated, even absorbed, into the norms of society.

With the non-occurrence, or non-event, of the trip, *Querida Nélida* maintains, in short, an elusive sense of queerness in the shadows, but also a hauntingly rich imaginary for queer futures. Muñoz, for whom queerness exists on the horizon, sees striving for queer utopia as a collective project. His 'queerness as collectivity' (2006: 825) and futurity as sociality point to a move beyond the obsessiveness of sitting opposite each other — which could be read as a confrontation, a paradoxical reiteration of binary logic of opposition — to an engagement with the world. It is in the spirit of turning outward from the isolated, specular, and dyadic act of sitting opposite one other that I move on to *Melalcor*. Turning to face one's environment need not mean becoming absorbed in its dominant logic, as Nélida seems to fear. *Melalcor*, for example, presents people who have been chastised by the religious morality of a rural Catalan village reaching out to and for others, proposing a community not only beyond the family, but also beyond the couple.

Part II: Improper Affinities in *Melalcor* (2000)

> where I love you, I don't care about the lineage
> of our fathers and their desire for imitation men.
> And their genealogical institutions. Let's be neither
> husband nor wife, do without the family, without roles,
> functions, and their laws of reproduction.
>
> — IRIGARAY ([1976] 1980: 72)

Melalcor, set largely in the fictionalised Catalan village of Santa Canar dels Montons, is punctuated by what is referred to in the novel as 'La Gran Culpa' [The Great Guilt]; the guilt-laden power of religious convention. Torras has read the name 'Montons' as a reference to the French word 'moutons', meaning sheep or docile ones (2008: 230); indeed, many in the village seem to be unquestioning followers of tradition. The majority of the villagers follow the example of the 'Savalt' family (an anagram of 'salvat', meaning 'saved' in Catalan), headed by the unnamed protagonist's parents 'els senyors Savalt'. The Savalt parents uphold religion in the village, and their family business also keeps the village economy afloat. Guided by 'La Gran Culpa', many of the villagers exclude and violently attack the property of those who challenge the reign of the 'Força Creadora' [Creative Force]. The 'Força Creadora' is clearly a reference to God, but in the novel it refers also to the societal pressure to procreate.

   Melalcor describes the relationship between the protagonist-narrator and a character who is sometimes referred to as Mel ('la mel' — feminine — means 'honey' in Catalan) and sometimes as Cor ('el cor' — masculine — means 'heart' in Catalan), both of whom are genderqueer or genderfluid, as signalled by Company's switching between masculine and feminine pronouns and adjectives for the same character, and, indeed, her non-adherence to norms of gender agreement between nouns/ pronouns and adjectives in the novel. Following the increasingly common preferred non-binary pronouns in English, I use the pronouns 'they' and 'their' to refer to the genderqueer characters in my analysis of the novel. The use of pronouns perceived of as plural to refer to individuals — which is actually common in spoken English when the gender of the speaker is not known — disrupts the norms of written grammar and thus may interrupt conventional reading practices, as Company's play with gender and language does in the novel. Such linguistic disruptions to the gender binary, and how the unaccustomed reader or listener might respond to them, are a reminder of how deeply ingrained the binary is in conventional language and consciousness, more so in Spanish than in English due to the grammatical gendering of adjectives and nouns as well as pronouns.

In the village, procreation is considered to be the axis around which everyone's life should revolve. The characters' place in the procreative line of the family is often the main marker of their identity. For example, the protagonist refers to their parents as 'engendradors' (55) [breeders] and to their brother as 'el primogènit' (149) [the firstborn]. So related, people are reduced to their position in the family and/or their procreative capabilities. The function of the family thus appears to be self-perpetuation and, by implication, the production of more and more sheeplike followers or 'moutons'. The oppressive force of religious tradition, bound to a procreative imperative, generates, so to speak, by affinity, groups comprised of those excluded or condemned by its rules. It is on these 'outcasts' that the novel focusses much of its attention, similar to *La nave*'s focus on those cast out from the worldview of the tapestry.

Mel/Cor and the protagonist's relationship is prohibited by their parents and condemned by the village at large. As they strive to find like-minded people in the face of their oppressive family and village environment, the protagonist and Mel/Cor meet other unconventional characters who are vilified in the village, such as Robert, who is English, and hence an outsider or foreigner, known by the villagers as 'La Gran Puta' [The Great Whore], a name which they have reclaimed. Robert is a transnational figure who lives in a *masia*, i.e. a large rural house, on the outskirts of the village. Robert lives with Casilda, known in the village as 'La Pobre Minyona de la Gran Puta' [The Poor Maid of the Great Whore]. Aged eighteen, the protagonist was introduced to Robert by their 'Tia Conca' [Aunt Conca], who has since died — I will return to the figure of the aunt in Part III of this chapter. In the days before their relationship, Mel/Cor and the protagonist stay in the *masia* with Robert and Casilda during their visits to the village from the city where they are studying. Eventually, all of these characters have sexual relationships with each other. The *masia* is destroyed in an arson attack by the villagers, leading Robert and Casilda to flee the village to live first in an unspecified city referred to simply as 'la Ciutat' [The City] (perhaps Barcelona), before going to Newport in the UK, where they are eventually joined by Robert's children, who had assumed Robert was dead. On the day that Mel/Cor is to marry the protagonist's brother, the protagonist, who has previously claimed not to feel love or desire, tells Mel they love them and they too leave the village and flee to Paris.

Company depicts various forms of non-monogamy in the novel, including long-term relationships between people who might be considered lovers, though the novel explicitly questions the concept of love, as I explore below. She also includes what might be considered to be more 'promiscuous' relationships with passing acquaintances. In a sense, the unnamed status of the protagonist hints at the unnamed status of any number of people who engage in promiscuity, in pleasure for the sake of pleasure, counter to the dominant discourse of monogamy, marriage, fidelity, and procreation that the novel impugns. Company's vision of a multiplicity of sexual encounters, loving and otherwise, resonates with Epps's 'ética de la promiscuidad' (2005) [ethics of promiscuity], a 'counter-ethics' to a conventional emphasis on purity, as manifested in exclusionary nationalist, xenophobic, racist, homophobic discourses. Indeed, in a story that el senyor Savalt tells the protagonist when he is a child, el senyor Savalt uses colours to illustrate why the 'Força Creadora' triggered the age of 'la Gran Culpa'. In words that echo John 1:1 — 'In the beginning was the Word, and the Word was with God, and the Word was God' — and conjure images of light and darkness, and of race, he says:

> Al principi de tot, quan el nostre món va començar gràcies al verb diví, tot era o bé blanc o bé negre. La puresa dels blancs i dels negres era l'orgull de la Força Creadora de l'univers bi-color [...]. Tot un grup de rebels, la majoria dels éssers que existien, van decidir seguir el seu impuls i es van barrejar. (32)

> [In the beginning, when our world was formed thanks to the Divine Word, everything was totally white or totally black. The purity of white and black was the pride of the Creative Force of the bicoloured universe [...]. A group of rebels, the majority of beings in existence, decided to follow their impulse and they mixed.]

In the novel, it was precisely 'promiscuity' or 'mixing' that triggered humanity's fall from grace; from an allegedly pure original state.

Fluid Bodies, Sticky Hearts

There are many possible interpretations of the title of the novel beyond a mere reference to the character Mel/Cor. 'Mel al cor', which in Catalan means 'honey at heart' or 'honey in the heart', might signal the fluidity of conceptions of the body, but also, how the body sticks; honey is, after all, more viscous than blood. The few other critics who have written on *Melalcor* have focussed on issues of gender and corporeality, drawing on theories of gender performativity, such as those of Butler.[3] Acedo Alonso, for example, explicitly links the honey of the title with a fluid conception of the body in a chapter titled 'Melalcos: nuevas manera de sentir mundos' (2008a). Ironically, her approach refuses the figurative dimension of 'heart' for what I would argue is an excessively corporeal one. Like all of the criticism on the novel to date, its focus is on the *body* in the text and its state of flux.

The reading experience described by these critics reveals the persistence of the gender binary to identity, how deeply ingrained the binary is even amongst readers who work to destabilise gender preconceptions and write about gender performativity. Paradoxically, their insistence on the body hypostasises, even fetishises, it, fixes it, ironically, even as it claims to track its flows. For example, despite acknowledging that Company pushes readers to think beyond the binary by switching between masculine and feminine pronouns and adjectives and by not adhering to normative gender-agreements, Gutiérrez Pardina nonetheless devotes a large part of her analysis to speculations about the genders of the narrator-protagonist and Mel/Cor. While Company's disruption of gender — and genre — in the novel is compelling, though not original, I will focus my reading of the novel on what it suggests about desire and relationality.

Although critics have rightly recognised that the novel challenges the violent force of the nuclear family, the gender binary, and heteronormativity, many of them have stopped short of commenting on the novel's critique of compulsory monogamy, whether heterosexual, homosexual, or otherwise. The chapter titled 'La família' starts with an oft-cited description of the family: 'La família és una institució caduca i demencial' (85) [The family is an outdated and deranged institution]. The sentence is immediately followed by 'Com la parella' (85) [Like the couple]. The reference to couples is clearly significant, and it is significant that it tends to be overlooked by critics.

Throughout the novel, the protagonist-narrator sleeps with many people — some lovers, others not — and the novel's utopian close is a joyful celebration of promiscuity and of love in and amidst promiscuity. In the final chapter we discover that Mel/Cor and the narrator-protagonist have moved away from the oppressive and suffocating village to Paris, a longtime symbol of unconventional sexualities, as we saw in the figure of Vivien and her milieu in Chapter One. Literal movement in space is linked with a figurative shift in perspective. Of Paris, the protagonist-narrator states, 'Hi ha més diversitat. Però això deu ser perquè hi ha més espai als carrers i potser als cervells' (60) [There's more diversity. But that must be because there is more space in the streets and perhaps also in people's heads]. The following sentences on the final page of the novel are telling: 'És curiós fins a quin punt canvia la visió de la promiscuïtat quan estimem algú. Que canviï la visió, però, no vol dir que canviïn els actes' (232) [It is interesting to see the degree to which our perspective on promiscuity changes when we love someone. While our perspective might change, it doesn't mean that our behaviours do too]. Love is associated with facilitating a change in vision, particularly of promiscuity. The narrative suggests that by the end of the novel the protagonists are able to fully embrace their 'promiscuity' without feeling the power of 'La Gran Culpa'. Earlier in the novel, Meravin, one of the narrator's lovers asserts that 'la gent que no sap jugar, tampoc no sap estimar' (52) [people who don't know how to play don't know how to love either]. Love, then, is associated with playfulness not mere procreation.

In the light of the novel's depiction of joyful non-monogamous relationships, I read the 'honey at heart' as a challenge to ideas of love — often represented by a heart, of course — as constant and enduring. Romantic monogamous love, most frequently accompanied by notions of unwavering affection, by the 'til death do us part' of the marriage contract, is presented as often involving dishonesty about or disconnection from one's feelings. The vision of monogamy as the *sine qua non* for sanctified procreation brings to mind another heart: the Sacred Heart of Christ in Catholicism. The protagonist challenges this vision of 'faithful' monogamous love, commenting that

> [Mel] tenia una fe absurda en l'Amor — Mel ho deia en majúscules, i jo entre cometes, perquè quan et penses que ja ets gran comences a posar-les a tot el que dius — ; havia llegit massa novel·les del segle XIX, i del segle XX també. Jo crec que l'amor no és sa, no és normal, no és ètic, no és humà. És una imposició cultural per fer-nos anar a tots de dos en dos. (60)

> [Mel [...] had an absurd faith in Love — Mel used to capitalise love and I used to put it in inverted commas, because when you think you have grown up you start putting everything you say in inverted commas — she had read too many

nineteenth-century novels, and twentieth-century ones too. I don't think that
love is healthy or normal, ethical or humane. It is a cultural imposition to make
us all go around in pairs.]

Mel's absurd faith in Love echoes Sara T.'s reference to the 'absurda fidelitat a un
interès pretèrit' [absurd loyalty to a past interest] mentioned in Chapter One, which
characterises both her experience of love and her search for Vivien.

The protagonist of *Melalcor* simultaneously questions an 'absurd faith' in love,
dogmatic faiths, the Love of Christ, and the compulsory 'faithfulness' of monogamy.
The protagonist is also suspicious of the rhetoric and ideology of happiness and
its pursuit, and feels 'aquella temptació gairebé perpètua de qüestionar les coses
i, entre elles, el concepte de felicitat' (59) [that almost perpetual temptation to
question things, including the concept of happiness]. As we saw in the last chapter,
the disciplinary force of happiness serves to normalise monogamous heterosexual
romance and marriage. In *Melalcor*, the couple is portrayed as a normalised cultural
imposition that should be challenged and 'Love' as an ideology that upholds
disciplinary religious ideology.

While in a relationship with Mel/Cor, the protagonist continues to have sexual
encounters with other people, including some former lovers, such as Johnny Dos
Daus. While conventional monogamous relationships demand the forgetting of
exes, of previous relationships and sexual encounters, in the case of the novel non-
monogamy acknowledges the stickiness of past loves, relations, encounters, and
sexual contacts. The characters' relationships chime with Rodríguez's critique of
the common wisdom of artificially forgetting or erasing one's sexual past:

> The narrative of a singular defining, lifelong committed relationship, be it
> amorous, familial, or national, enforces an odd formulation of temporality —
> marking and remarking when a lifetime begins. Heterosexual social norms
> generally demand that we erase past loves, naming them (at best) developmental
> phases on the path to true love and communion, or (at worst) mistakes we
> would rather forget. (2014: 52)

Rodríguez continues to describe previous encounters as 'loves', and, in my own
writing I have had to battle a tendency to refer to all of the protagonists' sexual
encounters as encounters with 'lovers', a term that, while usually connoting a more
casual commitment than, say, partner, in its root implies a loving relationship. The
persistence of the term in my own writing about a novel that calls into question
the notion of 'love' is perhaps testament to the very stickiness of romantic, loving
concepts of sexual relationality.

The protagonist has a number of sexual encounters with characters whom they
do not deem to be lovers. Counter to the idealisation of the monogamous, loving
couple, the novel celebrates people and relationships that accept, even embrace, the
fluidity in their feelings, their affinities, and their desires. These loves, contacts,
and encounters, are viscous like honey and *stick* with the characters, obsessing them,
perhaps, but they also *shift*. The novel thus depicts a mutable conceptualisation of
desire that does not demand the constancy of a single lover or a claim to know one's
present *and future* selves and desires.

The novel's celebration of non-monogamy and promiscuity goes hand-in-hand with a conception of love and relationality in which no one possesses another — possess in the sense of owning another, rather than haunting them, though these might go hand in hand, as I explored in Part I on *Querida Nélida*. The transient relations between the characters, like the errant, erratic wandering of Equis and his often ephemeral encounters with others, offer a vision of desire and relationality that is not centred on possession or obedience. The protagonist and Robert/La Gran Puta have the following discussion:

> — [...] Sé que sóc miserable. No posseixo cap desig. [...]
> — Tens una empresa. *You are a businessomething.* Ha, ha, ha!
> — Encara no, Robert. Encara no és meva. A més a més... ¿i què? Jo parlo del desig, de posseir-ne un i d'obeir-lo.
> — T'equivoques, *my dear* — diu La Gran Puta — . Ningú no posseeix cap desig. És exactament al contrari. (141)

> > ['I know that I'm miserable. I don't possess a single desire. [...]
> > 'You have a business. *You are a businesssomething.* Hahaha!'
> > 'Not yet, Robert, It's not mine yet. Anyway... what's that got to do with anything? I'm talking about desire, about possessing and obeying a desire.'
> > 'You are wrong, *my dear*,' says The Great Whore. 'No one possesses desire. It's precisely the opposite.']

The protagonist, who wants to possess and obey a desire, describes Robert/La Gran Puta as someone from whom they have learnt a great deal. In this exchange, Robert reveals a vision of desire as involving expropriation, rather than possession. 'Improper' affinities are not based on the notion of possession of another, but, more loosely, on the acknowledgement that in reality one does not even possess one's self.

Marta Segarra advocates a counter-ideal of community that contests the more entrenched notion of community as plenitude, identity, completion, and purity. Drawing on Jean-Luc Nancy and Hannah Arendt, she sees community 'no como algo que "rellena" la brecha que existe entre los individuos sino como aquello que se sitúa en ese creux o vacío, en el "entre"' (2012: 9) [not as something that fills the gap between individuals, but something that is situated in that space, in the in-between]; in Segarra's analysis, community *requires* distance and difference between people. Her reading of community recalls Foucault's fragmented genealogy, the unravelling of the tapestry in *La nave* and the gaps in Sara T.'s sketch of Vivien and, for that matter, in Sappho's fragments. Segarra draws on the Italian philosopher Roberto Esposito who highlights the etymology of community — from the Latin *cum* meaning 'with' and *munus* meaning a 'duty', 'load', or 'compulsory gift' (Segarra 2012: 10). Crucially, for Esposito's analysis, a *munus* is a gift given, not received, not an expected or obliged exchange but a willing loss, which leads Esposito to suggest that the common 'begins where what is proper ends' (ibid). Therefore, in Esposito's vision of community, the sense of an individual as an undivided, self-sufficient total-ity gives way to vulnerable 'expropriation' of the self in an 'intimate diaspora' (ibid.).

The narrator-protagonist comments on efforts to theorise plenitude and coherence by way of German mathematician Georg Cantor's set theory (or 'teoria dels conjunts' in Catalan). The protagonist summarises the theory as an effort to bring together knowledge in a coherent whole: 'un llenguatge unificat amb el qual es pogués expressar tota la matemàtica i, potser, tot el coneixement' (81) [a unified language with which one could express all of mathematics and, perhaps, all knowledge]. Writing of their supportive relationship with their aunt, Mel/Cor states:

> Conca i jo constituíem un conjunt. Una mena de conjunt, si prenem la teoria dels conjunts des d'un punt de vista heterodox, que és el que s'hauria de fer amb totes les teories i, principalment, amb totes les lleis. Però per ser heterodox, s'ha d'estar en desacord. I per estar en desacord, s'ha de saber ser lliure. I *la llibertat és incòmoda, perquè és el més difícil d'organitzar que hi ha al món.* (85, my emphasis)

> [Conca and I made a set. A sort of set, if we approach set theory from a heterodox point of view, which is what one should do with all theories and, principally, with all laws. But in order to be heterodox, one has to be in disagreement. And to be in disagreement, one has to know how to be free. And *freedom is uncomfortable, because it is the most difficult thing in the world to organise.*] (my emphasis)

The comment that freedom is difficult and requires work suggests that relationality based on negotiations and desire rather than obligations may be difficult, complex work, but it is paradoxically required if human beings are to live as freely as possible.

Counter to the apparent security of possessing and obeying an imposed desire, Rodríguez values the 'precarious bonds' of queer community. With respect to a queer collective 'we', she writes: 'Rather than define itself through the exclusion of its others, this 'we' is continually coming together and coming undone, a precarious bond that performs its own disarticulation of desire and discontent' (2014: 1). The 'coming together and coming undone' recalls Nélida and Celia's sense of a fractured self in their (con)fusion with each other. Rodríguez queries the ideal of community as an extension of a normalised monogamy based on cohesion and closure. Referring to other ways of relating and forming communities, with alternatives to the nuclear family, she writes:

> investments in *lifelong*, monogamous attachments foster fictions of *linearity* and cohesion while denying the *simultaneity* of lived experience. Queers have a long history of loving and living differently, spinning out social and sexual networks and *coextensive* bonds with other temporal moments of affection and desire. In reality, our lives are always beginning anew, our lifetime is always the *new now* [...] we can enter 'committed' relationships over and over again, committing to the *forever*, to the now, to fidelity, to openness, to honesty, to caring, to pleasure, not always everything, always something else besides. These are the contracts of love in all its forms, contracts that are rewritten, undone, and renewed in time. (53, my emphasis)

Rodríguez proposes different ways of understanding temporality and relationality, beyond the constancy of monogamy. The contracts to which Rodríguez refers recall the exchange of letters in *Querida Nélida* that take the place of a single signed document. While Rodríguez refers to many different relationships as manifestations of love, unlike *Melalcor*, which questions the very idea of love, her reference to multiple relationships without set timelines nonetheless resonates with the many different relationships in *Melalcor*.

In the chapter titled 'El joc i la vida' [The Game and Life], the protagonist describes his/her/their understanding of Chinese solitaire, the game in which one jumps over marbles with other marbles in order to remove them from the board, the aim being to be left with just one marble on the board. The narrator comments:

> He tardat molt de temps a aconseguir una sola victòria. I ha estat precisament avui, el dia que he entès que no es tractava pas d'una victòria sinó del triomf de *la solidaritat més anònima*. Cap peça no té més importància que les altres. Avui he comprès que no s'eliminen ni es mengen entre elles, sinó que se *serveixen de pont, de contacte amb les altres*, de baules per mantenir-se al tauler fins que deixen de ser imprescindibles. (37)

> [It took me ages to achieve a single victory. And it was precisely today that I came to understand that it was not about victory but about the triumph of the most anonymous solidarity. No piece is more important that the others. Today I understood that the pieces do not eliminate or eat each other, but act as bridges, contact points with the other pieces, as links to keep themselves on the board until they are no longer essential.]

Their interpretation of the game is a prelude to the form of affinity they experience through Robert and Casilda, both of whom are their lovers at some point, and to other sexual contacts. It seems to be an acknowledgement and understanding that people appear, disappear, and reappear in each other's lives and that all of these people are important. It is a utopian vision of solidarity through love and an attempt to overcome hierarchical visions of human relationality in which one's partner is prioritised over everything and everyone else. In the multiplicity of timelines that both Rodríguez and the novel evoke through describing relationships that are ephemeral, simultaneous, interrupted, a simple vision of fidelity considered in terms of the longevity of the relationship is contested.

Fidelity is instead construed of as being true to one's desires and sincere in one's affections, rather than in terms of constancy at all costs, i.e. committing to being with someone in the same way forever. The protagonist admires Robert who 'havia estat capaç de deixar enrere tota una institució social. La Gran Puta no es movia segons el punt de vista. La Gran Puta tenia autèntics sentiments, i jo en fugia' (92) [had been able to leave behind an entire social institution. The Great Whore did not act in accordance with a point of view. The Great Whore had authentic feelings, and I ran away from them]; the protagonist admires Robert's embraces of a sticky, shifting heart. The form of the 'novel·la', with its forty-eight chapters across 232 pages that make it seem more like a series of vignettes, underscores its emphasis on ephemerality and interruption. Rather than the connected prose more characteristic of a conventional novel, the text's brief chapters, some of which are shorter than a page, are broken up with blank pages and title pages between each chapter; the novel's form reflects its challenge to constancy, longevity, and plenitude.

One of Rodríguez's comments on the duration of friendships, which she does not differentiate from romantic relationships, is particularly relevant to Company's depiction of friendship amongst Mel/Cor, Robert, Casilda, and the protagonist. Rodríguez writes: '[c]apable of lasting a lifetime or defined in a single moment, the corporeal intimacy of friendship blurs the lines used to separate the romantic, the sexual, and the social' (2014: 186). Honey, at heart, blurred and blurry lines of honey — shifting, but sticky. The entanglement of friendship and love is even greater in Romance languages; *amor, amistat* and David Vilaseca (2010) has explored poignantly the relevance of this for queer intimacy in male friendship.

We have seen the power of fleeting queer possibilities for a sociality based on desires that are fluid but sticky. These are 'improper' affinities, which involve joining with others but not considering them possessions. Whereas the family is depicted in the novel as going hand in hand with property and propriety, with the forces of procreation and guilt, with the aim of perpetuating and replicating itself, the queer affinities in the novel have promiscuity and ephemerality at their heart.

However, Robert and Casilda, after having lived in and through affinities beyond the family, are presented at the end of *Melalcor* as living with Robert's children back in the UK, where Robert was born. For Robert, then, the shedding of family and nation is partial and temporary. The ephemeral utopia of their lives in the house that was destroyed by the villagers could be considered in the light of Michael O'Rourke's readings of queer temporalities, via Muñoz: 'That not-yet-hereness (as well as an already-goneness) represents perverse temporalities in which glimpses of other possibilities and potentialities appear *fleetingly*' (2014: 34). However, like an 'interruption', like a chance encounter, a *fleeting* possibility may radically alter the status quo of relationality. Company's literary trajectory can also be described as evoking potentialities *fleetingly*. Having depicted affinities beyond the biological family and nation in *Querida Nélida*, *Melalcor*, and other works, in her more recent texts Company turns *to* the biological family and to the country where she was born.

Part III: Beyond Identity and Back Again in *Volver antes que ir* (2012) and *Por mis muertos* (2014)

Company's book-length autobiographical poem *Volver antes que ir* (2012) contains her reflections on a trip back to Buenos Aires, where both she and her late mother were born. In the poem, Company grapples with the tensions between a desire for a sense of belonging that may be appealing and comforting at times of disorientation or grief, and the apparent freedom of non-belonging, or impertinence, in a globalised age. I draw on Esposito's conception of community as entailing an *expropriation* of ourselves, as mentioned in Part II, to suggest that despite the turn to family and nation, in her later works Company continues to link impertinence not with non-belonging but with community, as in *Melalcor*.

In parts, the poem strives to conjure a coherent national identity through visions of a romanticised childhood in Argentina, which was emphasised in a performance of the poem at the Ateneu Barcelonès that I attended in June 2015. In that event, Company, as author-cum-performer, combined piano accompaniment, video footage shot by her father in Buenos Aires of a happy family gathering that appears to be a birthday of the young Company (aged one or two), her voice as she recited the poem, and audience participation through the collective reading of the extracts from Wikipedia and the Encyclopaedia Britannica that feature in *Volver antes que ir*. In the text, Company expresses a totalising desire — 'quiero todo' (36) [I want everything] — a longing for roots — 'Viajar a mi país de origen, ¿mis raíces?, era parte de la escritura' (10) [Travelling to my country of origin (my roots?) was part of the writing process] — and a wish to synthesise her life through poetry (13). She initially posits roots and synthesis as a foundation for belonging. However, the total forms that she alleges to seek are frustrated through the form and content of the poem.

Drawing on Butler's assertion in 'Giving an Account of Oneself' (2001) that the fractured self is an ethical basis for relating to others, I will explore how Company reconciles her desire for a sense of belonging with an awareness of the changeability of the self and the impossibility of fully knowing oneself. After doing so, I will turn briefly to Company's semi-autobiographical collection of short stories *Por mis muertos* (2014) to consider the queering of family inheritance via the figure of the aunt in two short stories. In the stories, rather than striving to move beyond family or to reclaim a coherent sense of national and familial identity through memories of her mother and childhood, Company turns to figures who were missing or removed from her life/the lives of the characters in the stories.[4]

On Impertinence and Rooting

As mentioned in Part II, in *Melalcor* the narrator describes the family as an outdated institution. The epigraph to *Querida Nélida* from Deuteronomy calls on believers to kill friends who tempt them from their family, nation, and God. The utopian move — or attempt to move — beyond family, nation, and religion in both *Querida Nélida* and *Melalcor* accords with a number of declarations Company has made in interviews: 'No me siento especialmente vinculada con ningún grupo y desde luego con ninguna patria ni con ninguna família ni religión' (Company 2014a) [I don't feel particularly linked with any group, let alone with any nation, family, or religion]. Much like Nélida's proud declaration to Celia that she is not a slave to societal structures, Company's assertion of her autonomy is clearly an overstatement: these structures persist and continue to trap us.

In contrast to her radical dismissal of kinship ties in interviews and her depictions of relations beyond the traditional Catholic family in *Querida Nélida* and *Melalcor*, Company returns to her own biological family in her more recent literary creations. The shift seems to align with Kaminsky's assertion that, in the diaspora, 'new ways of living are complicated by a sense of identity that persists in connecting the individual with the homeland' (1999: 17). *Volver antes que ir* is an exploration of parts of the author's identity that are inextricably and often uncomfortably linked to her childhood in Argentina. During the trip to Argentina that inspired the writing of the poem, Company read her deceased mother's childhood diary that her mother had written, aged twelve, in 1952 on her first trip to Spain to the hometown of her father — Company's grandfather — in Catalonia. Company made her own journey from Buenos Aires to Catalonia some twenty years later, for reasons not given in the poem, but possibly political given the timing of the move in 1973.[5]

The move to Barcelona from Argentina was evidently traumatic for the young Company. She describes her resentment vis-à-vis the feeling of foreignness prompted by her parents' decision, which she presents as evasive:

> ven el problema y lo esquivan
> se van a otro país por ejemplo
> y son extranjeros el resto de sus vidas (69)

> [they see the problem and dodge it
> they go to another country, for example
> and are foreigners for the rest of their lives]

Company as narrator here displays an acute awareness of what was lost in the move and nostalgia for a feeling of belonging, which is aligned in the poem with a clear sense of national identity.[6] In many respects, she thus essentialises the condition of being foreign in contrast to Peri Rossi's mobilization of it in *La nave*. In Company's nostalgic rendition of her return to Argentina and her remembrance of things past, we hear what Kaminsky describes as 'a discourse of desire, a desire to recuperate, repair, and return' (1993: 33), which is frequently present in texts written in exile.

One of the motivating factors for Company's return to Argentina appears to be a desire to lay bare the 'lies' she says she was told as a child prior to her family's move to Barcelona: 'La mentira, eso sí, te permite volver a empezar. Tanto trayecto por desandar, digamos, para llegar hasta la primera, para atreverte a mirarla y desnudarla' (17) [The lie, yes, the lie enables you to start over. There are so many steps to retrace to reach the first lie, to dare to look it in the eye and undress it]. For her, life in Barcelona is permeated by the lies that she was told by her family and she longs to return to her 'roots' in order to reach the truth. It is, of course, interesting that Company as the narrator in the poem, here expresses such a negative opinion of lying, given that Company is a writer of fiction. The naïve tone, especially at the beginning of the poem, seems crafted to reflect the perspective of a child; Company was nine when her family left Argentina.

Through the form of the poem and the prologue to *Por mis muertos*, Company nuances the somewhat naïve approach to truth and lies expressed at the beginning of *Volver antes que ir*. In the prologue to *Por mis muertos*, titled 'El abuelo de Andrea' [Andrea's Grandfather] (Andrea seems to be an alter-ego for Company), the narrator writes about Andrea's disappointment upon realising that many of the supposedly autobiographical stories that her grandfather tells her turn out to be 'mentira de principio a fin' (13) [lies from start to finish]. Her grandfather, the representative of family history, indeed, of genealogy, defends himself:

> la vida es aquello que narramos que es la vida, es lo que la gente cuenta, el modo en que la organiza con las palabras y con la imaginación; la vida por sí misma no es nada. La realidad es la ficción que cada cual elige. (ibid.)

> [life is what we narrate as life, the stories people tell, the way in which people organise life with words and imagination; life in itself is nothing. Reality is the fiction that each of us chooses.]

In the poem Company takes advantage of the power of fiction to shape 'reality' by willing into being an Argentine identity that she both narrates to 'los otros', i.e. other Argentines, and also fragments through the form of the poem:

> el primer avión fue una trampa que me tendieron
> *los míos* y así me separaron de *los otros*,
> pero yo siempre los quise, a *los otros*,
> los quiero,
> *los otros* son *los míos*,
> yo soy de *los otros* y *los otros* lo saben,
> o van a saber, van sabiendo, *yo les cuento*,
> *les voy contando*. (28–29, emphasis mine)

> [the first plane was a trap that *my people* set for me
> and in that way they separated me from *the others*,
> but I always loved them, *the others*,
> I love them,
> *the others* are *mine*,
> I belong to *the others* and *the others* know it,
> or they will know soon, they are discovering it, *I tell them*,
> *I'm telling them*.] (my emphasis)

Through the repetition of 'los míos' and 'los otros', she yet again essentialises national identity and belonging and points to a marked difference between those who stayed in Argentina and those who left, like she did. As well as her story-telling, Company also strives to make her sense of belonging in Argentina more concrete and tangible. While in Buenos Aires, she takes photos of the signs of street signs about which she has heard her mother, uncle, and grandmother speak, one of which appears in the prologue to the poem (11). Her effort to create a shared memory thus involves an indexical prop that serves to align name, image, and place to create a more concrete memory to back up her narrated belonging.

Company's turn to biological family is accompanied, moreover, by a turn to poetry, a genre that she has not previously cultivated. In the prologue to the poem, she writes, 'Por primera vez decido publicar versos, por primera vez escribo en argentino' (13) [For the first time I have decided to publish poetry, for the first time I am writing in Argentine]. The sense of recuperation of a lost Argentine identity is reflected in the fact that as well as being Company's first published poem, she declares it to be her first work to be published in 'argentino', her mother tongue. Given that the differences between the Argentine variety of Spanish and other varieties are relatively minor, Company's distinction between Spanish, a language in which she has previously published, and 'argentino', highlights her investment in recuperating a sense of difference. She hopes to regain the sense of belonging in Argentina that she believes she felt in the early years of her life, which she spent in Buenos Aires. She thus traces a matrilineal inheritance through at least three interrelated returns: to the biological mother, to the mother tongue, and to the motherland.

Company's shift from narrative to poetry mirrors, in inverse form, Marçal's shift from poetry to narrative described in Chapter One. Interestingly, despite the poetic penchant for elliptical, even fragmentary expression, Company deploys it to convey a sense of wholeness, rootedness, and belonging in the midst of feelings of loss and disorientation. As already mentioned, Company describes her turn to poetry in the prologue as an attempt to reach 'synthesis': 'el único modo de hablar de aquel tránsito serían los versos, los versos que permitieran las imágenes, las imágenes que permitieran la síntesis, la síntesis que procurara un modo de intentar decirlo todo con apenas casi nada' (13) [poetry was the only way to speak about that trip, poetry that could create images, images that could enable synthesis, synthesis that could find a way of trying to say everything with almost nothing]. Synthesis, from the Greek *suntithenai*, 'to place together', chimes with the root of 'poetry' as a 'piling up'; both terms hint at the bringing together of disparate elements. The subtle difference between a 'piling up' and 'a placing together' emphasises the tension in Company's poem between a harmonious joining or fitting into place (with her roots, perhaps) and the disorder and disharmony in thrusting things together that do not quite fit, as in a 'pile-up'.

Company's desire for synthesis, her need to 'decirlo todo' [say everything], can be read in the light of Kaminsky's suggestion that in order to move on from their pasts, diasporic subjects often need to contain the past through concrete memories. With echoes of Freud's notion of a healthy process of mourning, which I touched on in Part I, Kaminsky writes that '[t]he lost place of origin needs to be contained, to become manageable as memory' (1999: 42). In a sense, Kaminsky is describing a need to 'volver antes que ir', to return to the past and process it in order to move on. Company's desire to contain her whole person through the poetic form could be read as an attempt to enact the process Kaminsky describes. Company writes:

> Sé que todo
> está contenido en cada parte y sin embargo no me sirve
> cada parte
> : quiero todo. (38)

> [I know that everything
> is contained in each part and yet
> each part
> is not useful to me
> : I want everything.]

Yet again, the repeated reference to wholeness recalls Oliverio's total artwork, Sara T.'s search for a complete image of Vivien, and the idea of harmony as recomposing the complete tapestry in *La nave*. For the narrating voice in this poem, parts are not sufficient. In the prologue, Company also describes a desire for symmetry in her return to Argentina, a journey she planned to undertake by boat '[p]ara darle al diario de mi madre un regreso simétrico. Ella lo había escrito durante su travesía a España, jornada tras jornada, y yo lo leería durante mi travesía a la Argentina, jornada tras jornada también' (10) [to give my mother's diary a symmetrical return. She had written it on her voyage to Spain, day after day, and I would read it during my voyage to Argentina, day after day as well]. Along with the desire to repeat her mother's journey in reverse, as if closing a circle, she publishes the book when she is forty-nine, the age her mother was when she died. Company's concern for symmetry and repetition can be linked with the desire for order, comfort, and completeness that the narrator in *La nave* sees emblematised in the tapestry. The desire for completeness differs from the 'sketched' trip that was not taken in *Querida Nélida*, but the need for temporal order recalls Nélida's rigid schedule for the trip in one of her notebooks.

Scattered Subjectivities and Time Lags

Although Company deploys signifiers of desire that are typically linked to conservatism (order, comfort, completeness), she nonetheless troubles a straightforward return to her roots. On the one hand, she describes feeling at home in Argentina: 'Busqué códigos, claves. Entendí complicidades, ironías. Me sentí rodeada, allí también, de mi tribu' (11) [I looked for codes and keys. I understood their in-jokes and irony. I felt surrounded, there too, by my tribe]; on the other hand, she describes feeling like a foreigner: 'Sos una extranjera' (15) [You are a foreigner]. Once again, Kaminsky's comments are here germane: 'At first glance, it appears that those most insistent on remembering are those who *remained outside the country*' (20, my emphasis). Company notes that those to whom she wants to narrate her belonging — 'mi tribu', 'los míos' — are now scattered across the world:

> Los otros están en todas partes, es verdad
> : soy yo la que necesita estar acá (29)
>
> [The others are everywhere, it's true
> : it's me who needs to be here]

Company asserts a need to be in Argentina and thus to 'learn' how to be Argentine again. With an ironic tone, she refers to narratives of triumphant nationhood, such as the national anthem and celebrations of independence. She also describes her need to learn to 'speak again' i.e. to speak 'argentino', signalled mainly by the use of the 'vos' second person singular form in place of the 'tú' form in the poem. She refers to wanting to 'recuperate' her 'complete' self through words:

> aprender a hablar otra vez es el principio de todo [...] son palabras recuperadas, que están en vos, que te persiguieron hasta acá, fieles a su misión, a su intención de recuperarte completa, ambiciosas, patrióticas ellas, como de 25 de mayo y de bicentenario y de himno, oíd, mortales (16)
>
> [learning to speak again is the start of everything [...] they are recuperated words that are inside you, that followed you here, faithful to their mission, to their intention to recuperate you whole, they are ambitious, patriotic, like those of the 25th of May and of the bicentenary, and of the national anthem, 'hear, mortals']

Foucault criticises the oft-fetished notion of the 'inviolable identity' of 'origin' (1984a: 79). He specifically refers to the *illusion* of a homeland to which one can return:

> The purpose of history, guided by genealogy, is not to discover the roots of our

> identity, but to commit itself to its dissipation. It does not seek to define our
> unique threshold of emergence, the homeland to which metaphysicians promise
> a return; it seeks to make visible all of those discontinuities that cross us. (95)

In line with Foucault's 'discontinuities', Company highlights the role of chance in identity formation, which Foucault describes as 'the exteriority of accidents' (81): 'Te tiraron al aire, fuiste a parar a otro hemisferio, rodaste, rodaste de canto tanto tiempo y tu naturaleza te lleva a aterrizar del lado en que te conociste' (16) [They threw you up in the air and you ended up in another hemisphere, you rolled, rolled on your side for so long and your nature led you to land on the side on which you discovered yourself]. Company expresses the contradictory sentiments she feels: she longs not to feel out of place in the nation, but she is aware that one's belonging to one nation or another is often the result of chance and occurrences beyond one's control.

Despite her desire for synthesis in the poem and its performance, Company signals the impossibility of such mastery. In this way, she complicates totalising representations, as Peri Rossi did with the tapestry in *La nave* and with Oliverio's map in *El libro*, and as Marçal did through Sara T.'s script in *La passió*. In the poem, the partial frustration of wholeness occurs through the interruption of her written text with texts from the internet and elsewhere and through the use of semi-colons throughout the poem, interrupting its flow. The Wikipedia articles scattered throughout the poem enact the interruption of globalised media in a poem about the nation and national belonging that is at once nostalgic and ironic. The Wikipedia articles are on souvenirs (objects that fetishise places, as the poem does), on migration (which Company has experienced first hand), and on Facebook — the social media platform through which Company cultivates a virtual community of readers. I will return to the author in virtual space later.

Reflecting the fragmented form of the poem, in its multimedia performance Company enacted a disruption of totality, completion, and situatedness in one time and place. She interrupted the recital by projecting video footage (of herself taken by her father) onto a large screen on the stage. She accompanied the footage with live piano; Company is a classically trained pianist. The evocation of the joy of her childhood in Buenos Aires, pieced together through text, video, and live music, contrasted with the vexed tone of her reading of the poem in the recital. She stopped playing the piano and paused the video to read parts of the poem from different places on the stage, literally scattering the pages on the stage after she read them, a gesture that highlighted her diasporic poetics. As mentioned earlier, the word 'diaspora' derives from the Greek *diaspeirein* meaning to 'scatter across'.

In the poem itself, Company stages the frustration of her desire for synthesis through describing the breakdown of an indivisible self. She refers to herself as 'vos' and 'yo', claiming not to understand herself and her desires. She then questions whether or not one needs to have a coherent narrative of who one is:

> hacés preguntas que no entendés ni vos.
> (Hay que ponerse de acuerdo en lo que es vos,
> o yo, o vos y/o yo). (O no). (27)

> [you ask questions that even you don't understand.
> (You have to agree on what is you,
> or me or you and/or me). (Or not).]

In the words of Foucault, each person contains 'many mortal souls' (1984a: 94), which are unable to be mastered by the powers of *synthesis*' (ibid., my emphasis). Striving for coherence and totality, for the synthesis that Company seeks through writing, is in itself an approach that Butler questions:

> Is the task to cover over the breakage, the rupture, which is constitutive of the 'I' through a narrative means that quite forcefully binds the elements together in a narration that is enacted as if it were perfectly possible, as if the break could be mended and defensive mastery restored? (2001: 36)

Part and parcel of the fracturing of a 'synthesis' of the self is a sense of temporal disruption that Company experiences alongside her spatial displacement:

> Es una sucesión cronológica desordenada,
> cosas que ocurren después tendrían que ser antes,
> hay hechos que deberían pasar y no les da tiempo (34)

> [It a disordered chronological succession,
> things that happen afterwards should have happened before,
> there are things that should happen, but they don't have time]

This chronological disorder is an example of what flores conceptualised as 'inter-ruqción', a queer interruption which may trigger dramatic change, as discussed in Chapter Two. An openness to what initially may be an unsettling sense of the unpredictability of events links with Equis's wandering in *La nave*, the unsigned contract in *Querida Nelida*, and the protagonists leaving the village to start a different life elsewhere in *Melalcor*. For Butler, the disruption of teleology and constancy is a characteristic of autobiographical narration, which she links with loss and impossible recuperation, noting that the story necessarily 'begins *in medias res*' (2001: 27). Butler writes: 'My account of myself is partial, haunted by that for which I have no definitive story' (27). She criticises the normative goal of psychoanalysis 'to produce a coherent narrative' (32), suggesting that narrative interruption rather than 'narrative reconstruction' (32) are the basis for ethical community. If the self accepts that it cannot know itself, it is more likely to accept the unknown within the other (27).

The holes or gaps in a poem (and in the performance of a poem) that is a self-proclaimed search for identity bring to mind Segarra's conceptualisation of the 'sujeto agujereado' (2012: 19) [pierced subject]. With echoes of her comments on community that I drew on in my discussion of *Melalcor*, Segarra posits that the 'sujeto agujereado' is the counter-ideal for a basis for community that may overcome entrenched notions of plentitude, purity, and completion. She writes of a 'sujeto agujereado' as the ideal building block — or perhaps 'sieve' is more appropriate, following De Certeau, as outlined in the last chapter — of community. Segarra writes:

> la escritura no constituirá nunca una cadena que ate los fragmentos de 'viven-cias' en un yo coherente, sino que muestra esta falta, este vacío constitutivo del

sujeto, impidiendo que tanto la poeta como sus lectoras nos refugiemos en un relato reconfortante que nos dé cohesión y sentido. (2012: 17)

[writing will never constitute a chain that ties together the fragments of lived experience in a coherent self, rather it shows this lack, this gap that is constitutive of the subject, preventing both the poet and readers from taking refuge in a comforting tale that gives us meaning and cohesion.]

The references to a chain and to tying or binding recalls religion, the family, and traditional conceptions of genealogy. Perhaps, then, Company's interruption and frustration of 'wholeness' indicates not the *failure* of the search for community, but, as in *Melalcor*, the sticky grounds for its ethical possibility.

While Company hopes to synthesise a coherent identity through her poem, she is evidently aware of the illusory nature of any such coherence. She dedicates the book to the patron saint of illusionists. At the end of the poem, she writes: 'vio la luz, impreso, el día de la onomástica de San Juan Bosco, Patrono de los Magos, Ilusionistas y Cineastas' (84) [this book saw the light, in printed form, on the Day of Saint John Bosco, the Patron Saint of magicians, illusionists, and film-makers]. The reference could be read as an ironic indication that the fictions through which we represent ourselves are illusions that we conjure to comfort ourselves and to make sense of an often disorientating and complex world. Company writes:

> : un país no es,
> de ningún modo,
> el lugar donde nacemos
> : un país, si acaso, es el tablero que se elige
> para vencer los miedos de vivir (50)

> [: a country is not,
> in any way,
> the place where we are born
> : a country, if anything, is the drawing board that one chooses
> to overcome the fear of living]

But who is the illusionist in the poem? During the performance, as well as scattering the physical pages of text across the stage, Company also orchestrated the scattering of the spoken word across the room. In an authorial play and ploy, she enjoined the audience to participate in the recital through reading aloud in unison the four extracts from Wikipedia and the Encyclopaedia Britannica that are included in the text (she gave print-outs of the extracts to the audience). Company told the audience to enact a sense of 'vulnerability' through reading aloud in English without attempting to disguise their 'foreign' accents. She was of course assuming that no one in the audience was a native English speaker or had an 'English' accent, ironically homogenising her audience through her attempt to stage difference. The performance also staged the *appearance* of the author letting go of her authorial authority through the interruption of her authorial voice with voices from all over the room. However, Company was still in control, directing the audience on how, when, and what to read. The effect in the performance recalls Bourdieu's oracle effect, which I mentioned in relation to *El libro*, in which, through multiplying the singularity of the authorial voice, the author paradoxically reasserts her authority all the more. Once again we return to Peri Rossi's authorial conundrum of how to contest authority without being authoritarian. Authority and power are at play in Company's increasing engagements with the virtual world — which is often regarded as potentially more democratic and less hierarchical than the offline world — in both the poem and *Por mis muertos*.

A Turn to the Virtual

As well as a turn to family and to her place of birth, *Volver antes que ir* and *Por mis muertos* involve a turn to virtual spaces and online platforms. The texts are directly connected as the prologue to *Volver antes que ir*, titled 'Secreto', appears with the same title as a section of *Por mis muertos*. We have already seen that Company uses a variety of media and that she performs her work in different fora, creating communities of readers, observers, and participants who may be physically present in the same place or may engage with her and others in virtual space such as on her blog or Facebook page. *Por mis muertos* directs the reader from the physical text to online content through scannable QR codes. If readers scan the codes with a smartphone, the codes take them to online content such as Company's blog, photos, her sister's website, Wikipedia, and images online. The inconspicuous presence of the codes in the book encourages the reader to interact with the book through a device; the reading process is therefore mediated by technology.

Company's drawing the reader online to her blog further blurs the already hazy lines between fiction and autobiography. The photo of Company and her then wife on the front cover of *Por mis muertos* and the prologue to the collection already encourage the reader to approach the stories in the light of events in Company's life, which perhaps narrows their readings to the biographical; or, more accurately, what the reader *believes to be* the biographical. In the use of new information technologies and new media, does the role of the author change radically? Is the virtual space more open, more collaborative, somehow truer?

The virtual space may seem more democratic, but virtual platforms such as blogs and social networks can also conceal power imbalances and the manipulation of content, perhaps even more so than the printed word, precisely because they often allege to be more shaped by anonymous users than by specific figures of authority. In *Volver antes que ir* Company juxtaposes an outdated, heteronormative entry from the Encyclopaedia Britannica on 'Human Reproduction', which is described as the '...ability of an individual or couple to reproduce through normal sexual activity' (42). In the printed Encyclopaedia, knowledge appeared fixed and dictated from an authority. She juxtaposes the entries with Wikipedia articles, in which the information is provided by many people, is subject to frequent changes, and is frequently signalled within the articles themselves as being incomplete and partial. The juxtaposition of the encyclopaedia entries and more 'progressive' perspectives in the Wikipedia articles chosen by Company might lead the reader to deduce that Wikipedia is part of a world in which knowledge can be shaped by more people, better reflect diverse perspectives, and *perhaps* be more up-to-date. However, this is a dangerous comparison. The virtual encyclopaedia, for its very openness, is prone to 'fake news' and moral relativism. We should consider Company's engagement with readers in the virtual space of Facebook and her blog with similar suspicion.

In *Por mis muertos*, the reader of Company's fiction is sent to engage with Company's posts allegedly about her own life, complete with photos, on her blog. Readers might have the impression that with the book alone they are not getting the full picture for there is always other material on other media to explore. However, they cannot get the full picture going online either. In Company's aforementioned interview with GAYLES.TV in 2014, Company expressly reminders viewers and readers that one cannot be sure whether information online is true or not. In so doing she entreats the reader to be suspicious of her own authorial truths; ironically, this could be read as another way of directing readers' textual engagement. An author's blog that seems to offer information about their personal life may well be as fictional as their fiction. The QR codes and the websites to which they link might give the impression of providing some factual background to the text, but truth is not guaranteed. Like the narrator in *La nave* who tells readers to guess which real cities the initials in the novel denote, Company seems to enjoy playing such games with readers who are keen to align fiction directly with reality.

In *Volver antes que ir* and its performance, there is a constant tension between, on the one hand, a turn to the concrete origin of identity in Company's journey back to Buenos Aires and the presence of readers/spectators at the performance of *Volver antes que ir* — that Company did not want recorded so the experience would be a one off, only to be experienced by those physically in attendance — and, on the other hand, the deterriorialisation of community and belonging through virtual interactions. The virtual interactions in *Volver antes que ir* and *Por mis muertos*, and the participative performance of the former, mark a simultaneous opening up of the creative process on the one hand, and the reemergence of the present, visible, overseeing figure of the author on the other. The texts therefore point to shifts in authorial authority in a virtual age, at once reduced (through collaborative creations between authors and their readers) and emphasised (through a proliferation of biographical sources online and virtual channels of communication through which writers might communicate with their readers and vice versa). Paradoxically, perhaps, the interactive virtual space in which readers can offer their comments on Company's work marks the rebirth of the author; a reconfigured author, but an author all the same.

From the Maternal to the Materteral

The rebirth of the author in Company's later texts is concurrent with Company's turn, or return, to the family. In the 'Herencia y elección' [Inheritance and Choice] part of *Por mis muertos*, Company explores alternatives to matrilineal and patrilineal inheritance through stories of aunts, biological and otherwise. She had already gestured towards such inheritance through *Melalcor*'s Tía Conca who defends Robert and Casilda and introduces the protagonist to them. The word to describe the attitude of an aunt to their nieces and nephews (i.e. the equivalent of the more commonly used 'avuncular', relating to uncles) is 'materteral'. That the term 'materteral' is decidedly rarer, more pedantic, and more humorous than 'avuncular' perhaps hints at the dismissal or overlooking of this alternative female line of transmission. 'Herencia y elección' points to the influence of the family history that we inherit, the ways we might choose to escape it, and how this escape is always incomplete. The stories in this part of the collection narrate the possibility of tracing alternative relational configurations that existed alongside patriarchal models of the nuclear family. I will explore two of the three stories here: 'La carta perdida de Andrea Mayo' (henceforth 'La carta') and 'Dos cuentos de amor' (henceforth 'Dos cuentos'). Both texts involve the inheritance or discovery of texts after the death of someone in the family, as in *Volver antes que ir*.

In 'La carta perdida', the aunt figure, Andrea Mayo, is a writer and past lover of the narrator's late mother and was present when Inés, the narrator, was ('artificially') conceived. After her mother's death, Inés discovers a letter that her 'aunt' had sent to her, which her mother had withheld. Mayo's imagining of her relationship with her ex-lover's child reveals her belief in the possibility of a genealogy expressed in familial terms but unrelated to biology, child-rearing, or a relationship through the law. She recalls in her letter that she was present, touching Inés's mother at the moment of conception: 'Justo ese día se te antojó empezar a existir. Y yo estaba allí, con la mano de Sara entre las mías' (94) [On that very day you decided to start existing. And I was there, with Sara's hand within mine]. She conceptualises her affective bond with Sara and Inés in familial terms, referring to what she sees as the position she ought to fill as Inés's 'tía'.

Mayo imagines what her relationship with her 'niece' would be like if Sara had allowed her to be involved in Inés's upbringing: 'pienso de pronto en el futuro, en un futuro no tan lejano, algo así como dentro de veinte años, y me resulta difícil concebir que tú y yo no seremos la sobrina y la tía que deberíamos ser' (91) [all of a sudden I think about the future, a not very distant future, within about twenty years, and it is difficult to conceive of the idea that you and me won't be the niece and aunt that we should be]. Despite not being a presence in Inés's life, Mayo believes that she has an unbreakable bond with the child that she saw conceived:

> Aunque nunca llegues a conocerme [...] formo parte de tu vida. [...Sara y yo] vivimos juntas las cosas más importantes de nuestras vidas, y eso está ahí como una herida en mi caso y tal vez como un virus en la suya, pero está ahí, indeleble. (101)

> [Even if you never meet me [...] I am part of your life. [...Sara and I] experienced the most important things in our lives together, and this remains as a wound in my case and perhaps as a virus in hers, but it is there, inerasable.]

Describing her history with Sara as a wound or a virus emphasises the long-lasting memory of pain. These are ruptures that, perhaps paradoxically, bind. For Mayo, her relationship with Sara is formative and cannot be erased, despite the solitude they have experienced and the breakdown of their relationship: 'Estuvimos bastante solas — la soledad es una de las principales características de la homosexualidad en su primera etapa' (97) [We were quite alone; solitude is one of the primary characteristics of the first stages of homosexuality]. Isolation is an issue that was addressed, to differing degrees, in the novels I analysed in Parts I and II of this chapter. The story ends with Inés trying to get in touch with Mayo. It is telling that we do not know the narrator's name until it is mentioned affectionately by Mayo in the final lines of her letter — this emphasises, again, her part in the bringing into being of Inés.

In 'Dos cuentos', two women are on honeymoon and one of them tells the other a story of an aunt with whom she is barely in touch as the aunt became estranged from the family as they were disapproving of her sexuality. The narrator had felt close to her aunt when she was younger and wanted to keep seeing her, but her parents would not let her because, as the narrator explains, '[e]staban más atentos a la educación que a la alegría' (123) [they were more attentive to moral upbringing than to happiness]; part of their 'education' of their daughter was to keep her away from the influence of her aunt. The narrator explains that when she was older, her requests to see her aunt were met with lies, as she was told that her parents had lost touch with her aunt. She remarks: 'Estoy segura de que pensaron que iba a ser una mala influencia para mí. No entienden que la única sexualidad que se impone o se contagia por miedo a lo desconocido es la heterosexualidad' (125) [I'm sure that they thought that she was going to be a bad influence on me. They don't understand that the only sexuality that is imposed or contagious due to fear of the unknown is heterosexuality]. The narrator notes that the force of 'compulsory heterosexuality', which supposedly sustains the sacred family, required, in the case of her aunt's 'excommunication', its partial breakdown.

Upon returning to Barcelona after their honeymoon the women are able to track down the narrator's aunt, Tía Malena, and 'su eterna novia' [her eternal girlfriend], Enriqueta. The newlyweds visit the elderly couple a few times, enchanted by the story of what they lived through in order to be together. The narrator and her wife learn that Tía Malena and Enriqueta were both forced to marry men, but that they also remained in a relationship, conducting their own secret ceremony just after their marriages to men: 'Se casaron primero con los hombres. Y después ellas, en una ceremonia simbólica, a escondidas, y escribieron sus votos en dos trozos de tela que recortaron de la sábana en que las violaron la noche de bodas' (125) [First they married the men. Then, in a secret symbolic ceremony, they wrote their vows on two piece of cloth that they cut from the sheets on which they were raped on their wedding nights]. The text(ile)s constitute the material of a queered inheritance. When Tía Malena dies, Enriqueta gives the women the pieces of bedsheet on which they wrote their vows. The bedsheet, a site of violence, is resignified to mark the bond between Malena and Enriqueta and, later, their bond across time with future lesbian lovers. The narrator notes that when Enriqueta hands over the pieces '[i]ba a decirnos algo, pero prefirió que lo imaginásemos' (126) [she was going to say something to us, but she preferred to let us imagine it]; their queer textual inheritance, as in the other texts, is open to their imaginations.

Indeed, in both of these stories, what is handed down does not constitute a complete, single, linear inheritance. Crucially, the piece of cloth embroidered with Tía Malena and Enriqueta's vows is a scrap torn or cut from the wedding night bedsheets of the aunt's heterosexual marriage, which symbolises a relationship that was implicated in patriarchy rather than separate to it. In 'La carta perdida', the letter from the narrator's 'aunt' is lost, used for different ends, found many years later; its deliverance is not simple. The two stories thus reflect Ohi's claim that 'thwarted transmission is both a locus of queer eroticism and a way of rethinking literary and cultural transmission' (2015: 4).

Through both stories, Company points to conceptions of queer kinship beyond *and* within the confines of relationships determined by blood and law. Once again, rather than dismissing the family as antithetical to the queer, a queer family history is posited as a validating force for alternative personal genealogies. The book, dedicated to Company's (now ex-)wife Inma and featuring a photo from their wedding on the front cover, marks the author's apparent renewed faith in alternative family configurations within the framework of traditional institutions such as marriage. In addition, a return to or resurgence of family members who have died in both stories — as was the case with the poem — signals that just as the queer haunts the family, the family haunts the queer. I could say, indeed, that the queer remains obsessed by the family, and the family by the queer.

Company's oeuvre points to the ambiguities and complexities within the family, the nation, and the queer, which are inflected within each other. Her vision of identity, affinity, and community across the works studied here demonstrates that the 'queer insists' (O'Rourke 2014) and 'be-longs', as Freeman has so eloquently argued in her reading of a false etymology of belonging as 'being long' through time, i.e. persisting (2011: 299). But just as the queer insists and persists, so do the family and nation. Vital to Company's project is the engagement with multiple and coexisting temporalities. The family and nation cannot be, and are not, dismissed entirely. Instead, they are queered, twisted, turned, morphed, and even reborn — just like the figure of the author.

Notes to Chapter 3

1. John's Gospel describes Christ as God's 'Word made flesh'. Given that the epigraph to the novel is taken from Deuteronomy, the biblical references are significant: Nélida's word runs counter to the words in the epigraph, which are a commandment not to travel beyond the bounds of family, nation, and religion.

2. The Biblioteca Nacional de Catalunya took its current name in 1981, the same year Company wrote *Querida Nélida*, following the Llei de Biblioteques of April 1981, passed by the Generalitat de Catalunya. It was first opened at the Biblioteca de l'Institut d'Estudis Catalans and, under Franco, from 1940, it was the Biblioteca Central. <http://www.bnc.cat/Coneix-nos/Cronologia> [accessed 4 August 2019].

3. See Acedo Alonso 2008a and 2008b; Torras 2008; Gutiérrez Pardina 2006.

4. Company deliberately blurs fiction and reality in *Por mis muertos*. In an interview with GAYLES.TV she says that people often ask her if all the stories in *Por mis muertos* are true. She comments that in the collection she deliberately wants to highlight the subjectivity of truth and how easy it can be to make fiction appear true (Company 2014a). As I note in Chapter Two, for Foucault the author represents societal 'fear [of] the proliferation of meaning' (1984: 119). Company seems to be playing with the tendency of some readers to limit meaning by seeking some 'truth' through biographical details of the author, particularly in texts that seem (or are alleged to be) partly autobiographical.

5. The Chilean military dictatorship presided by General Augusto Pinochet lasted from 1973 to 1990 and the dictatorship in Uruguay from 1973 to 1985. Argentina's military junta held power from 1976 to 1983, though tensions existed prior to this date, as in the other Southern Cone countries, and some date the beginning of the highly repressive period that led to the so-called 'Proceso de Reorganización Nacional' to 1969.

6. My slippage between Company the author and Company the narrator is inevitable in the analysis of an autobiographical work in which Company deliberately plays with the slippage between fiction and reality. Where it seems like Company is adopting the perspective of her younger self or someone else, I have endeavoured to indicate this. Much of the poem has an ironic tone in which Company seems to be gently mocking her own desires and hopes, or those of her younger self. Perhaps in believing that I can differentiate between Company the narrator and Company the author I am falling into precisely the trap into which Company hopes to draw her readers, as evident in her aforementioned comments on GAYLES.TV.

CODA

> no one set of practices or relations
> has the monopoly on the so-called radical,
> or the so-called normative [...]
> it's the binary of normative/transgressive
> that's unsustainable,
> along with the demand that anyone
> live a life that's all one thing
> — NELSON (2016: 91–93)

Fittingly, it has been a challenge to complete a book on the potential in fragment-ation, on the limitations of mastery and coherence, on the provocative and erotic force of the unfinished work, on the disruptive pleasures of unravelling and interrupting texts and textiles, or, indeed, 'interruqting' them, following flores's rendering of queer/cuir interruptions as 'interruqciones' (2013). To end a book concerned with queer genealogies with a 'coda', from the Latin for tail, seems more appropriate than to follow it with a 'conclusion', from the Latin for 'to shut completely'. Although perhaps to shut a book concerned with futurity completely would be to (re)inscribe precisely the sort of contradiction that is so dear to the queer.

The queer, with its twists and turns, does not turn away from contradiction. It is an anti-institutional movement, born in the streets, which has been theorised, and institutionalised, in the Academy. Queer theory seeks to be attentive to the minoritarian, the peripheral, and the deviant, and yet, as an umbrella term, it paradoxically replicates some of the effects of Anglophone hegemony. It is a move-ment against reductionist labels that has become a label proudly worn. Where the queer sticks to fluid anti-identitarian positions, it makes a 'fetish of fluidity' (Epps 2001) and becomes, paradoxically, cryptoessentialist (Fuss 1990). Many queers protest the exclusions of heteronormativity even as we lament inclusion as a loss of a radicality and decry 'homonormativity'. Queer writers and critics thus invoke an incoherence that ironically comes to cohere, a tarrying with kaleidoscopic, fragmentary, imperfect, unravelling, and interrupted forms that *brings together* the works that I have studied in this book.

My monograph structure traces an increasingly diasporic scattering. Each chapter looks at more texts than the previous one, but the proliferation of texts falls into a pattern of its own, forming a Trinity, twice over: Chapter One in one part, Chapter Two in two parts, Chapter Three in three parts. Given that all of the writers come from a Catholic background, as is reflected in their works and intertexts (in Peri Rossi the Tapestry of Creation depicting Genesis; in Marçal the Passion and the

'Introit'; in Company *Querida Nélida's* epigraph from Deuteronomy and the 'Gran Culpa' in *Melalcor*, as well as the Sacred Heart that the title evokes), perhaps a queer trinity is appropriate: mothers, daughters... holey spirits? Or, perhaps, especially given the importance of Sappho in this book, the two tripartite structures reflect the dialectic triangulation of pre-Christian Attic philosophy. Possible lines for future inquiry might pay closer attention to plurilingualism in Barcelona through a more diverse corpus in linguistic, religious, and economic terms.

Queer genealogies explore how relationality is *written* and how it interacts with the biological, the familial, the temporal, the national, the authorial, with relations that cannot be eliminated completely. We may try to escape such structures and norms, as Nélida does, but they continue to leave their mark on us. For instance, even as I have challenged the universalising, allegedly objective, authoritative subject, I have continued to conjure the plural 'we' of readers, a rhetorical convention. We can endeavour to write over and amongst the marks left by our relations, but in doing so we create palimpsests, haunted by the spectral traces of prior people, places, and things.

All of the texts analysed constantly navigate contradictions. The authors and their characters often reveal the perils of the family, yet seek the family, albeit a reconfigured one, despite themselves: Marçal searches for symbolic mothers amongst her literary predecessors; Peri Rossi depicts an alternative inheritance through cousins; Company returns to the motherland, the mother tongue, and her mother's writing. Similarly, the authors challenge the violence of national identity in their texts, yet are caught in its webs, despite themselves: Vivien renounces her English identity to be reborn as French; Federico flees the family home and joins a guerrilla movement that is suspicious of foreignising influences; Company as narrator in *Volver antes que ir* longs to feel belonging as she returns to her 'roots' in Argentina. The texts are at once utopian — pointing to both no place and a better place, a 'Terra de Mai', in Marçal's words — and grounded in particular, if disrupted, locations. Utopian Lesbos is mobilised in *La passió* and reterritorialised in Paris and in Barcelona. Equis's journey with no fixed route passes through vague, yet concrete, locations. The guerrillas in *El libro*, set in the Southern Cone in the 1960s, live amongst the mountains and the streams of an unspecified country that appears on a map that Oliverio defaces. Two women in Barcelona plan a trip to nowhere in *Querida Nélida*, a trip that obsesses them long after its possibility has faded.

Castle laments the ghostly lesbian, wanting to 'bring the lesbian back into focus' (1993: 2), but the texts in my corpus suggest that the ghost may be a figure of desire, one that engages with the past, the future, and the present. My readings of the texts show that they are attuned to different but interrelated temporalities: simultaneity, ephemerality, spectrality, and futurity, amongst others. Given the themes of haunting and obsession that recur in this book, it is not surprising that I maintain that previous alliances cannot be swept away, fully and finally, with a gesture of the will. The family, the nation, and the city are present in the texts; fractured, altered, but lingering all the same. What is at play is the difference between utopia and reality, between a *formless* no-place that we can shape with our desires and imagination — our 'relatos' — and the *forms* of compromise that visibility in the world entails in — our 'relaciones'.

We have seen that Marçal calls for a genealogy of women writers that is contingent and collaborative. It is possible to recuperate texts and to (re)create an inheritance, but without creating a complete counter-tradition. It is a *moving* tradition, in that it shifts and in that it *moves* others, inciting them to partake in its creation. My response to the not uncommon lament that lesbian texts are mutilated, censored, and fragmented, that they are not affirmative enough, not explicit enough, has been to grapple with *why* desire is often troubled or *implicit*. I ask what implicit, fragmented texts suggest about queer transmission. The texts are *implicit* because the writers, for all their differences, recognise that readers, as human beings, are enfolded and entwined, *implicated*, in the lives and stories of others.

As I mentioned in the introduction, Peri Rossi presents the reader and writer as desiring subjects. They transmit, translate, and transpose new modes of relationality through literature. Collaborative creations permeate the texts: in *La passió* the reader navigates lines from Vivien, Sappho, and Marçal via Sara T.; in *La nave* Peri Rossi's narrator dialogues with the anonymous creators of the tapestry; in *El libro* Federico creates texts with his cousins Oliverio and Aurelia; in *Querida Nélida* Nélida and Celia write together; and in *Volver antes que ir* Company engages with her mother through the poem's main intertext — her mother's childhood diary. Such collaborative endeavours comprise a 'patchwork', as Otero Vidal (2011) has remarked, made of scraps from multiple places, in keeping with Halberstam's 'scavenger methodology' (1998). Like scholars of Sappho, those involved in the creations will look in the ruins of art, the rubbish heaps of history, and the debris of their own disciplines.

The book title refers to 'transnational Barcelona' and pays attention to the circulation of texts, ideas, and people across and between places. However, the texts also point to how transnational circulation is inextricably entangled in the movement of capital. Marçal, a working-class Catalan writer turns to wealthy cosmopolitan heiresses in Paris in *La passió*. The disciplinary happiness that Peri Rossi critiques in *La nave* is a force that is often at the service of capitalism and the *degree* to which one can afford to be nomadic, to move beyond family and nation — literally and metaphorically — depends on one's economic and cultural capital. *El libro* is set largely in an aristocratic house and the background to the political inheritance of Oliverio from Federico is that of the Marxist guerrilla movement confronting the right-wing old guard. In *Querida Nélida*, Celia and Nélida grapple in their epistolary exchanges with an uneven economy of desire. Nélida decries the structures that bind her and others, writing of her power to operate beyond such structures, in words that echo calls for free-market neoliberalism.

The Catalan capital, in some ways a victim of this neoliberalism, is at once central and incidental to the study, at once insistent and elusive. In the introduction, I mention Hernández's analysis of an 'autonomous' or 'indigenous tradition' of lesbian literature in Catalonia, centred on Barcelona and formed by authors such as Riera, Moix, and Tusquets. The idea of lesbian literature — and lesbian identity, whatever that of the authors — reveals, as noted, a concern with origin. However, as I have shown through my readings of these texts, genealogy does not have to remit to a pure origin, tracing continuous lines from it, as in arborescent conceptions of trunks and branches, centres and peripheries. Genealogy may also pay attention to the nuances of texts and contexts, their movements and impurities, their promiscuous plays, their excesses, omissions, and gaps. Foucault's words, quoted in the epigraph and in the introduction of this book, bear repeating at its close: 'Genealogy is gray, meticulous, and patiently documentary. It operates on a field of entangled and confused parchments, on documents that have been scratched over and recopied many times' (1977: 76).

In contrast to Hernández's concern with an 'indigenous' or 'autonomous' tradition, the texts in my corpus form transnational queer genealogies that call into question the very notions of autonomy, indigeneity, and origin through complex webs of entangled and confused transnational intertexts, translations, and transpositions. Marçal draws on Sappho's paradigmatically fragmented extant works to map a fractured genealogy through Sappho's peripheral — Aeolic rather than Attic — voice and the peripheral (for little known) works of transnational Vivien. Marçal mixes her words with theirs through including in her novel translations into Catalan of their poetry. Peri Rossi writes her diasporic characters in *La nave* into the frayed origin story of the Tapestry of Creation. In *El libro*, despite Abuela Clara and the uncles' attempts to keep the outside world out, it intrudes into the aristocratic house in an unspecified city that seems to be Montevideo. Company's works shuttle between Barcelona and Buenos Aires, as well as rural Catalonia, Paris, and the UK. And *yet* the texts recognise and stage the allure of coherence, or a comforting sense of completion.

The tensions in the texts between, on the one hand, wholeness, coherence, and clarity and, on the other hand, fragmentation, incoherence, and ambiguity translate onto the very tensions that have repeatedly resurfaced between the often comforting notions of pure and simple origins that are often violently at odds with disordered and disorderly implications with others (other people, other nations). These tensions lie at the heart of the contemporary global landscape. The resonances of the Ship of Fools with boats of migrants in the Mediterranean trying to reach the shores of places such as Lesbos in an era of nations striving to be 'great again', is a reminder that it is a 'greatness' built on xenophobia and set notions of who belongs where. The genealogies that we trace and create, and the ways in which we trace and create them, have implications for how we see the relations between ourselves and others. It is ever more imperative that we pay close attention to the queer kaleidoscopic bringing together of disparate fragments if we are to navigate difference in an increasingly entwined and yet ever more fractious world.

BIBLIOGRAPHY

Acebrón, Julián, and Rafael Mérida Jiménez (eds.). 2007. *Diàlegs gais, lesbians i queer/ Diálogos gays, lesbianos, queer* (Lleida: Edicions de la Universitat de Lleida)

Acedo Alonso, Noemí. 2008a. 'Melalcos: nuevas maneras de sentir mundos', in *Escribir con el cuerpo*, ed. by Beatriz Ferrús and Núria Calafell (Barcelona: Editorial de la Universitat Oberta de Catalunya), pp. 81–88

——2008b. 'Carta abierta a Flavia Company. Una propuesta de lectura de *Melalcor*', *Lectora: Revista de dones i textualitat*, 14: 115–22

Agamben, Giorgio. 2007. *Profanations*, trans. by Jeff Fort (New York: Zone Books)

Aguado, Neus. 2000. *Aldebarán* (Barcelona: Lumen)

Aguilar, Gonzalo. 2009. *Episodios cosmopolitas en la cultura argentina* (Buenos Aires: Arcos)

Ahmed, Sara. 2000. *Strange Encounters: Embodied Others in Post-Coloniality* (London and New York: Routledge)

——2010. *The Promise of Happiness* (Durham and London: Duke University Press)

Altman, Janet. 1982. *Epistolarity: Approaches to a Form* (Columbus: Ohio State University Press)

Amado, Ana, and Nora Domínguez (eds.). 2004. *Lazos de familia: Herencias, cuerpos, ficciones* (Buenos Aires, Barcelona, México: Paidós)

Anzaldúa, Gloria. 2012. *Borderlands / La Frontera: The New Mestiza* (San Francisco: Aunt Lute)

Apter, Emily. 2006. *The Translation Zone: A New Comparative Literature* (Princeton: Princeton University Press)

Austin, Kelly. 2011. 'Southern Cone (South America)', in *The Encyclopedia of the Novel*, ed. by Olakunle George, Susan Hegeman, Efraín Kristal and Peter Melville Logan (Chichester: Wiley-Blackwell), pp. 780–91

Averis, Kate. 2014. *Exile and Nomadism in French and Hispanic Women's Writing* (Oxford: Legenda)

Back, Les. 2016. *Academic Diary: Or Why Higher Education Still Matters* (London: Goldsmiths Press)

Barthes, Roland. 1977. 'The Death of the Author', in *Image Music Text*, trans. by Stephen Heath (London: Fontana Press), pp. 142–48

Bassnett, Susan. 1998. *Comparative Literature: A Critical Introduction* (Oxford and Massachussetts: Blackwell)

de Beauvoir, Simone. 2011. *The Second Sex*, trans. by Constance Borde and Sheila Malovany-Chevallier (New York: Vintage)

Benítez Burgos, Geoconda. 2015. *De condición femenina, inmigrante y excluida: La mujer latinoamericana en España* (Madrid: Biblioteca Nueva)

Benjamin, Walter. [1923] 1999. 'The Task of the Translator', in *Illuminations*, ed. by Hannah Arendt, trans. by Harry Zorn (London: Pimlico), pp. 70–82

——2009. *The Origin of German Tragic Drama*, trans. by John Osborne (London and New York: Verso)

Bishai, Linda S. 2004. *Forgetting Ourselves: Secession and the (Im)possibility of Territorial Identity* (Lanham: Lexington Books)

BLEJMAR, JORDANA. 2012. '1969: Youth and Rebellion in *Diario de la guerra del cerdo* and *Invasión*', in *Adolfo Bioy Casares: Borges, Fiction and Art* (Cardiff: University of Wales Press), pp. 371–419

BOURDIEU, PIERRE. 1991. *Language and Symbolic Power*, ed. by John B. Thompson, trans. by Gino Raymond and Matthew Adamson (Cambridge: Harvard University Press)

BRAIDOTTI, ROSI. 1994. *Nomadic Subjects: Embodiment and Sexual Difference in Contemporary Feminist Theory* (New York: Columbia University Press)

——2014. *Thinking as a Nomadic Subject*, online video recording, ERRANS (ICI Berlin), 7 October 2014 <ici-berlin.org/events/rosi-braidotti> [accessed 6 August 2019]

BUTLER, JUDITH. 1997. *Excitable Speech: A Politics of the Performative* (New York: Routledge)

——2001. 'Giving an Account of Oneself', *Diacritics*, 31.4: 22–40

——2003. 'Afterword: After Loss, What Then?', in *Loss: The Politics of Mourning*, ed. by David L. Eng and David Kazanjian (Berkeley, Los Angeles, and London: University of California Press), pp. 467–74

——2011. *Gender Trouble: Feminism and the Subversion of Identity* (New York: Routledge)

CABRÉ, MARIA ÀNGELS. 2011. 'Plomes de paper: Representació de les lesbianes en la nostra literatura recent', in *Accions i reinvencions: Cultures lèsbiques a la Catalunya del tombant de segle XX–XXI*, ed. by Meri Torras (Barcelona: Editorial UOC), pp. 17–40

CALZADA I OLIVERAS, JOSEP. 1980. 'El mosaic de la sinagoga de Beth-Alfa i El Tapís de la Creació de la Catedral de Girona', *Revista de Girona*: 173–205

CAMPI, TERESA. 1983. *Sul ritmo saffico: la vita e le opere di Renée Vivien* (Rome: Bulzoni)

CAMPT, TINA M. 2017. *Listening to Images* (Durham: Duke University Press)

CANO, VIRGINIA. 2015. *Ética tortillera: ensayos en torno al êthos y la lengua de las amantes* (Buenos Aires: Editorial Madreselva)

CARSON, ANNE. 2003. 'Introduction', in *Fragments of Sappho*, Sappho (London: Virago), pp. ix–xiii

CASTLE, TERRY. 1993. *The Apparitional Lesbian: Female Homosexuality and Modern Culture* (New York: Columbia University Press)

CATALÀ, VÍCTOR. 1948. 'Carnestoltes', in *Caires vius*, Editorial Selecta (Barcelona), pp. 185–201

DE CERTEAU, MICHEL. 1984. *The Practice of Everyday Life*, trans. by Steven Rendall (Berkeley and Los Angeles, California: University of California Press)

CLIMENT, LAIA. 2013. *Maria-Mercè Marçal, Veus entre onades* (La Canyada: Tres i Quatre)

COMPANY, FLAVIA. 1988. *Querida Nélida* (Barcelona: Montesinos)

——2000a. 'Carta inventada', in *M'escriuràs una carta?* (Girona: Museu d'Art de Girona), p. 205

——2000b. *Melalcor* (Barcelona: Edicions 62)

——2012. *Volver antes que ir* (Madrid: EugenioCanoEditor)

——2014a. 'Flavia Company, la alquimia de la literatura'. GAYLES.TV. May 8. https://www.youtube.com/watch?v=VdGMO5EZXmM [accessed 6 August 2019]

——2014b. *Por mis muertos* (Madrid: Páginas de Espuma)

'Comitè d'Escriptores Centre Català del Pen Club'. N. d. Nodo 50. <http://www.nodo50.org/mujeresred/cescriptores-pen_catala.html#2> [accessed 30 September 2014]

'Constitución de la República'. N. d. *Parlamento del Uruguay*. <https://parlamento.gub.uy/documentosyleyes/constitucion> [accessed 4 August 2019].

CÓRDOBA GARCÍA, DAVID. 2005. 'Teoría queer: Reflexiones sobre sexo, sexualidad e identidad. Hacia una politización de la sexualidad', in *Teoría queer: Políticas bolleras, maricas, trans, mestizas*, ed. by David Córdoba, Javier Sáez and Paco Vidarte (Barcelona and Madrid: Editorial EGALES), pp. 21–66

CORNEJO PARRIEGO, ROSALÍA and KAY SIBBALD. 2010. 'Introducción: Estudios LGTB hispánicos: un espacio queer — Queer Space', *Revista Canadiense de Estudios Hispánicos*, 35.1: 1–10

COWAN, BAINARD. 1981. 'Walter Benjamin's Theory of Allegory', *New German Critique*: pp. 109–22

CRAWFORD, MARGO NATALIE. 2016. 'The Inside-Turned-Out Architecture of the Post-Neo-Slave Narrative', in *The Psychic Hold of Slavery: Legacies in American Expressive Culture*, ed. by Soyica Diggs Colbert, Robert J. Patterson and Aida Levy-Hussen (New Brunswick, New Jersey, and London: Rutgers University Press), pp. 69–85

DE LAURETIS, TERESA. 1991. 'Queer Theory: Lesbian and Gay Sexualities', *Differences: A Journal of Feminist Cultural Studies*, 3.2: iii–xviiii

——1994. 'Habit Changes', *Differences: A Journal of Feminist Cultural Studies*, 6.2/3: 296–313

DEJBORD, PARIZAD TAMARA. 1998. *Cristina Peri Rossi: escritora del exilio* (Buenos Aires: Editorial Galerna)

DELEUZE, GILLES, and FÉLIX GUATTARI. 1986. *Kafka: Toward a Minor Literature*, trans. by Dana Polan (Minneapolis: University of Minnesota Press)

——1987. *A Thousand Plateaus: Capitalism and Schizophrenia*, trans. by Brian Massumi (Minneapolis and London: University of Minnesota Press)

DEMA, VERÓNICA. 2011. 'Las huellas de la tortura en el casino de oficiales de la esma'. *La Nación*. 28 March. <https://www.lanacion.com.ar/1359808-las-huellas-de-la-tortura-en-el-casino-de-oficiales-de-la-esma> [accessed 15 January 2019].

DERRIDA, JACQUES. 1979. 'Living On', in *Deconstruction and Criticism*, trans. by James Hulbert (New York: The Seabury Press), pp. 75–176

——1981. *Dissemination*, trans. by Barbara Johnson (London: The Athlone Press)

'Desaparecidos'. N.d. <http://www.desaparecidos.org/arg/> [accessed 4 August 2019].

DÍAZ VICEDO, NOÈLIA. 2014. *Constructing Feminine Poetics in the Works of a Late-20th-Century Catalan Woman Poet: Maria-Mercè Marçal* (London: The Modern Humanities Research Association)

DINSHAW, CAROLYN. 1999. *Getting Medieval: Sexualities and Communities, Pre- and Postmodern* (Durham: Duke University Press)

——2001. 'Got Medieval?', *Journal of the History of Sexuality*, 10.2: 202–12

——2007. 'Temporalities', in *Oxford Twenty-First-Century Approaches to Literature: Middle English*, ed. by Paul Strohm (Oxford and New York: Oxford University Press), pp. 107–23

DUBOIS, PAGE. 1995. *Sappho is Burning* (Chicago: University of Chicago Press)

DUFFY, CAROL ANN. 2009. 'Preface', in *Stung with Love: Poems and Fragments*, Sappho (London: Penguin Classics), pp. vii–viii

EDELMAN, LEE. 2004. *No Future: Queer Theory and the Death Drive* (Durham and London: Duke University Press)

ELLIS, ROBERT RICHMOND. 2010. 'Spanish Constitutional Democracy and Cinematic Representations of Queer Sexuality, or, Saving the Family: *Los novios búlgaros, Reinas*, and *Fuera de carta*', *Revista Canadiense de Estudios Hispánicos*, 35.1: 67–80

ENGELS, FRIEDRICH. 2016. *The Origin of the Family, Private Property, and the State*, trans. by Ernest Untermann (Wroclaw: Pantianos Classics)

EPPS, BRAD. 1995. 'Virtual Sexuality: Lesbianism, Loss, and Deliverance in Carme Riera's "Te deix, amor, la mar com a penyora"', in *¿Entiendes?: Queer Readings, Hispanic Writings*, ed. by Paul Julian Smith and Emilie L. Bergmann (Durham: Duke University Press), pp. 317–45

——1999. 'A Writing of One's One: Carme Riera's *Qüestió d'amor propi*', in *Moveable Margins: The Narrative Art of Carme Riera*, ed. by Kathleen Mary Glenn, Mirella D'Ambrosio Servodidio and Mary Seale Vásquez (Lewisburg: Bucknell University Press), pp. 104–52

——2001. 'The Fetish of Fluidity', in *Homosexuality and Psychoanalysis*, ed. by Tim Dean and Christopher Lane (Chicago: University of Chicago Press), pp. 412–31

——2005. 'La ética de la promiscuidad: Reflexiones en torno a Néstor Perlongher', *Iberoamericana*, V.18: 145–62

——2008. 'Retos, riesgos, pautas y promesas de la teoría queer', *Revista Iberoamericana*, LXXIV.225: 897–920

FERNÀNDEZ, JOSEP-ANTON. 2000. *El gai saber: Introducció als estudis gais i lèsbics* (Barcelona: Llibres de l'Índex)

FERRARIO, ELBIO. 2015. 'Museo de La Memoria', leaflet (Montevideo: Centro Cultural Museo de la Memoria)

FLORES, VALERIA. 2013. *Interruqciones. Ensayos de poética activista: escritura, política, educación* (Neuquén: Editora La Mondonga Dark)

FOUCAULT, MICHEL. 1984a. 'Nietzsche, Genealogy, History', in *The Foucault Reader: An Introduction to Foucault's Thought*, ed. by Paul Rabinow, trans. by Donald F. Bouchard and Sherry Simon (New York: Pantheon Books), pp. 76–100

——1984b. 'What is an Author?', in *The Foucault Reader: An Introduction to Foucault's Thought*, ed. by Paul Rabinow, trans. by Josué V. Harari (New York: Pantheon Books), pp. 101–20

——2005. *Madness and Civilization*, trans. by Richard Howard (London and New York: Routledge)

FOUZ-HERNÁNDEZ, SANTIAGO. 2010. 'Assimilation and its Discontents: Representations of Gay Men in Spanish Cinema of the 2000s', *Revista Canadiense de Estudios Hispánicos*, 35.1: 81–104

FRECCERO, CARLA. 2006. *Queer/Early/Modern* (Durham: Duke University Press)

——2007. 'Queer Times', *South Atlantic Quarterly*, 106.3: 485–94

FREEMAN, ELIZABETH. 2005. 'Time Binds, or, Erotohistoriography', *Social Text*, 23.3–4: 57–68

——2010. *Time Binds: Queer Temporalities, Queer Histories* (Durham: Duke University Press)

——2011. 'Still After', in *After Sex? On Writing since Queer Theory*, ed. by Janet Halley and Andrew Parker (Durham and London: Duke University Press), pp. 27–33

——2015. 'Queer Belongings: Kinship Theory and Queer Theory', in *A Companion to Lesbian, Gay, Bisexual, Transgender, and Queer Studies*, ed. by George E. Haggerty and Molly McGarry (Oxford: Wiley Blackwell), pp. 295–314

FREUD, SIGMUND. 1971. 'Mourning and Melancholia', in *The Standard Edition of the Complete Psychological Works of Sigmund Freud: Volume XIV (1914–1916)* (London: The Hogarth Press), pp. 243–58

FUSS, DIANA. 1990. *Essentially Speaking: Feminism, Nature & Difference* (London and New York: Routledge)

GALEANO, EDUARDO H. 2006. *Nosotros decimos no: crónicas (1963/1988)* (Madrid: Siglo XXI de España)

GAVRAS, KONSTANTINOS. 1972. *État de siège* (Cinema 5 Distributing)

GORDON, PAMELA. 2002. 'Introduction', in *Poems and Fragments*, Sappho (Indianapolis: Hackett), pp. v–xxv

GOUJON, JEAN-PAUL. 1983. 'Nota Introduttiva', in *Sul ritmo saffico: La vita e le opere di Renée Vivien*, ed. by Teresa Campi (Rome: Bulzoni), pp. 11–14

GRAMSCI, ANTONIO. 1992. *Selections from the Prison Notebooks* (New York: International Publishers)

GREENE, ELLEN (ed.). 1996. *Re-Reading Sappho: Reception and Transmission* (Berkeley and Los Angeles, California: University of California Press)

GUTIÉRREZ PARDINA, EVA. 2003. 'Viaje de amor y de muerte: *Querida Nélida*, de Flavia Company', *Versátil: Cuaderno de Letras / Quadern de Lletres*, 1: 42–46

——2006. *Cuatro caras de Hermes en la obra narrativa de Flavia Company* (Thesis, Tarragona: Universitat Rovira i Virgili) <http://tdx.cesca.cat/handle/10803/8787> [accessed 3 October 2013]

HALBERSTAM, J. JACK. 1998. *Female Masculinity* (Durham: Duke University Press)

—— 2005. *In a Queer Time and Place: Transgender Bodies, Subcultural Lives* (New York and London: New York University Press)

—— 2015. 'Forgetting Family: Queer Alternatives to Oedipal Relations', in *A Companion to Lesbian, Gay, Bisexual, Transgender, and Queer Studies*, ed. by George E. Haggerty and Molly McGarry (Oxford: Wiley Blackwell), pp. 315–24

HALLEY, JANET, and ANDREW PARKER (eds.). 2011. *After Sex? On Writing Since Queer Theory* (Durham and London: Duke University Press)

HARRIS, ROBERT G. Undated. 'Good Housekeeping Illustration'. *Wikiart: Visual Art Encyclopedia* <https://www.wikiart.org/en/robert-g-harris/good-housekeeping-illustration> [accessed 31 July 2017]

HERNÁNDEZ, WILFREDO. 2003. 'From the Margins to the Mainstream: Lesbian Characters in Spanish Fiction (1964–79)', in *Tortilleras: Hispanic and U.S. Latina Lesbian Expression*, ed. by Lourdes Torres and Inmaculada Pertusa (Philadelphia: Temple University Press), pp. 19–34

HOOKS, BELL. 1990. *Yearning: Race, Gender, and Cultural Politics* (Boston: South End Press)

INVERNIZZI SANTA CRUZ, LUCÍA. 1995. 'Entre el tapiz de la expulsión del Paraíso y el tapiz de la creación: múltiples sentidos del viaje a bordo de "La nave de los locos" de Cristina Peri Rossi', in *Cristina Peri Rossi: papeles críticos*, ed. by Rómulo Cosse (Montevideo: Librería Linardi y Risso), pp. 127–57

IRIGARAY, LUCE. 1980. 'When Our Lips Speak Together', *Signs*, 6.1, trans. by Carolyn Burke: 69–79

—— 1985. 'This Sex Which Is Not One', in *This Sex Which Is Not One*, trans. by Claudia Reeder (Ithaca: Cornell University Press), pp. 23–33

JAMESON, FREDRIC. 2002. *The Political Unconscious: Narrative as a Socially Symbolic Act* (London and New York: Routledge)

JAY, KARLA. 1988. *The Amazon and the Page* (Bloomington: Indiana University Press)

JOHNSON, BARBARA. 1981. 'Translator's Introduction', in *Dissemination*, by Jacques Derrida (London: The Athlone Press), pp. vii–xxxiii

JOSEPH, MIRANDA. 2002. *Against the Romance of Community* (Minneapolis: University of Minnesota Press)

JULIÀ, LLUÏSA. 2000. 'Utopia i exili en la poesia de Maria-Mercè Marçal', in *El gai saber: Introducció als estudis gais i lèsbics*, ed. by Josep-Anton Fernàndez (Barcelona: Llibres de l'Índex), pp. 353–71

—— 2002. 'Inventari del Fons Maria-Mercè Marçal' (Biblioteca de Catalunya)

—— 2013. '*La passió segons Renée Vivien*: un espai d'experimentació formal', in *IV Jornades Marçalianes: i en el foc nou d'una altra llengua*, ed. by Mireia Calafell, Heura Marçal and Meri Torras (Sabadell: Fundació Maria-Mercè Marçal), pp. 165–87

—— 2017. *Maria-Mercè Marçal: una vida* (Barcelona: Galaxia Gutenberg)

KAMINSKY, AMY. 1987. 'Gender and Exile in Cristina Peri Rossi', in *Continental, Latin American and Francophone Writers: Selected Papers from the Witchita State University Conference on Foreign Literature 1984–1985*, ed. by Eunice Myers and Ginette Adamson (London: University Press of America), pp. 149–59

—— 1999. *After Exile: Writing the Latin American Diaspora* (Minneapolis and London: Minnesota University Press)

KAMINSKY, AMY K. 1993. *Reading the Body Politic: Feminist Criticism and Latin American Women Writers* (Minneapolis and London: University of Minnesota Press)

KANTARIS, ELIA GEOFFREY. 1995. *The Subversive Psyche: Contemporary Women's Narrative from Argentina and Uruguay*, Oxford Hispanic Studies (Oxford: Clarendon)

KAUFFMAN, LINDA S. 1992. *Special Delivery: Epistolary Modes in Modern Fiction* (Chicago and London: The University of Chicago Press)

KRAFFT-EBING, RICHARD VON. 1901. *Psychopathia sexualis*, trans. by F. J. Rebman (Chicago: Keener)

KRISTEVA, JULIA. 2012. *Hatred and Forgiveness* (New York: Columbia University Press)

LINDSAY, CLAIRE. 2003. *Locating Latin American Women Writers: Cristina Peri Rossi, Rosario Ferré, Albalucía Angel, and Isabel Allende* (New York and Oxford: Peter Lang)

LLORCA ANTOLÍN, FINA. 2004. '"Terra on arrelar": la construcció de genealogia literària femenina segons Maria-Mercè Marçal', *Lectora: Revista de dones i textualitat*, 10: 217–29

LOMBARDO, STANLEY. 2002. 'Translator's Notes' in *Poems and Fragments*, Sappho (Indianapolis: Hackett), pp. xxvi–xxvii

LORENZ, PAUL. 1977. *Sapho 1900, Renée Vivien* (Paris: Julliard)

LOVE, HEATHER. 2007. *Feeling Backwards: Loss and the Politics of Queer Theory* (Cambridge, Massachusetts, and London: Harvard University Press)

——2008. 'Compulsory Happiness and Queer Existence', *New Formations*, 63: 52–64.

MACARTHUR, ELIZABETH J. 1990. *Extravagant Narratives: Closure and Dynamics in the Epistolary Form* (Princeton and Oxford: Princeton University Press)

MARÇAL, MARIA MERCÈ. 1995. 'El retorn', *Àmica*, 27: 171–75

——2008. *La passió segons Renée Vivien* (Barcelona: Edicions 62)

——2014a. *The Body's Reason*, trans. by Montserrat Abelló and Noèlia Díaz Vicedo (London: Francis Boutle)

——2014b. *El senyal de la pèrdua: escrits inèdits dels últims anys* (Barcelona: Editorial Empúries)

——2017. *Llengua abolida: poesia completa 1973–1998* (Barcelona: Edicions 62)

MARÇAL, MARIA-MERCÈ, and LLUÏSA JULIÀ. 1998. 'En dansa obliqua de miralls: Pauline M. Tarn (Renée Vivien) — Caterina Albert (Víctor Català) — Maria Antònia Salvà', in *Cartografies del desig: Quinze escriptores i el seu mon*, ed. by Maria-Mercè Marçal (Barcelona: Proa), pp. 21–52

MARKS, LAURA U. 2000. *The Skin of the Film: Intercultural Cinema, Embodiment, and the Senses* (Durham: Duke University Press)

MARTÍNEZ-EXPÓSITO, ALFREDO. 2013. 'Queer Literature in Spain: Pathways to Normalisation', *Culture & History Digital Journal*, 2(1): e010. doi: http://dx.doi.org/10.3989/chdj.2013.010

MASSUMI, BRIAN. 1987. 'Translator's Foreword', in *A Thousand Plateaus: Capitalism and Schizophrenia*, Gilles Deleuze and Félix Guattari (Minneapolis and London: University of Minnesota Press), pp. ix–xv

MATUTE, ANA MARÍA. 2013. *Los soldados lloran de noche* (Barcelona: Austral)

MCCLENNEN, SOPHIA A. 2004. *The Dialectics of Exile: Nation, Time, Language, and Space in Hispanic Literatures* (West Lafayette: Purdue University Press)

MEDHURST, ANDY, and SALLY MUNT (eds.). 1997. *Lesbian and Gay Studies: A Critical Introduction* (London and Washington: Continuum International)

MEESE, ELIZABETH A. 1992. *(Sem)erotics. Theorizing Lesbian : Writing* (New York and London: New York University Press)

MÉRIDA JIMÉNEZ, RAFAEL. 2011. 'Viratges, visibilitats i reminiscències de Maria-Mercè Marçal', in *Accions i reinvencions: cultures lèsbiques a la Catalunya del tombant de segle XX–XXI*, ed. by Meri Torras (Barcelona: Editorial UOC), pp. 99–105

MIDDEKE, MARTIN, and CHRISTINA WALD (eds.). 2011. *The Literature of Melancholia: Early Modern to Postmodern* (Basingstoke: Palgrave Macmillan)

MOIX, ANA MARÍA. 1972. *Julia* (Barcelona: Seix Barral)

MOIX, TERENCI. 1972. *Siro o la increada consciencia de la raça* (Barcelona: Edicions 62)

MORA, GABRIELA. 1995. 'Cristina Peri Rossi: *La nave de los locos* y la búsqueda de armonía', in *Cristina Peri Rossi: papeles críticos*, ed. by Rómulo Cosse (Montevideo: Librería Linardi y Risso), pp. 159–71

MULVEY, LAURA. 1975. 'Visual Pleasure and Narrative Cinema', *Screen*, 16.3: 6–18

MUÑOZ, JOSÉ ESTEBAN. 2006. 'Thinking beyond Antirelationality and Antiutopianism in Queer Critique', *PMLA*, 121.3: 825–26

——2009. *Cruising Utopia: The Then and There of Queer Futurity* (New York and London: New York University Press)

——2015. 'Queerness as Horizon: Utopian Hermeneutics in the Face of Gay Pragmatism', in *A Companion to Lesbian, Gay, Bisexual, Transgender, and Queer Studies,* ed. by George E. Haggerty and Molly McGarry (Oxford: Wiley Blackwell), pp. 452–63

NARVÁEZ, CARLOS RAÚL. 1983. *Critical Approaches to Cristina Peri Rossi's El libro de mis primos* (Thesis, Ann Arbor: University Microfilms)

NELSON, MAGGIE. 2016. *The Argonauts* (London: Melville House UK)

NIETZSCHE, FRIEDRICH. 1989. *Beyond Good and Evil: Prelude to a Philosophy of the Future,* trans. by Walter Kaufmann (New York: Vintage)

OHI, KEVIN. 2015. *Dead Letters Sent: Queer Literary Transmission* (Minneapolis and London: Minnesota University Press)

O'ROURKE, MICHAEL. 2014. *Queer Insists (for José Esteban Muñoz)* (Brooklyn: Punctum Books)

OTERO VIDAL, MERCÈ. 2011. 'Patchwork lèsbic', in *Accions i reinvencions: Cultures lèsbiques a la Catalunya del tombant de segle XX–XXI,* ed. by Meri Torras (Barcelona: Editorial de la Universitat Oberta de Catalunya), pp. 41–46

PELS, DICK. 1999. 'Privileged Nomads: On the Strangeness of Intellectuals and the Intellectuality of Strangers', *Theory, Culture & Society,* 16.1: 63–86

PÉREZ, JORGE. 2010. 'Pensamiento y no solo acción: sobre la valiosa aportación peninsular a la teoría queer', *Revista Canadiense de Estudios Hispánicos,* 35.1: 141–61

PÉREZ-SÁNCHEZ, GEMA. 2007. *Queer Transitions in Contemporary Spanish Culture: From Franco to LA MOVIDA* (Albany: State University of New York Press)

——2010. 'Transnational Conversations in Migration, Queer, and Transgender Studies: Multimedia Storyspaces', *Revista Canadiense de Estudios Hispánicos,* 35.1: 163–84

PERI ROSSI, CRISTINA. 1981. *Indicios pánicos* (Barcelona: Editorial Bruguera)

——1984. *La nave de los locos* (Barcelona: Editorial Seix Barral)

——1989a. *El libro de mis primos* (Barcelona: Ediciones Grijalbo)

——1989b. *La nave de los locos* (Barcelona: Biblioteca de Bolsillo)

——2002. *Panic Signs,* trans. by Angelo A. Borrás and Mercedes Rowinsky-Geurts (Waterloo: Wilfrid Laurier University Press)

——2005a. *Poesía reunida* (Barcelona: Lumen)

——2005b. *El pulso del mundo, artículos periodísticos: 1978–2002,* ed. by Mercedes Rowinsky-Geurts (Mexico City: Universidad Autónoma de la Ciudad de México)

——2007a. *Cuentos reunidos* (Barcelona: Random House Mondadori)

——2007b. 'Lectura comentada', in *Diàlegs gais, lesbians, queer/Diálogos gays, lesbianos, queer,* ed. by Julián Acebrón and Rafael Mérida Jiménez (Lleida: Edicions de la Universitat de Lleida), pp. 15–36

——2014. *La noche y su artificio* (Palencia: Cálamo Poesía)

PERRIAM, CHRIS. 2013. *Spanish Queer Cinema* (Edinburgh: Edinburgh University Press)

PI-SUNYER, ORIOL. 1995. 'Under Four Flags: The Politics of National Identity in the Barcelona Olympics', *Political and Legal Anthropology Review,* 18.1: 35–56

PLATERO MÉNDEZ, R. LUCAS. 2005. '¿Invisibiliza el matrimonio homosexual a las lesbianas? Una crítica feminista sobre la construcción y representación del matrimonio homosexual en España', *Orientaciones: revista de homosexualidades,* 10: 103–20

POOCHIGIAN, AARON. 2009. 'Introduction and Notes', in *Stung with Love: Poems and Fragments,* Sappho (London: Penguin Classics), pp. xi–xlvi

POORE, FEDERICO. N.D. 'Una recorrida por el lugar de los hechos'. <https://www.pagina12.com.ar/diario/elpais/1–158422–2010–12–10.html> [accessed 15 January 2019].

PRINS, YOPIE. 1996. 'Sappho's Afterlife in Translation', in *Re-Reading Sappho: Reception and Transmission*, ed. by Ellen Greene (Berkeley and Los Angeles, California: University of California Press), pp. 36–67

PROBYN, ELSPETH. 2015. *Outside Belongings* (New York and London: Routledge)

PUAR, JASBIR. 2007. *Terrorist Assemblages: Homonationalism in Queer Times* (Durham: Duke University Press)

QUELART, RAQUEL. 2010. 'En Catalunya nos consideramos como el ombligo del mundo'. *La Vanguardia*. 8 March. <https://www.lavanguardia.com/cultura/20100308/53897204222/en-catalunya-nos-consideramos-el-ombligo-del-mundo.html> [accessed 4 August 2019].

REYNOLDS, MARGARET. 2000. *The Sappho Companion* (London: Chatto & Windus)

RIBA SANMARTÍ, CATERINA. 2015. 'Maria-Mercè Marçal: Tradició/traducció/creació', *Estudis Romànics*, 37: 471–81

RICH, ADRIENNE. 1980. 'Compulsory Heterosexuality and Lesbian Existence', *Signs*, 5.4: 631–60

——1994. *Blood, Bread, and Poetry: Selected Prose, 1979–1985* (New York and London: Norton)

RIERA, CARME. 2004a. *Te deix, amor, la mar com a penyora* (Barcelona: Proa)

——2004b. 'Maria-Mercè Marçal, autora de contes', *Lectora: revista de dones i textualitat*, 10: 251–58

——2005. *Te deix, amor, la mar com a penyora* (Barcelona: Columna Edicions)

RIVIERE, JOAN. 1929. 'Womanliness as Masquerade', *The International Journal of Psychoanalysis*, 9: 303–13

RODRÍGUEZ, JUANA MARÍA. 2014. *Sexual Futures, Queer Gestures and Other Latina Longings* (New York: New York University Press)

DE RODRÍGUEZ, MERCEDES M. 1989. 'Oneiric Riddles in Peri Rossi's *La nave de los locos*', *Romance Languages Annual*, 1: 521–27

ROIG, MONTSERRAT. 2001. *Digues que m'estimes encara que sigui mentida* (Barcelona: Edicions 62)

ROMERO BACHILLER, CARMEN. 2005. 'Poscolonialismo y teoría queer', in *Teoría queer: Políticas bolleras, maricas, trans, mestizas*, ed. by David Córdoba, Javier Sáez y Paco Vidarte (Barcelona and Madrid: EGALES), pp. 149–64

ROOF, JUDITH. 1991. *A Lure of Knowledge: Lesbian Sexuality and Theory* (New York: Columbia University Press)

ROSENCOF, MAURICIO. 1993. 'On Suffering, Song, and White Horses', in *Repression, Exile, and Democracy: Uruguayan Culture*, ed. by Saúl Sosnowski, trans. by Louise B. Popkin (Durham: Duke University Press), pp. 120–32

RUBIN, GAYLE. 2011. *Deviations: A Gayle Rubin Reader* (Durham and London: Duke University Press)

SABADELL-NIETO, JOANA. 2012. 'Feminismo y ética de las alianzas', in *Repensar la comunidad desde la literatura y el género,* ed. by Marta Segarra (Barcelona: Icaria), pp. 71–87

SANTANA, MARIO. 2000. *Foreigners in the Homeland: The Spanish American New Novel in Spain, 1962–1974* (Lewisburg: Bucknell University Press)

SAPPHO. 2002. *Poems and Fragments*, trans. by Stanley Lombardo (Indianapolis: Hackett)

——2003. *Fragments of Sappho*, trans. by Anne Carson (London: Virago)

——2009a. *Sapho*, trans. by Renée Vivien (Cassaniouze: ErosOnyx)

——2009b. *Stung with Love: Poems and Fragments*, trans. by Aaron Poochigian (London: Penguin Classics)

SARACENI, GINA ALESSANDRA. 2008. *Escribir hacia atrás: herencia, lengua, memoria* (Rosario: Beatriz Viterbo Editora)

SARTRE, JEAN-PAUL. 1949. *What is Literature?*, trans. by Bernard Frechtman (New York: Philosophical Library)

SCHIESARI, JULIANA. 1992. *The Gendering of Melancholia: Feminism, Psychoanalysis and the Symbolics of Loss in Renaissance Literature* (Ithaca: Cornell University Press)

SEDGWICK, EVE KOSOFSKY. 1993. *Tendencies* (Durham and London: Duke University Press)

SEGARRA, MARTA (ed.). 2012. *Repensar la comunidad desde la literatura y el género* (Barcelona: Icaria)

SMITH, PAUL. 1982. 'The Will to Allegory in Postmodernism', *Dalhousie Review*, 62: 105–22

SPIVAK, GAYATRI. 1993. *Outside in the Teaching Machine* (New York: Routledge)

TIERNEY-TELLO, MARY BETH. 1996. *Allegories of Transgression and Transformation: Experimental Fiction by Women Writing Under Dictatorship* (Albany: State University of New York Press)

TORRAS, MERI. 2007. 'Escriure el desig al cos del text. Escriptures i lectures lèsbiques a la literatura catalana contemporània', in *Diàlegs gais, lesbians, queer/Diálogos gays, lesbianos, queer*, ed. by Julián Acebrón and Rafael Mérida Jiménez (Lleida: Edicions de la Universitat de Lleida), pp. 133–50

——2008. 'Cuerpos interrogantes, reescrituras queer. *Melalcor*, de Flavia Company', *Scriptura* 19/20: 219–37

TORRAS, MERI, and MIREIA CALAFELL. 2013. 'Introducció: El foc de la reescriptura', in *IV Jornades Marçalianes: i en el foc nou d'una altra llengua*, ed. by Mireia Calafell, Heura Marçal and Meri Torras (Sabadell: Fundació Maria-Mercè Marçal), pp. 15–18

TORRES, LOURDES, and INMACULADA PERTUSA-SEVA (eds.). 2003. *Tortilleras: Hispanic and U.S. Latina Lesbian Expression* (Philadelphia: Temple University Press)

TUSQUETS, ESTHER. 1978. *El mismo mar de todos los veranos* (Barcelona: Anagrama)

——1979. *El amor es un juego solitario* (Barcelona: Anagrama)

——1980. *Varada tras el último naufragio* (Barcelona: Anagrama)

VERA ROJAS, MARÍA TERESA. 2012. 'Comunidades imposibles. En torno al concepto de comunidad en Gloria Anzaldúa y Cherría Moraga', in *Repensar la comunidad desde la literatura y el género*, ed. by Marta Segarra (Barcelona: Icaria), pp. 107–22

VILASECA, DAVID. 2010. 'Queer Ethics and the Event of Love in Álvaro Pombo's *Contra natura* (2005)', *Revista Canadiense de Estudios Hispánicos*, 35.1: 243–63

VIVIEN, RENÉE. 1982. *A Woman Appeared to Me*, trans. by Jeanette H. Foster (Tallahassee: Naiad Press)

——1983. *The Woman of the Wolf and Other Stories*, trans. by Karla Jay and Yvonne M. Klein (New York: Gay Presses of New York)

——1997. *La Vénus des aveugles* (Charlieu: La Bartavelle Editeur)

VOSBURG, NANCY, and JACKY COLLINS (eds.). 2011. *Lesbian Realities/Lesbian Fictions in Contemporary Spain* (Lewisburg: Bucknell University Press)

WEIGEL, SIGRID. 1985. 'Double Focus: On the History of Women's Writing', in *Feminist Aesthetics*, ed. by Gisela Ecker, trans. by Harriet Anderson (London: The Women's Press)

WINTERSON, JEANETTE. 1994. *Art & Lies: A Piece for Three Voices and a Bawd* (London: Vintage Books)

——2007. 'Introduction', in *Nightwood*, Djuna Barnes (London: Faber and Faber), pp. ix–xv

WITTIG, MONIQUE. [1973] 1975. *The Lesbian Body,* trans. by David Le Vay (London: Peter Owen)

WITTIG, MONIQUE, and SANDE ZEIG. 1979. *Lesbian Peoples: Material for a Dictionary* (New York: Avon)

YAÑEZ, RÚBEN. 1993. 'The Repression of Uruguayan Culture: A Response to the People's Response to the Crisis', in *Repression, Exile, and Democracy: Uruguayan Culture,* ed. by Saúl Sosnowski, trans. by Louise B. Popkin (Durham: Duke University Press), pp. 133–46

ZTARDUST, MORGAN. 2013. 'Aquí se escribe (y se corta) con la lengua', in *Interruqciones. Ensayos de poética activista: Escritura, política, educación,* valeria flores (Neuquén: Editora La Mondonga Dark), pp. 9–17

INDEX

Lightning Source UK Ltd.
Milton Keynes UK
UKHW031018200220
359006UK00004BA/42